Webber Artic Fun Sheets

Set One – S, R, L, S/R/L Blends & Z!

Cards created by Sharon G. Webber M.S., CCC-SLP

Written by Ashley Drennan, Karla Duncan, Clint Johnson, and Amy Jundi

Edited by Thomas Webber

Copyright ©2001, SUPER DUPER® PUBLICATIONS, a division of Super Duper®, Inc. All rights reserved. Permission is granted for the user to reproduce the material contained herein in limited form for classroom use only. Reproduction of this material for an entire school or school system is strictly prohibited. No part of this material may be reproduced (except as noted above), stored in a retrieval system, or transmitted in any form or by any means (mechanically, electronically, recording, web, etc.) without the prior written consent and approval of Super Duper® Publications.

www.superduperinc.com
1-800-277-8737

ISBN 978-1-58650-209-6

snowman
"S" blends

grapes
"R" blends

flag
"L" blends

sailor
"R" final

mouse
"S" final

tulips
"L" medial

apple
"L" final

Introduction

Webber® Artic Fun Sheets Set One – S, R, L, S/R/L Blends & Z – will help reinforce your students' production of target speech sounds at the word, phrase, and sentence levels. This book goes hand in hand with the **Webber® Articulation Set One** cards published by Super Duper® Publications.

Each of the **Webber® Artic Decks** comes with 32 matching pairs of cards, with target sounds in the initial, medial, and final positions of single words. **Webber® Artic Fun Sheets** use the same words and pictures found in the **Set One** cards, and display them in a worksheet format. You can use the activity sheets in therapy or for homework.

The activity pages work best with students ages 3 and up. As they complete each fun activity, your students will learn to accurately produce their target sounds at the word, phrase, or sentence level. Each page also builds vocabulary skills, and encourages following directions.

These pages provide a variety of amusing activities, including word searches, crossword puzzles, mazes, unscramble the sentence games, football games, memory games, cube rolls, matching questions to pictures, and more! Each **Webber® Artic Fun Sheet** provides an additional blank line so that you can add to or change directions. You also receive a parent letter, two different tracking forms, award certificates, and an answer key. Have fun!

Table of Contents

S Activites... **1-54**
   Initial S Words... 2-9
   Initial S Phrases 10-12
   Initial S Sentences.................................... 13-15
   Final S Words.. 16-21
   Final S Phrases 22-24
   Final S Sentences 25-27
   Medial S Words 28-34
   Medial S Phrases 35-37
   Medial S Sentences................................... 38-40
   Combo S Words.. 41-46
   Combo S Phrases...................................... 47-50
   Combo S Sentences 51-54

R Activites **55-110**
   Initial R Words 56-65
   Initial R Phrases 66-68
   Initial R Sentences..................................... 69-71
   Final R Words.. 72-77
   Final R Phrases 78-80
   Final R Sentences 81-83
   Medial R Words 84-89
   Medial R Phrases 90-92
   Medial R Sentences 93-95
   Combo R Words.. 96-102
   Combo R Phrases 103-106
   Combo R Sentences................................107-110

L Activities **111-164**
   Initial L Words.. 112-119
   Initial L Phrases 120-122
   Initial L Sentences..................................... 123-125
   Final L Words.. 126-131
   Final L Phrases 132-134
   Final L Sentences 135-137
   Medial L Words... 138-143
   Medial L Phrases 144-146
   Medial L Sentences................................... 147-150
   Combo L Words 151-156
   Combo L Phrases...................................... 157-160
   Combo L Sentences 161-164

Table of Contents

Z Activities **165-218**
    Initial Z Words 166-173
    Initial Z Phrases 174-176
    Initial Z Sentences 177-179
    Final Z Words 180-185
    Final Z Phrases 186-188
    Final Z Sentences 189-191
    Medial Z Words 192-197
    Medial Z Phrases 198-200
    Medial Z Sentences 201-204
    Combo Z Words 205-210
    Combo Z Phrases 211-214
    Combo Z Sentences 215-218

S, R, L Blends **219-272**
    S Blend Words 220-227
    S Blend Phrases 228-230
    S Blend Sentences 231-233
    R Blend Words 234-241
    R Blend Phrases 242-244
    R Blend Sentences 245-247
    L Blend Words 248-255
    L Blend Phrases 256-258
    L Blend Sentences 259-261
    S, R, L Blend Combo Words 262-265
    S, R, L Blend Combo Phrases 266-269
    S, R, L Blend Combo Sentences 270-272

Awards **273-278**

Answers **279-280**

Parent/Helper Letter

Date: _____

Dear Parent/Helper:

   Your child is currently working on _____ in Speech and Language Class.

   The attached worksheet(s) will help your child practice and reinforce skills reviewed in the classroom.

☐ Please complete these exercises with your child and return them signed and completed.

☐ Please complete these exercises with your child. You do not need to return them to me.

☐ _____
   _____
   _____

   Thank you for your support.

_____   _____
Speech-Language Pathologist   Parent/Helper's Signature

Tracking Sheet

_____   _____   _____
Name   SLP   Date

Date _____

Correct Responses/Total Percentage

_____Sound
Initial/Medial/Final/Blends

☐☐☐☐☐☐☐☐☐☐ = ____%

_____
Word/Phrase/Sentence Level

Date _____

Correct Responses/Total Percentage

_____Sound
Initial/Medial/Final/Blends

☐☐☐☐☐☐☐☐☐☐ = ____%

_____
Word/Phrase/Sentence Level

Date _____

Correct Responses/Total Percentage

_____Sound
Initial/Medial/Final/Blends

☐☐☐☐☐☐☐☐☐☐ = ____%

_____
Word/Phrase/Sentence Level

Date _____

Correct Responses/Total Percentage

_____Sound
Initial/Medial/Final/Blends

☐☐☐☐☐☐☐☐☐☐ = ____%

_____
Word/Phrase/Sentence Level

Progress Chart

Student Name _____

Date	Sound	I, M, F	W/P/S	✔ or -	%

S Sound

#BK-290 Webber® Artic Fun Sheets • ©2001 Super Duper® Publications • www.superduperinc.com • 1-800-277-8737

Color Scene

Directions: Answer the questions below. Say your answer aloud using your good S sound. Then, find and color the answers in the picture scene.

1. What shines in the sky? Color it yellow.

2. What two things can you wear on your feet? Color them red.

3. What number comes after 6? Color it blue.

4. What do you wear when riding in a car? Color it brown.

5. What animal has flippers and barks? Color it purple.

6. What has two slices of bread and is eaten for lunch? Color it orange.

Answers: 1. sun, 2. sandals/socks, 3. 7, 4. seatbelt, 5. seal, 6. sandwich.

Homework Partner   Date   Speech-Language Pathologist   Initial S Words

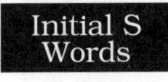

3 Games in 1

Directions: Say aloud the picture–words below, using your good S sound.
Then, play one of the following games:

☐ Lotto – Caller reads a word and student repeats the word and covers it with a token/chip.
☐ Tic–Tac–Toe – Each time you write an **X** or **O**, say the word you mark over.
☐ Memory – Cut out all the cards and place face down. Try to find matching pairs. Say aloud each word you find. Keep all matches.

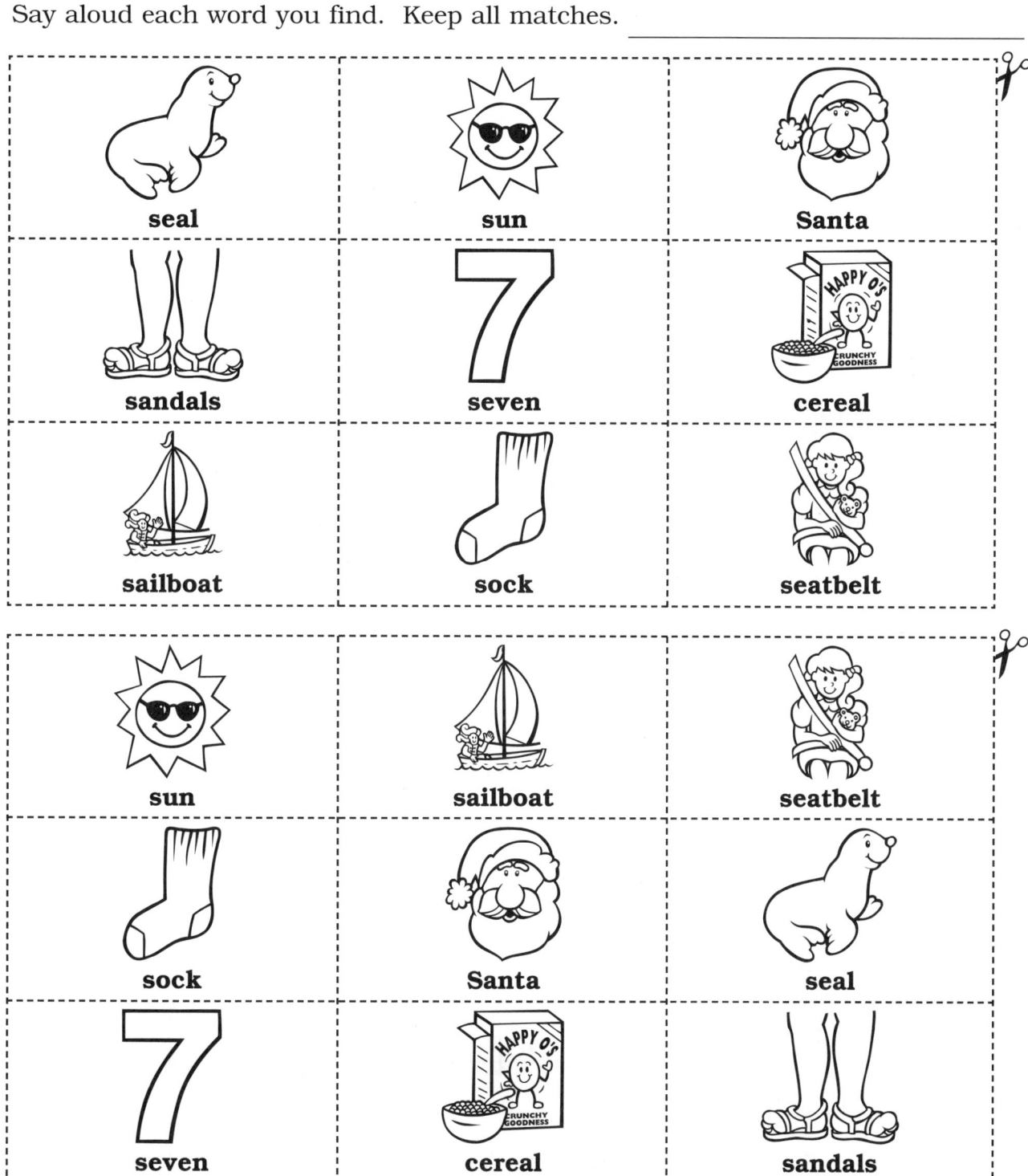

seal	sun	Santa
sandals	seven	cereal
sailboat	sock	seatbelt

sun	sailboat	seatbelt
sock	Santa	seal
seven	cereal	sandals

Homework Partner   Date   Speech-Language Pathologist

Initial S Word

#BK-290 Webber® Artic Fun Sheets • ©2001 Super Duper® Publications • www.superduperinc.com • 1-800-277-8737

3

Sound Sorter

Directions: Read/say each picture–word aloud. Listen to the first sound in each word. Cross out the picture and/or pictures that do not start with the S sound. Then, read/say aloud only the words that begin with the S sound.

sun	ball	sock
seal	seven	wagon
sandwich	sandals	camel
cereal	seatbelt	drink
Santa	sailboat	dog	sun
silly	seal	saw	book

Homework Partner   Date   Speech-Language Pathologist

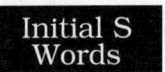

Initial S Words

Secret Word

Directions: Read/say aloud each picture–word below. Write the answers from the Word Bank in the blank spaces. The letters in the square will spell out a secret word. Use the Bonus Clue to help you. Say aloud the secret word, using your good S sound.

Word Bank

sun   Santa   sock   silly
cereal   seatbelt   sandwich   sailboat
saw   seven   seal

1. I shine during the day. ___ ___ ___
2. I can balance a ball on my nose. ___ ___ ___ ___
3. I am 3 + 4. ___ ___ ___ ___ ___
4. I have bread on both sides. ___ ___ ___ ___ ___ ___ ___ ___
5. You have me for breakfast. ___ ___ ___ ___ ___ ___
6. I keep you safe in the car. ___ ___ ___ ___ ___ ___ ___ ___
7. You can't act ___ in school. ___ ___ ___ ___ ___

Bonus Clue

I keep your feet cool in the summer.

Secret Word

☐ ☐ ☐ ☐ ☐ ☐ ☐
1 2 3 4 5 6 7

Answer Key on Page 279

Homework Partner   Date   Speech-Language Pathologist

Initial S Words

Crazy Crossword

Directions: Read/say the picture–words below. Then, complete the crossword puzzle by reading and answering the clues. Use the pictures to help you. Then, use your good S sound and read/say the S words aloud, as you fill in your answers.

sock sailboat seal cereal seatbelt sun saw silly seven sandals

Across

2. This number comes after six and before eight.
5. We wear this in the car to be safe.
6. What water animal has flippers and barks?
7. This keeps your foot warm.
8. We cut down trees with this.

Down

1. This shines in the sky.
2. This is another word for funny.
3. We wear these on our feet in the summer.
4. We eat this for breakfast.
5. This floats in the water and uses wind to move.

Answer Key on Page 279

Homework Partner   Date   Speech-Language Pathologist   Initial S Words

Guess It!

Directions: Practice saying aloud each S picture–word below. Then, read the riddles. Draw a line from the statements to the correct pictures. Remember to use your good S sound.

A.
1. I am round.
2. I am hot.
3. I am in the sky.

saw

cereal

E.
1. I keep you safe.
2. I go across your waist.
3. You wear me in the car.

B.
1. I go in a bowl.
2. You eat me with a spoon.
3. You pour milk on me.

seatbelt

Santa

F.
1. I come in a pair.
2. I keep feet warm.
3. I am not a shoe.

C.
1. I move fast in the wind.
2. I float in the water.
3. I have a tall sail.

seven

sailboat

G.
1. I am an odd number.
2. I am 3 + 4.
3. I come after 6.

D.
1. My last name is Claus.
2. I have a white beard.
3. I fly in a sled.

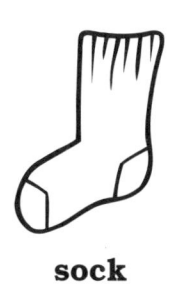

sock

sun

H.
1. I am sharp.
2. I am made of metal.
3. I cut down trees.

Answer Key on Page 279

Homework Partner   Date   Speech-Language Pathologist   Initial S Words

Name It!

Directions: Practice saying aloud each S picture–word. Then, read each statement in the middle. Name the item that goes with each statement. Draw a line from a sentence to each correct picture. Say the words again, using your good S sound.

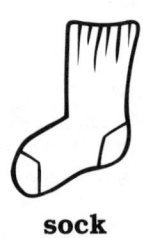

sock

Name something you wear.

seatbelt

sandwich

Name something you ride in.

cereal

sailboat

Name something that you put on your feet.

seven

saw

Name something you find in the water.

sun

Name something you find outside.

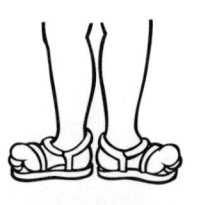

seal

sandals

Homework Partner   Date   Speech-Language Pathologist

Medial S Words

Which One Fits?

Directions: Choose the picture–word that best completes the sentence. Say that word aloud. Remember to use your good S sound.

1. I want a peanut butter and jelly _____ .

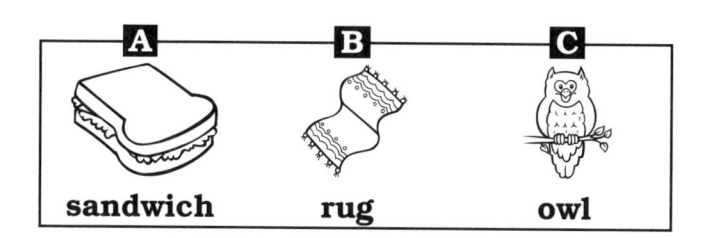

   A. sandwich   B. rug   C. owl

2. When I get in the car, I put on my _____ .

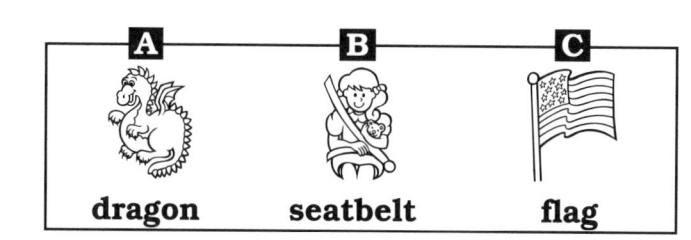

   A. dragon   B. seatbelt   C. flag

3. We cut the tree down with a _____ .

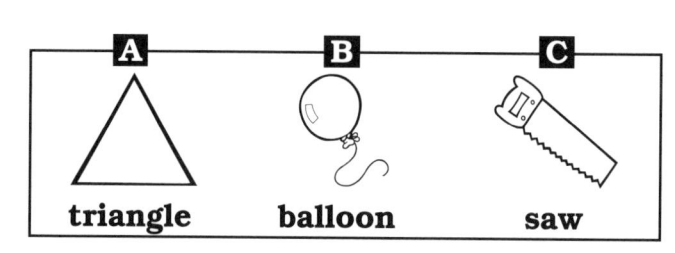

   A. triangle   B. balloon   C. saw

4. I poured milk on my _____ .

   A. plane   B. cereal   C. beard

5. We went out on the water in a _____ .

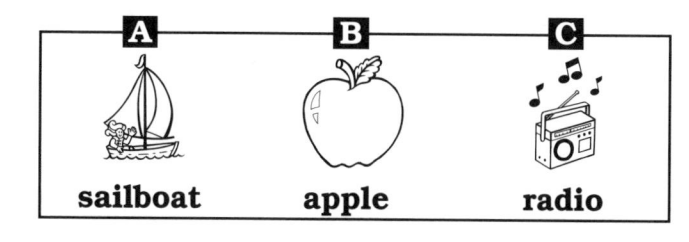

   A. sailboat   B. apple   C. radio

6. Tomorrow is my birthday and I will be _____ .

   A. fruit   B. laundry   C. seven

_____   _____   _____   Initial S Words
Homework Partner   Date   Speech-Language Pathologist

#BK-290 Webber® Artic Fun Sheets • ©2001 Super Duper® Publications • www.superduperinc.com • 1-800-277-8737

9

Descripto Match

Directions: Read/say aloud the picture–words on the right. Then, draw a line from the describing word on the left to a picture–word it describes. There may be more than one describing word for each picture. Then, read/say each phrase aloud. Remember to use your good S sound!

1. big

2. yellow

3. sharp

4. tall

5. gray

6. crunchy

7. red

8. yummy

9. noisy

10. cool

sailboat

saw

sandwich

seal

sun

Santa

cereal

Homework Partner   Date   Speech-Language Pathologist

Initial S Phrases

Search-A-Word

Directions: Read/say the picture–words aloud. Then, complete the phrases below. Use the picture–words for hints. Find and circle each word answer in the word search box. Then, read/say the complete phrases aloud. Use your good S sound.

cereal

saw

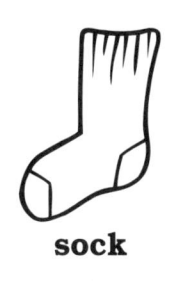

sock

sandwich

```
T L E B T A E S A S O C K W Z
N Q A U S R B T I F M A P U K
H W D E E A N X S B Q G R H U
K K N R A W S V P X S M R W
X F G Y S E J X L U A W P A Q
W C C J X C U M N S M X F L
K X Z B W R K X D I U R P V H
C Q B Z D N S W C K N W L Z W
N L E V S E I I H R L H K O I
E Z N B O C Q U O F F Q S E N
V N R I H A H B O P D W J W M
E S J J Q M P J Y Y F Q C X M
S R R I Z A B Z B C B K B O O C
J R H E N E A I K B J U X Y O
V D H R H N K B H H Z V M J X
```

Answer key on page 280

seatbelt

sun

Santa

seven

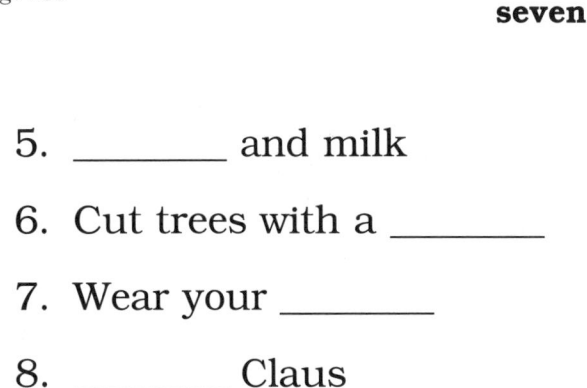

1. One shoe and one _____
2. _____ and moon
3. Peanut butter and jelly _____
4. 10, 9, 8, _____

5. _____ and milk
6. Cut trees with a _____
7. Wear your _____
8. _____ Claus

Homework Partner   Date   Speech-Language Pathologist

Initial S Phrases

#BK-290 Webber® Artic Fun Sheets • ©2001 Super Duper® Publications • www.superduperinc.com • 1-800-277-8737   11

Act It Out!

Directions: Practice each S phrase aloud. Then, cut the squares out and place them face down on a table. The students/helpers take turns picking a card, acting it out, and guessing what the actor is doing. Variations:
1. Pick two cards to act out to have the students use longer phrases ("acting silly and eating a sandwich").
2. Homework partner/teacher acts out all cards and student(s) guess the activities.

Putting on a sock	Eating a sandwich	Cutting with a saw
Putting on a seatbelt	Eating cereal	Acting like a seal
Acting silly	Counting to seven	Talking like Santa

Homework Partner   Date   Speech-Language Pathologist

Initial S Phrases

Say It Silly

Directions: Read/say each sentence aloud. In each set, use the other picture–word to make a silly sentence. ("The <u>sailor</u> flew in the <u>sock</u>.") Use your good S sound. _____

_____

1. The <u>sun</u> shines brightly.
   The ____ shines brightly.

   sailor **sun**

2. When I got out of bed I was only wearing one <u>sock</u>.
   When I got out of bed I was only wearing one ____.

   sock **seal**

3. I made a bologna and cheese <u>sandwich</u>.
   I made a bologna and cheese ____.

   sandwich **sailboat**

4. In the car I always wear my <u>seatbelt</u>.
   In the car I always wear my ____.

   seven **seatbelt**

5. The wind blew the <u>sailboat</u> over the water.
   The wind blew the ____ over the water.

   sailboat **Santa**

6. <u>Seven</u> is my lucky number.
   ____ is my lucky number.

   sandals **seven**

7. I eat <u>cereal</u> in the morning.
   I eat ____ in the morning.

   cereal **sun**

8. The <u>seal</u> barked and clapped for the crowd.
   The ____ barked and clapped for the crowd.

   sandwich **seal**

9. The lumberjack used his mighty <u>saw</u> to cut down the tree.
   The lumberjack used his mighty ____ to cut down the tree.

   saw **sock**

10. The chimney was filled with a very fat <u>Santa</u>.
    The chimney was filled with a very fat ____.

    sandwich **Santa**

Answers: 1-sailor, 2-seal, 3-sailboat, 4-seven, 5-Santa, 6-sandals, 7-sun, 8-sandwich, 9-sock, 10-sandwich

Homework Partner   Date   Speech-Language Pathologist   **Initial S Sentences**

Scrambled Sentences

Directions: Try to unscramble each sentence. Write it on the line below the egg. Then read/say the sentence aloud, using your good S sound.

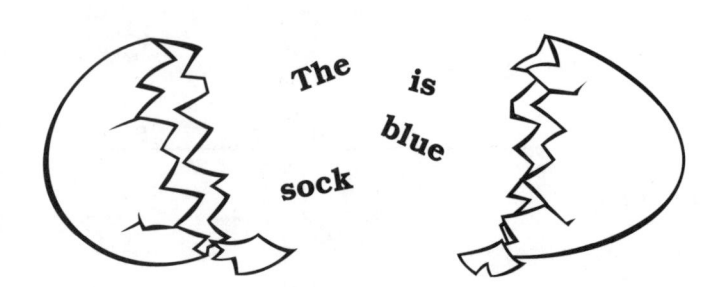

1. The sock is blue.

2. My dog had seven puppies.

3. I ate a bowl of cereal.

4. The silly clown was at the carnival.

5. I made a peanut butter and jelly sandwich.

6. You should wear your seatbelt in the car.

7. He wears sandals when it is hot.

8. I need a saw to cut the board.

Answer key on page 279

Homework Partner   Date   Speech-Language Pathologist

Initial S Sentences

14   #BK-290 Webber® Artic Fun Sheets • ©2001 Super Duper® Publications • www.superduperinc.com • 1-800-277-8737

Story Loop

Directions: Read/say aloud each picture–word. Make up a story using all of the pictures in the circle. You can start anywhere in the circle and go in either direction, but you must always end where you started to complete the loop. Say your story aloud, using your good S sound.

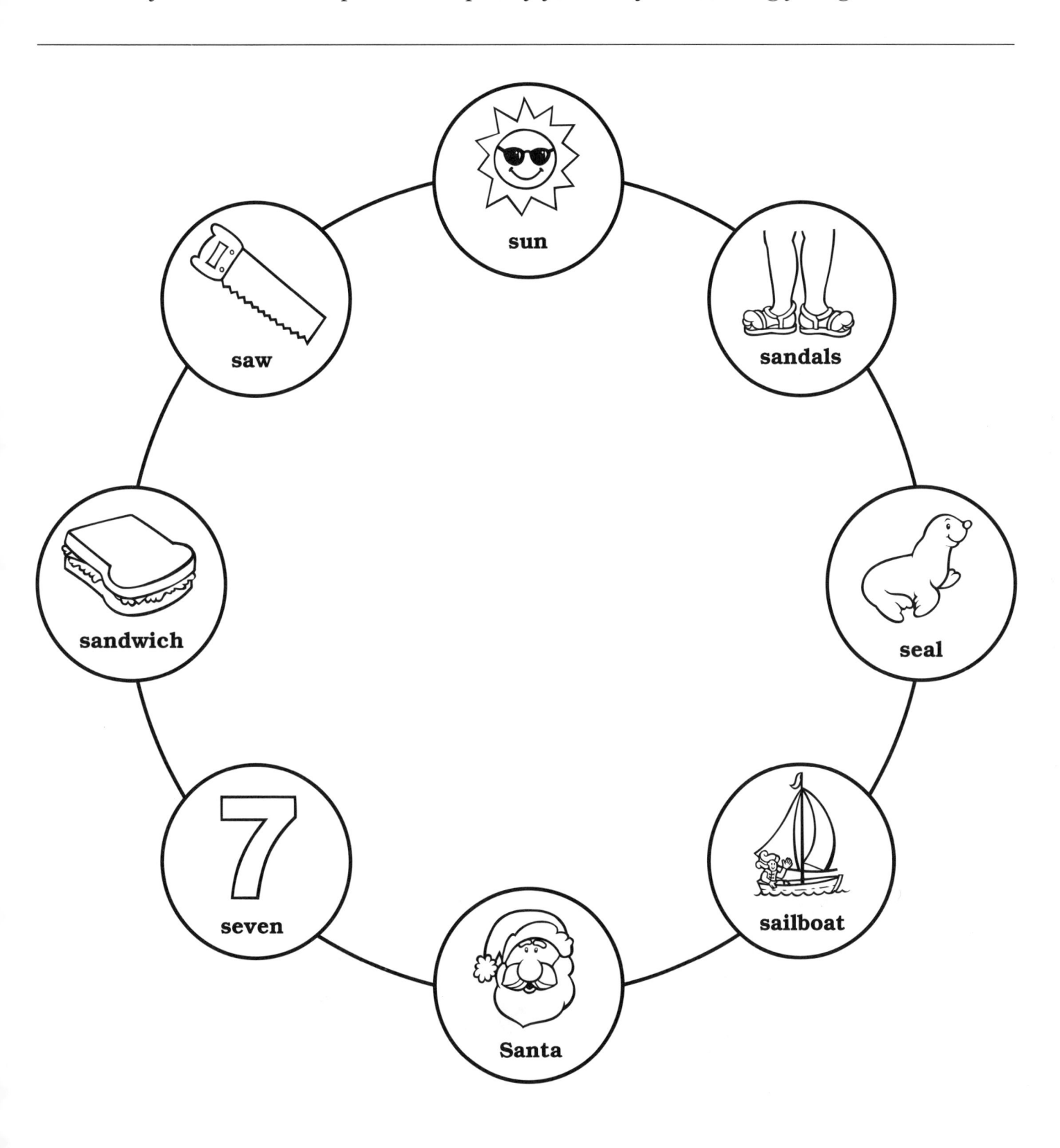

- sun
- sandals
- seal
- sailboat
- Santa
- seven
- sandwich
- saw

Homework Partner   Date   Speech-Language Pathologist

Initial S Sentences

Pyramid Power

Directions: Cut out the triangles at the bottom of the page. Read/say each word aloud. Then, place each triangle in the pyramid outline below. Use your good S sound! _____

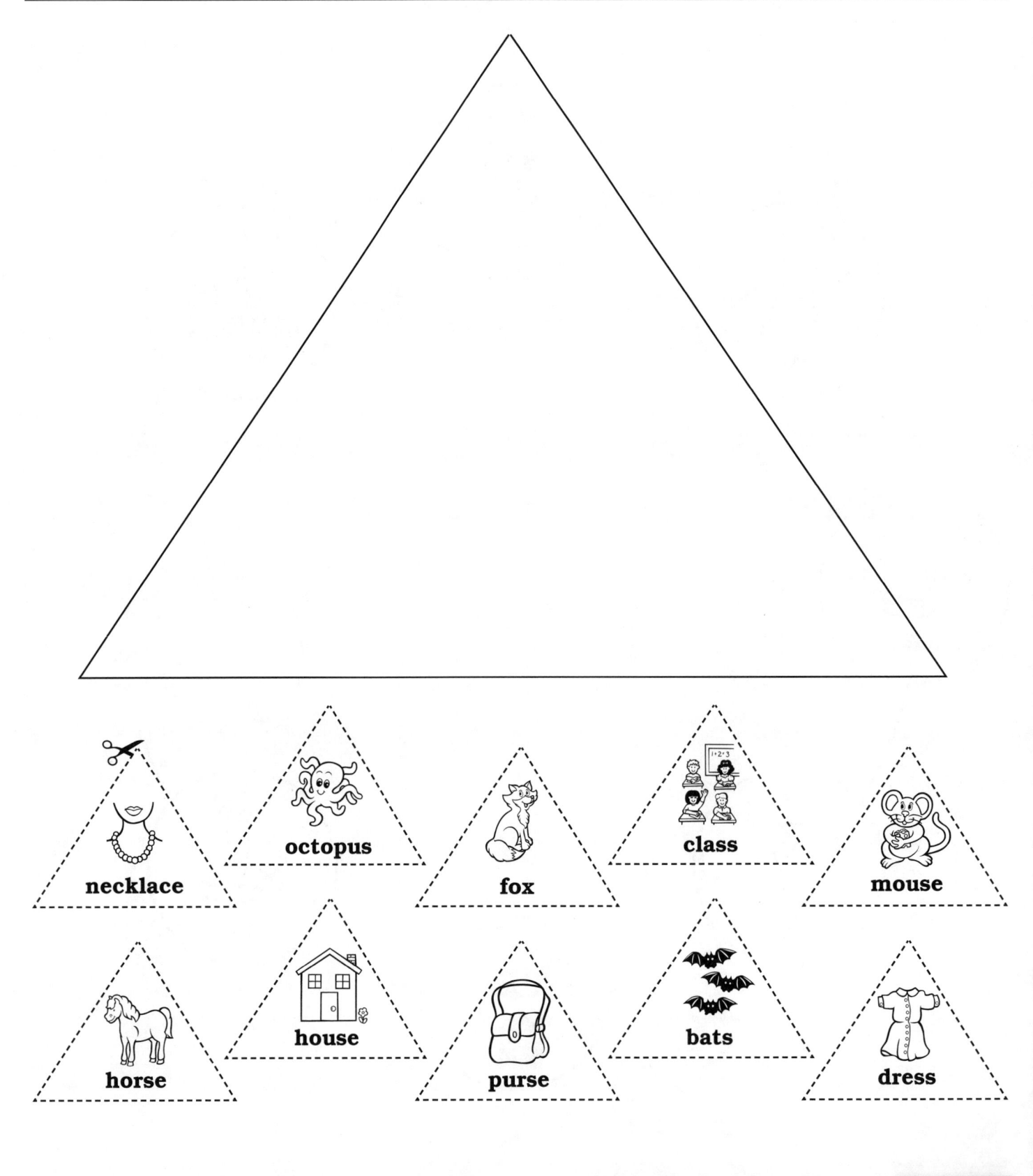

necklace

octopus

fox

class

mouse

horse

house

purse

bats

dress

Homework Partner   Date   Speech-Language Pathologist   Final S Words

Yo-De-Lay-De-Hoo Game

Directions: Read/say aloud the picture–words below. Then, cut out the markers. Flip a coin (heads=1, tails=2) to determine how many spaces to move. As you move, read/say each word aloud, using your good S sound. First player to reach the finish wins.

FINISH — pants — necklace — bats — octopus — purse — house — fox — class — mouse — glass — dress — horse — grapes — lips — princess — START

Homework Partner — Date — Speech-Language Pathologist — Final S Words

Guess It!

Directions: Look at each picture part and guess aloud what it is. Finish drawing the picture if you would like. Remember to use your good S sound.

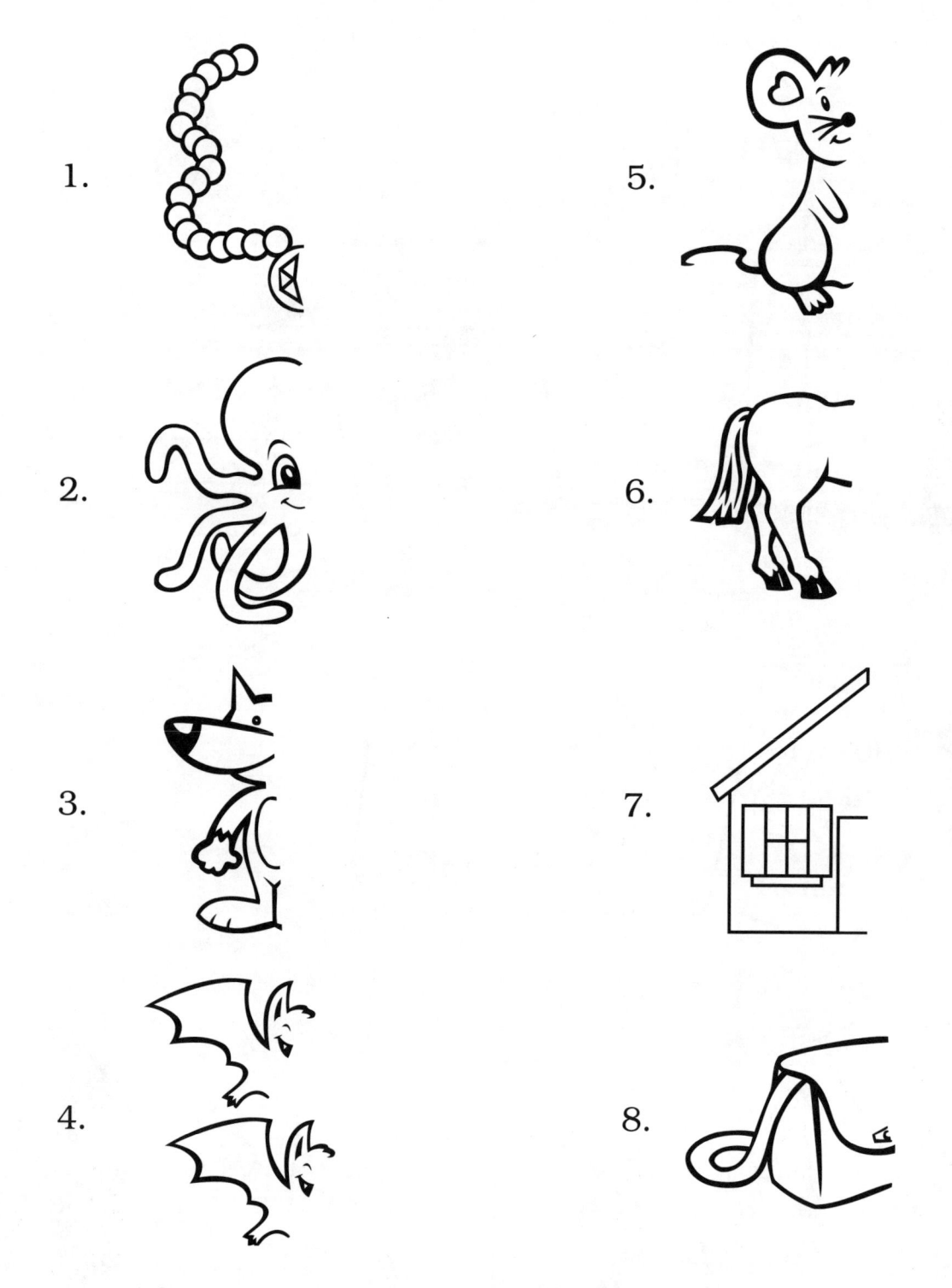

1.
2.
3.
4.
5.
6.
7.
8.

Answers: 1. necklace, 2. octopus, 3. fox, 4. bats, 5. mouse, 6. horse, 7. house, 8. purse

Homework Partner   Date   Speech-Language Pathologist

Final S Words

Memory Game

Directions: Read/say aloud each picture–word below. Cut out the pictures. Place all cards face down. Try to match the cards. Say each card as you pick it up, using your good S sound. Keep all matches. Most matches wins! _____

class	fox	purse	bats
octopus	necklace	house	mouse
pants	horse	class	fox
house	mouse	octopus	necklace
purse	bats	horse	pants

_____ _____ _____
Homework Partner Date Speech-Language Pathologist

Final S Words

Spinner Action

Directions: Read/say aloud the picture–words below. If you prefer, glue this page to construction paper for added durability. Cut out the arrow/dial. Use a brad to connect the dial to the circle. Spin the spinner. When you land on a picture, read/say the word aloud, using your best S sound.

- horse
- mouse
- house
- class
- necklace
- octopus
- pants
- fox

Homework Partner Date Speech-Language Pathologist

Final S Words

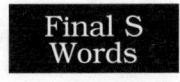

What Am I?

Directions: Read/say aloud each picture–word below. Then, read each question. Fill in the blank with the appropriate word. Read/say each answer aloud, using your good S sound.

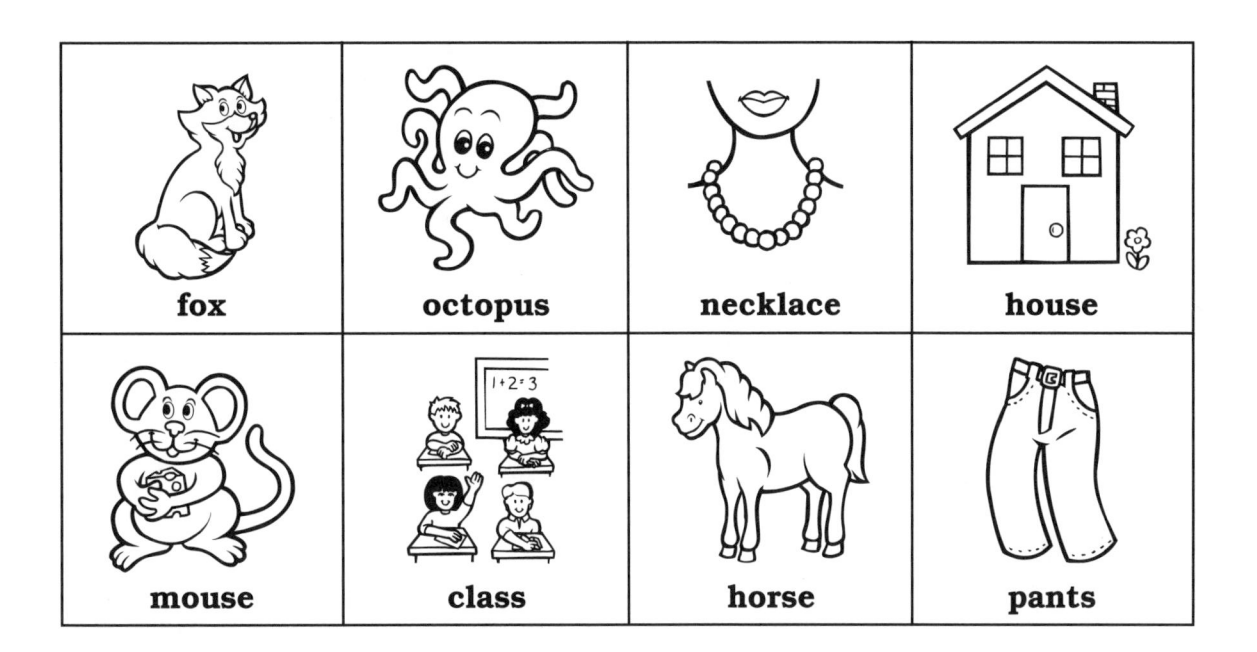

fox	octopus	necklace	house
mouse	class	horse	pants

1. What has eight arms? _____
2. What do you wear on your neck? _____
3. What has a door and windows? _____
4. Where do you find a teacher? _____
5. What can you ride? _____
6. What is holding the cheese? _____

   BONUS: These require more than one answer.

7. What has a tail? _____
8. What can you wear? _____
9. Where do you find people? _____
10. What has four legs? _____

Answers: 1. octopus, 2. necklace, 3. house, 4. class, 5. horse, 6. mouse, 7. horse, fox, mouse, 8. necklace, pants, 9. class, house, 10. fox, horse, mouse

Homework Partner   Date   Speech-Language Pathologist   **Final S Words**

#BK-290 Webber® Artic Fun Sheets • ©2001 Super Duper® Publications • www.superduperinc.com • 1-800-277-8737

Don't Leaf Me Hanging!

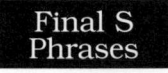

Directions: Read/say each picture–word below. Then, cut out all the leaf pictures below. Say aloud the phrase "_____ in a tree" using each leaf word ("<u>necklace</u> in a tree"). Use your good S sound. Glue/tape or place the pictures onto the tree. _____

necklace

bats

class

fox

octopus

pants

purse

horse

Homework Partner   Date   Speech-Language Pathologist

Final S Phrases

22   #BK-290 Webber® Artic Fun Sheets • ©2001 Super Duper® Publications • www.superduperinc.com • 1-800-277-8737

Mine or Yours?

Directions: Read/say each picture–word below. Cut out the pictures. At each turn, flip a coin. Heads means the student keeps the pictures and says, "My _____" ("My <u>octopus</u>"). Tails means that the student gives the picture to his partner and says, "Your _____" ("Your <u>octopus</u>"). Player with the most pictures at the end wins.

octopus	**necklace**
fox	**class**
mouse	**horse**
house	**purse**
bats	**pants**

Homework Partner   Date   Speech-Language Pathologist   Final S Phrases

Rev Up the Phrase!

Directions: Read/say aloud each S word below. Then, let's rev up the phrases below and make them more exciting! Use the descriptive words from the Word Bank to rev up the phrases. Then read/say them aloud, using your good S sound.

Word Bank

hungry	new	hopping	friendly
heavy	pretty	noisy	galloping
dirty	tall	clean	full
gigantic	happy	tiny	good

1. a _____ octopus _____

2. a _____ fox _____

3. a _____ class _____

4. a _____ necklace _____

5. a _____ mouse _____

6. a _____ horse _____

7. a _____ house _____

8. a _____ purse _____

9. _____ bats _____

10. my _____ pants _____

Homework Partner   Date   Speech-Language Pathologist

Final S Phrases

Clean-Up

Directions: Read/say aloud the picture–words below. Cut out pictures at the bottom of the page. Then, put each item in a drawer. Say aloud what you are doing. ("I'm putting the mouse in the middle drawer.") Use your good S sound!

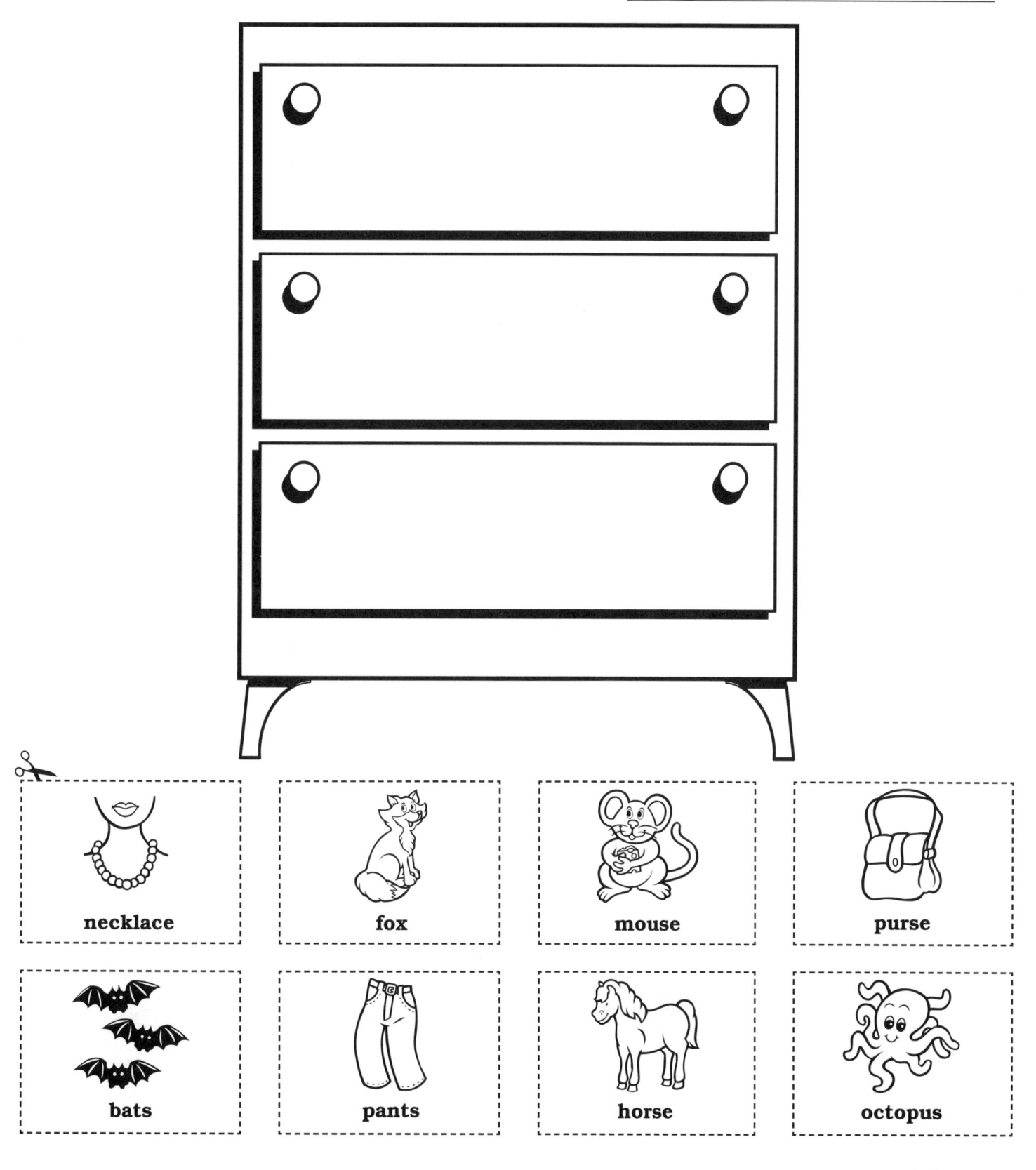

| necklace | fox | mouse | purse |
| bats | pants | horse | octopus |

Homework Partner   Date   Speech-Language Pathologist   Final S Sentences

Calendar!

Directions: Read/say aloud the picture–words below. Cut out the pictures at the bottom of the page. Then, place each picture on a certain day and say a sentence aloud. ("On Monday, I found the horse.") Remember to use your good S sound.

Monday	Tuesday	Wednesday	Thursday	Friday

octopus	pants	horse	house	mouse
purse	bats	necklace	class	fox

Homework Partner   Date   Speech-Language Pathologist

Final S Sentences

Silly S Choices

Directions: Read/say aloud each picture–word. Then, complete each sentence below by choosing one picture from Column A and one from Column B. ("At the fair, the <u>mouse</u> got a <u>necklace</u>.") Say each sentence aloud using your good S sound!

	A	**B**
1. In the closet, the		
2. In the dark cave, a	octopus	pants
3. After dinner, my	mouse	bats
4. On the roof, the		
5. During a bumpy boat ride, a	house	purse
6. In the barn, my	necklace	horse
7. At the fair, the		
8. While they were talking, their	fox	class

Homework Partner   Date   Speech-Language Pathologist   Final S Sentences

Finger Hopscotch

Directions: Read/say aloud the picture–words below. Then, slide a penny across the hopscotch board. Hop your finger to the square it lands on. Read/say the name of the picture–word again, practicing your good S sound. Play again until you have landed on all the words.

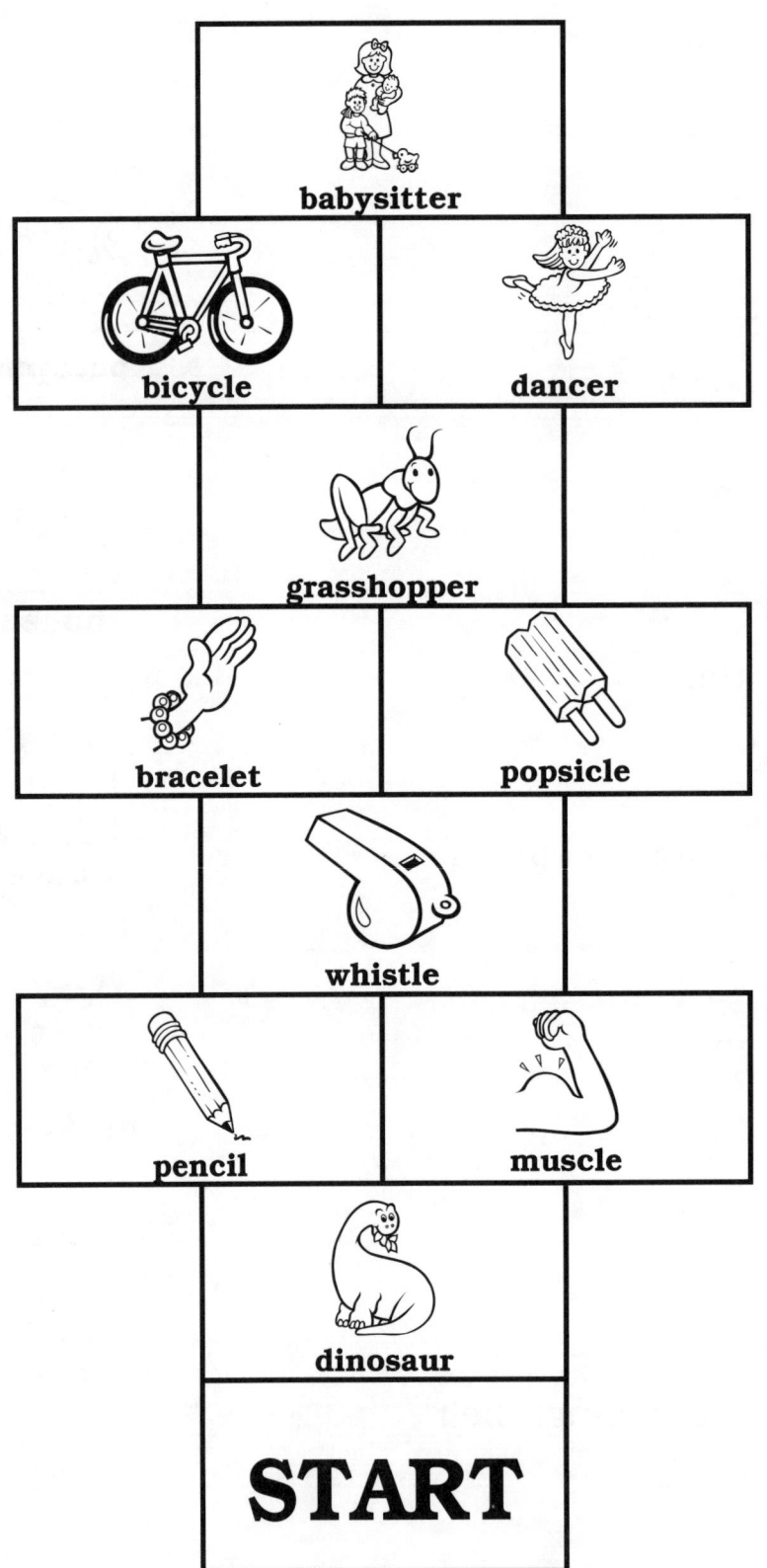

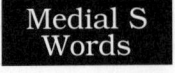

babysitter

bicycle | dancer

grasshopper

bracelet | popsicle

whistle

pencil | muscle

dinosaur

START

Homework Partner | Date | Speech-Language Pathologist

Medial S Words

Memory Game

Directions: Read/say aloud each picture–word below. Cut out the pictures. Place all cards face down. Try to match the cards. Say each card as you pick it up, using your good S sound. Keep all matches. Most matches wins!

pencil	muscle	popsicle	dinosaur
bracelet	grasshopper	bicycle	babysitter
dancer	whistle	pencil	muscle
popsicle	dinosaur	bracelet	grasshopper
bicycle	babysitter	dancer	whistle

Homework Partner   Date   Speech-Language Pathologist

Medial S Words

Football Mania!

Directions: Read/say aloud the picture–words. Cut out the footballs and place them at the 10 yard line on opposite sides of the field. First player flips a coin and moves 10 yards (heads) or 20 yards (tails). Say the word you land on aloud. Play continues in turn. First player to score a touchdown wins. Next time you play, switch sides. _____

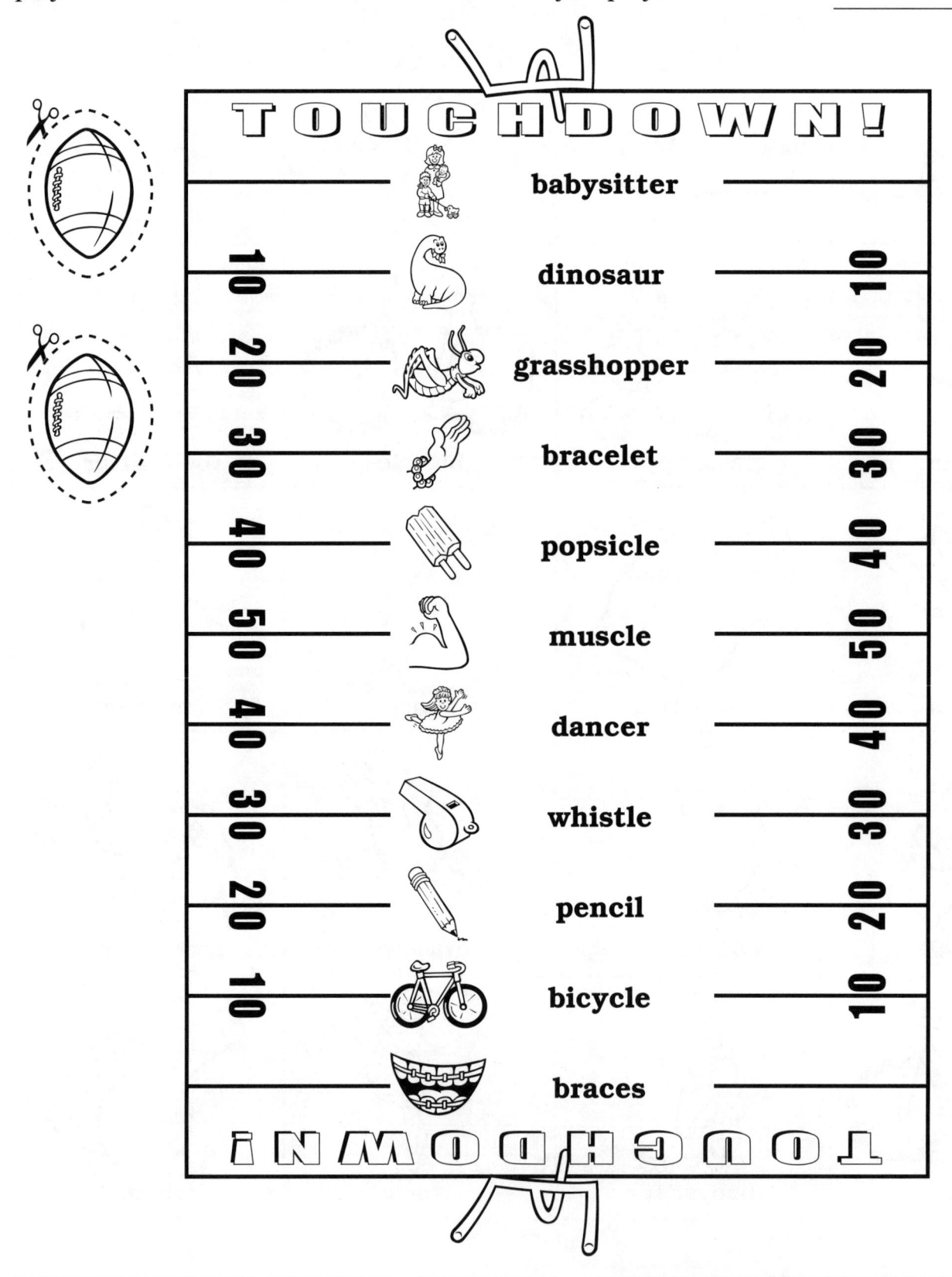

TOUCHDOWN!

- babysitter
- dinosaur
- grasshopper
- bracelet
- popsicle
- muscle
- dancer
- whistle
- pencil
- bicycle
- braces

TOUCHDOWN!

Homework Partner | Date | Speech-Language Pathologist

Medial S Words

X and O

Directions: Cut out each X and O below. Have each player/partner choose X or O. The first player reads/says a picture–word aloud and places an X or O on the square. Play continues in turn. The first person to get three in a row wins.

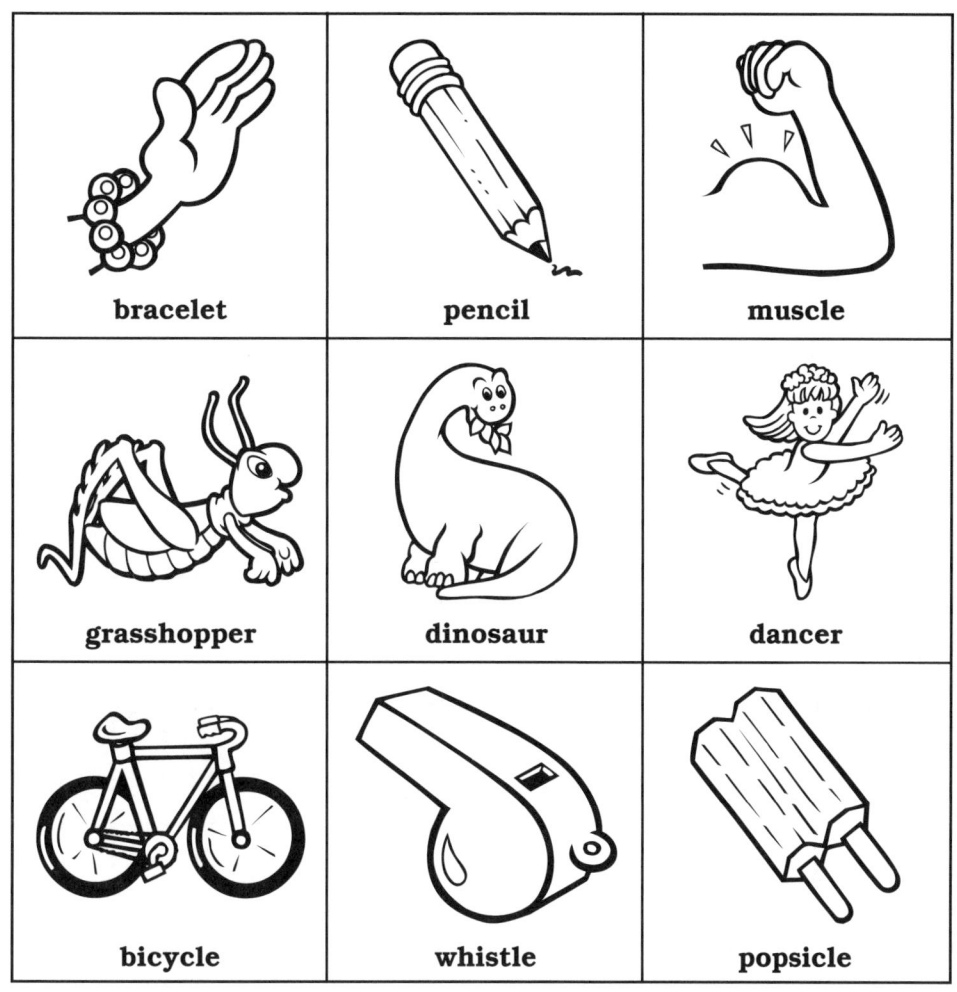

bracelet	pencil	muscle
grasshopper	dinosaur	dancer
bicycle	whistle	popsicle

X X X X X

O O O O O

Homework Partner   Date   Speech-Language Pathologist

Medial S Words

Amaze Me

Directions: You are a prince trying to save the princess who has been kidnapped!! Try to solve the maze to find her. Say aloud the name of each S word you come across as you try to solve the maze. Remember to use your good S sound. _____

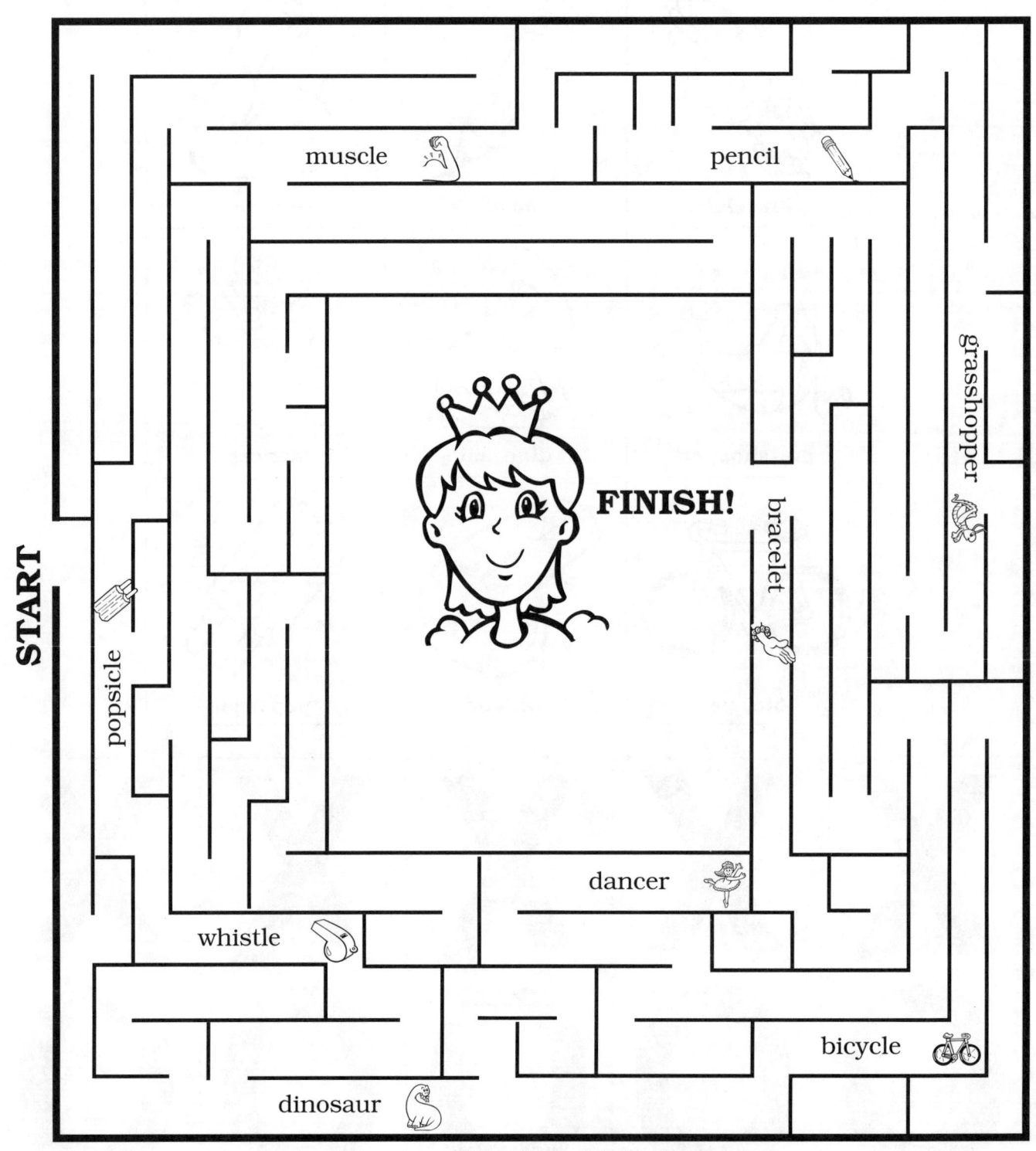

muscle   pencil

grasshopper

START

popsicle

FINISH!

bracelet

dancer

whistle

bicycle

dinosaur

Answer key on page 280

Homework Partner   Date   Speech-Language Pathologist   **Medial S Words**

32   #BK-290 Webber® Artic Fun Sheets • ©2001 Super Duper® Publications • www.superduperinc.com • 1-800-277-8737

Syllable Secrets

Directions: Read/say aloud each picture–word below. Then, check as many boxes as there are syllables (pencil – check 2 boxes). When you finish, write the letters from the boxes you checked on the line below to reveal the secret word. Say each word using your good S sound.

Words	Syllables
pencil	1 ☐ 2 ☐ 3 ☐ 4 ☐ Y O F P
popsicle	1 ☐ 2 ☐ 3 ☐ 4 ☐ U A R J
bracelet	1 ☐ 2 ☐ 3 ☐ 4 ☐ E A L P
whistle	1 ☐ 2 ☐ 3 ☐ 4 ☐ S U D M
grasshopper	1 ☐ 2 ☐ 3 ☐ 4 ☐ P E R K
dinosaur	1 ☐ 2 ☐ 3 ☐ 4 ☐ D U P Y
muscle	1 ☐ 2 ☐ 3 ☐ 4 ☐ E R Z F
babysitter	1 ☐ 2 ☐ 3 ☐ 4 ☐ W H I Z
bicycle	1 ☐ 2 ☐ 3 ☐ 4 ☐ K I D A
dancer	1 ☐ 2 ☐ 3 ☐ 4 ☐ ! ! B M

Secret Message: _____

Homework Partner   Date   Speech-Language Pathologist

Medial S Words

Riddle Detective

Directions: Read/say aloud the picture-words. Then, read the riddles below. Choose the correct answers from the Word Bank. Write the answers in the spaces. Read/say your answers aloud using your good S sound.

Word Bank

pencil   bracelet   bicycle

dinosaur   popsicle   dancer

1. You use me to write,
   And draw pictures too,
   I can be erased,
   I'm a useful tool.

   I am a _____.

2. I lived long ago,
   Before you were here,
   But time went by,
   And I disappeared.

   I am a _____.

3. I am some jewelry,
   That goes on your arm,
   I'm made of beads,
   Or sometimes have charms.

   I am a _____.

4. I am frozen,
   And good to eat,
   I am not ice cream,
   But I'm still a treat.

   I am a _____.

5. You have to balance,
   So you don't fall down,
   Put your feet on the pedals,
   And the wheels go around.

   I am a _____.

6. I twirl or jump,
   On the stage each day,
   Watch me tap,
   When music plays.

   I am a _____.

Answers: 1. pencil, 2. dinosaur, 3. bracelet, 4. popsicle, 5. bicycle, 6. dancer

Homework Partner   Date   Speech-Language Pathologist

Medial S Words

34   #BK-290 Webber® Artic Fun Sheets • ©2001 Super Duper® Publications • www.superduperinc.com • 1-800-277-8737

Silly Match-Ups!

Directions: Read/say aloud each picture–word. Then, draw a line from an adjective to an S noun. Make up phrases to say aloud using your best S sound ("purple grasshopper"). They can be silly or serious.

Adjectives **S Nouns**

Large... popsicle

Purple... grasshopper

Cold... whistle

Broken... pencil

Hungry... dinosaur

Heavy... bracelet

Pretty... bicycle

Homework Partner　　Date　　Speech-Language Pathologist

Medial S Phrases

Phrase Racing

Directions: Cut out the cars. Give one to the student and one to a race partner. Begin at the starting line. Use a coin to determine the number of spaces to advance (heads=2, tails=1). Read/say aloud each phrase as you land on it. First one to the Finish wins! Play again.

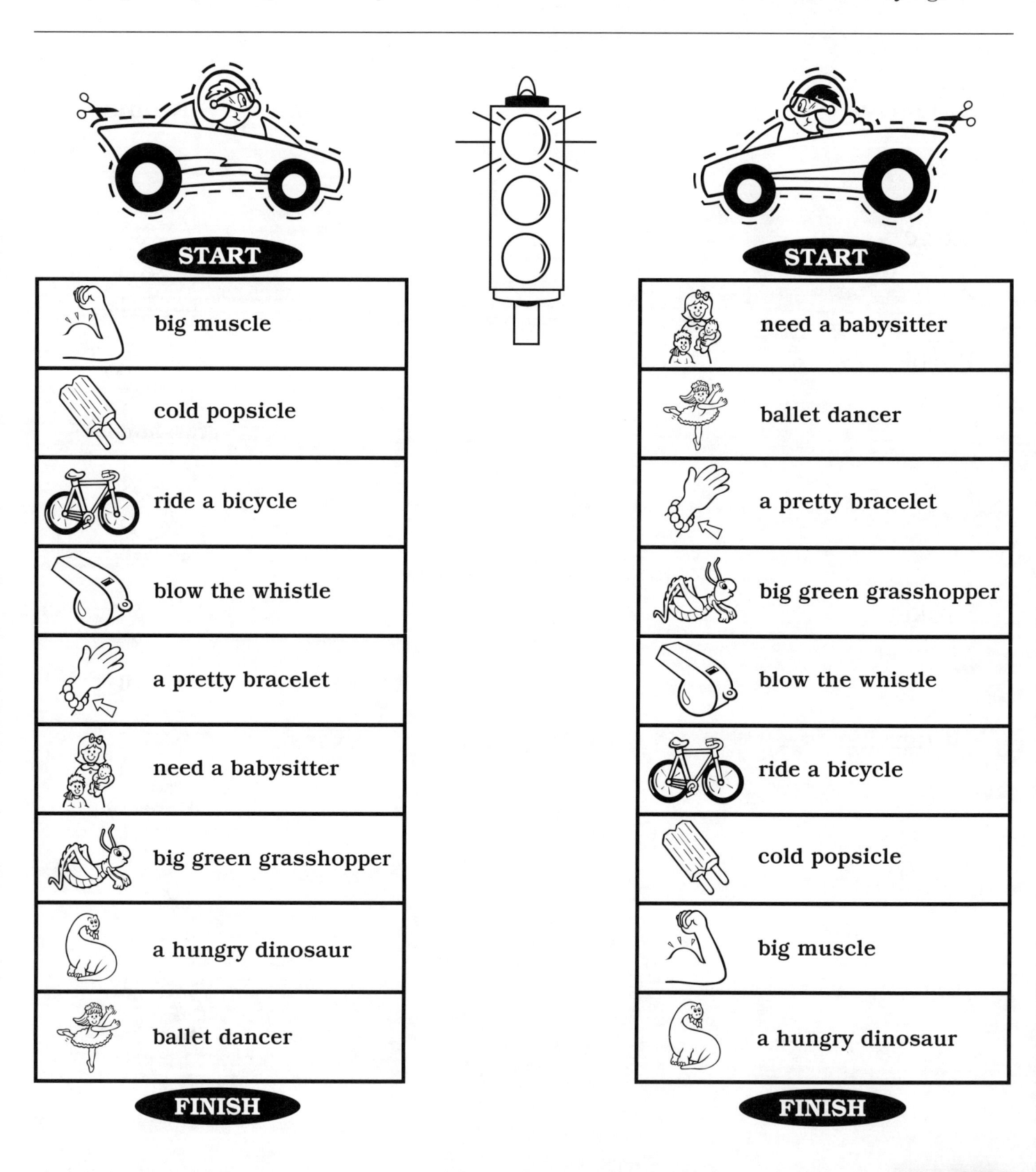

START (left track):
- big muscle
- cold popsicle
- ride a bicycle
- blow the whistle
- a pretty bracelet
- need a babysitter
- big green grasshopper
- a hungry dinosaur
- ballet dancer

FINISH

START (right track):
- need a babysitter
- ballet dancer
- a pretty bracelet
- big green grasshopper
- blow the whistle
- ride a bicycle
- cold popsicle
- big muscle
- a hungry dinosaur

FINISH

Homework Partner   Date   Speech-Language Pathologist

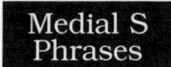

Medial S Phrases

Phrase Fill-In

Directions: Read/say aloud the phrases below, using your best S sound. Then, choose and say aloud a phrase to finish each sentence. Make it silly or serious.

Phrases

a baby grasshopper

a broken pencil

a melted popsicle

a tiptoeing dinosaur

a candy bracelet

a funny babysitter

a new bicycle

a pretty dancer

1. In my drawer I found _____.

2. I turned around when I heard _____.

3. I tripped and fell over _____.

4. I need to buy _____.

5. I was surprised to see _____.

6. Mom made me play with _____.

7. When I grow up, I want to be _____.

8. Inside my lunchbox was _____.

Homework Partner   Date   Speech-Language Pathologist

Medial S Phrases

Fire and Ice

Directions: Have your partner pick a picture on this page, but tell him/her not to tell you what it is. Then, try to figure out which picture your partner chose by asking questions ("broken pencil?"). If the picture you chose is close to target, your partner should say, "You are hot." If it is far away from the target he/she should say, "You are cold." Keep trying until you guess your partner's picture. Then, switch places.

The pencil is broken.	He dropped the popsicle.	The dinosaur is eating.
The bracelet is too big.	She likes to ride her bicycle.	The referee blew the whistle.
The grasshopper is eating a leaf.	She is a ballet dancer.	The babysitter talked on the phone.

Homework Partner   Date   Speech-Language Pathologist

Medial S Sentences

Word in a Word

Directions: Read/say aloud the picture–words on the left. Then, read a sentence and circle a word in the sentence that is part of the word on the left. ("**address:** We sent the (dress) to the wrong address.") Then, read the sentence aloud using your best S sound.

1. **whistle** — He blew his whistle.

2. **pencil** — You write with a pen or a pencil.

3. **grasshopper** — I found a grasshopper in my shop.

4. **popsicle** — Do you want a pop or a popsicle?

5. **dinosaur** — The dinosaur had no ears.

6. **bracelet** — He let me have the bracelet.

Answers: 1- his, 2- pen, 3- shop, 4- pop, 5- no, 6- let

Homework Partner   Date   Speech-Language Pathologist

Medial S Sentences

Crazy Crossword

Directions: Read/say the picture–words below. Then, complete the crossword puzzle by reading and answering the clues. Use the pictures to help you. Then use your good S sound and read/say the S sentences aloud, as you fill in your answers. _____

popsicle

bicycle

dancer

grasshopper

babysitter

whistle

bracelet

pencil

Across

2. On your arm you wear a _____.
4. A person who likes to move to music is a _____.
6. A toy you blow in to make a noise is a _____.
7. A green bug that jumps is a _____.

Down

1. You write with a _____.
2. You pedal to move a _____.
3. Children are taken care of by a _____.
5. A cold treat is a _____.

Answer on page 279

Homework Partner   Date   Speech-Language Pathologist   Medial S Sentences

3 Games in 1

Directions: Say aloud the picture–words below, using your good S sound.
Then, play one of the following games:

☐ Lotto – Caller reads out a word and student repeats the word and covers it with a token/chip.

☐ Tic–Tac–Toe – Each time you write an **X** or **O**, say the word you mark over.

☐ Memory – Cut out all the cards and place face down. Try to find matching pairs. Say aloud each word you find. Keep all matches.

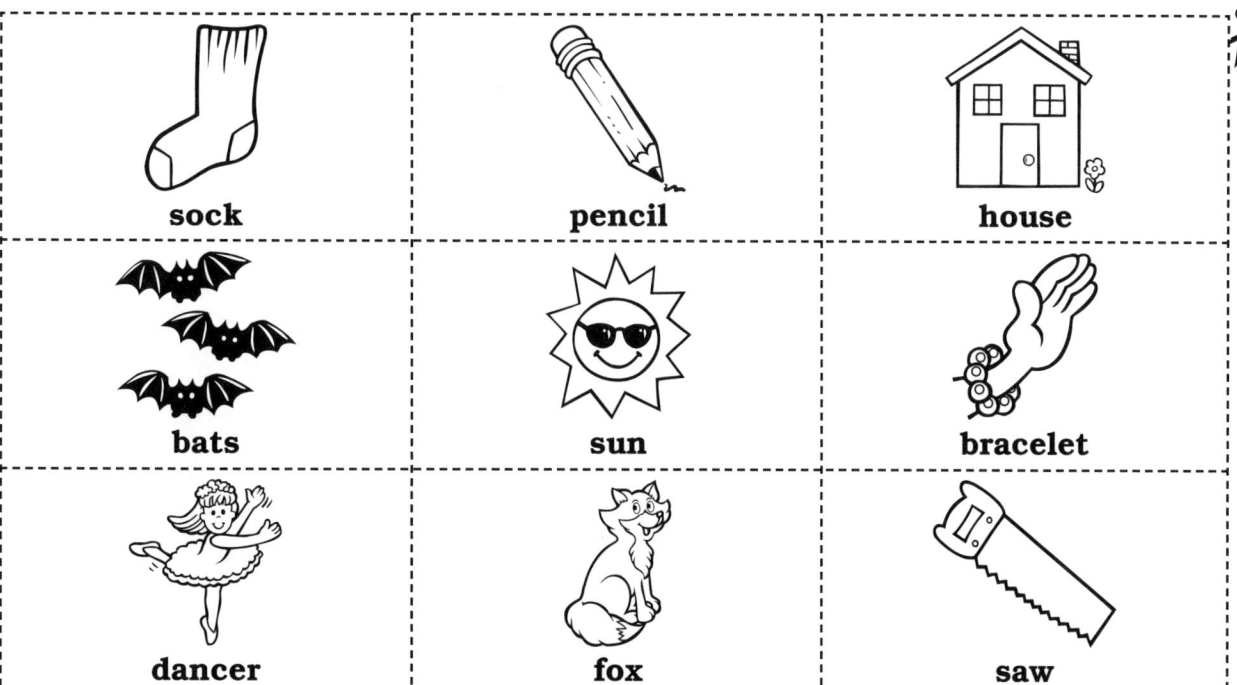

saw	dancer	pencil
house	sock	sun
bracelet	fox	bats
sock	pencil	house
bats	sun	bracelet
dancer	fox	saw

Homework Partner   Date   Speech-Language Pathologist

Combo S Words

Which Is?

Directions: Read/say the following questions aloud. Say the answers aloud, using your best S sound.

1. Which is heavier - a **grasshopper** or a **house**?

2. Which is smaller - a **whistle** or a **saw**?

3. Which is noisier - a **seal** or a **mouse**?

4. Which is lighter - a **sock** or a **dinosaur**?

5. Which is bigger - a **bicycle** or a **purse**?

6. Which is yummier - a **popsicle** or a **sandwich**?

Answers: 1. house, 2. whistle, 3. seal, 4. sock, 5. bicycle, 6. popsicle

Homework Partner   Date   Speech-Language Pathologist

Combo S Words

Spinner Action

Directions: Read/say aloud the picture–words. If you prefer, glue this page to construction paper for added durability. Cut out the arrow/dial. Use a brad to connect the dial to the circle. Spin the spinner. When you land on a picture, read/say the word aloud, using your best S sound.

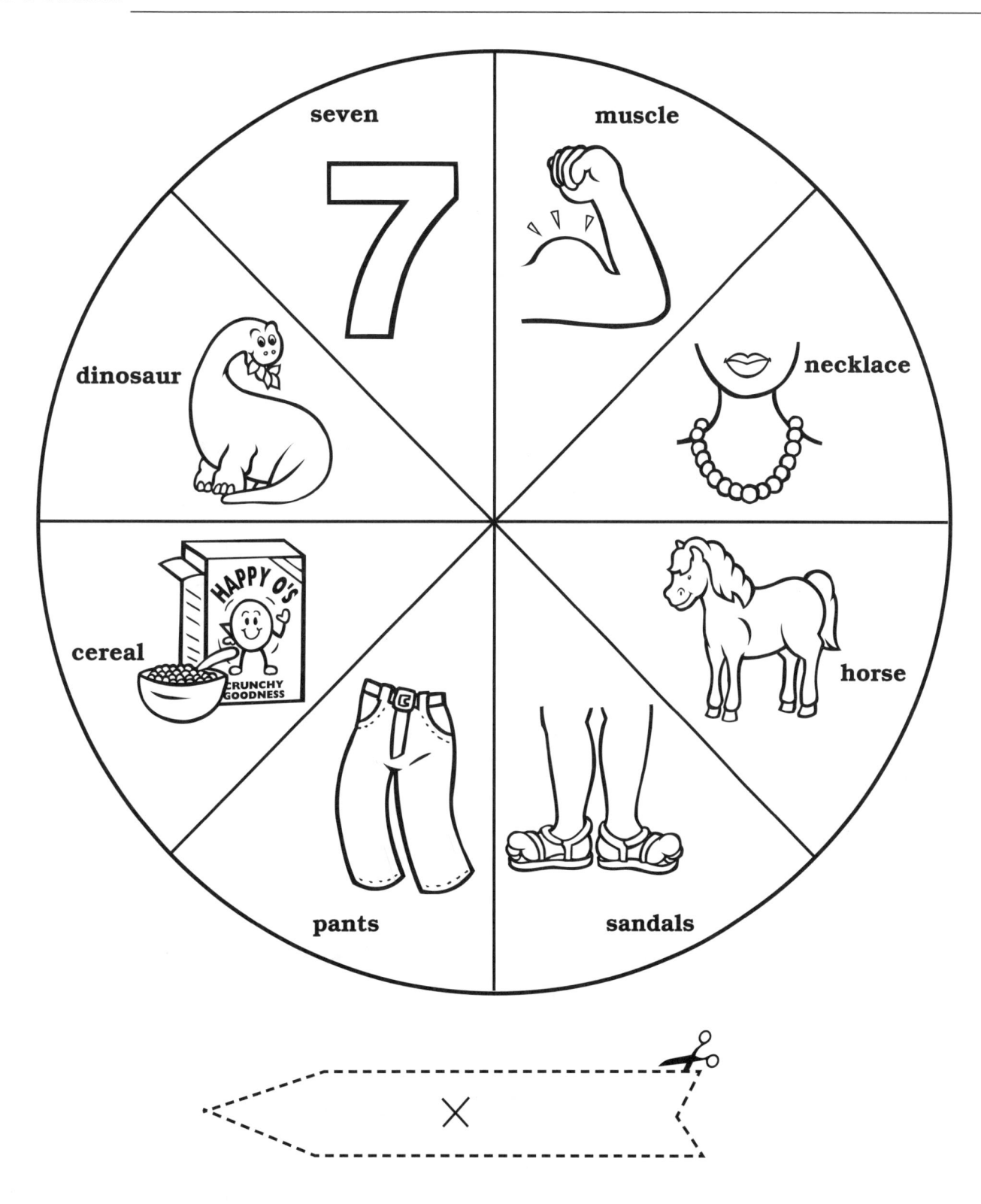

- seven
- muscle
- necklace
- horse
- sandals
- pants
- cereal
- dinosaur

Homework Partner Date Speech-Language Pathologist

Combo S Words

S Cube Roll

Directions: Assemble the cube as follows: Glue onto construction paper for added durability. Cut along the dotted lines. Fold on solid lines and glue as indicated. To play: Roll the cube. Read/say aloud the word you see using your best S sound.

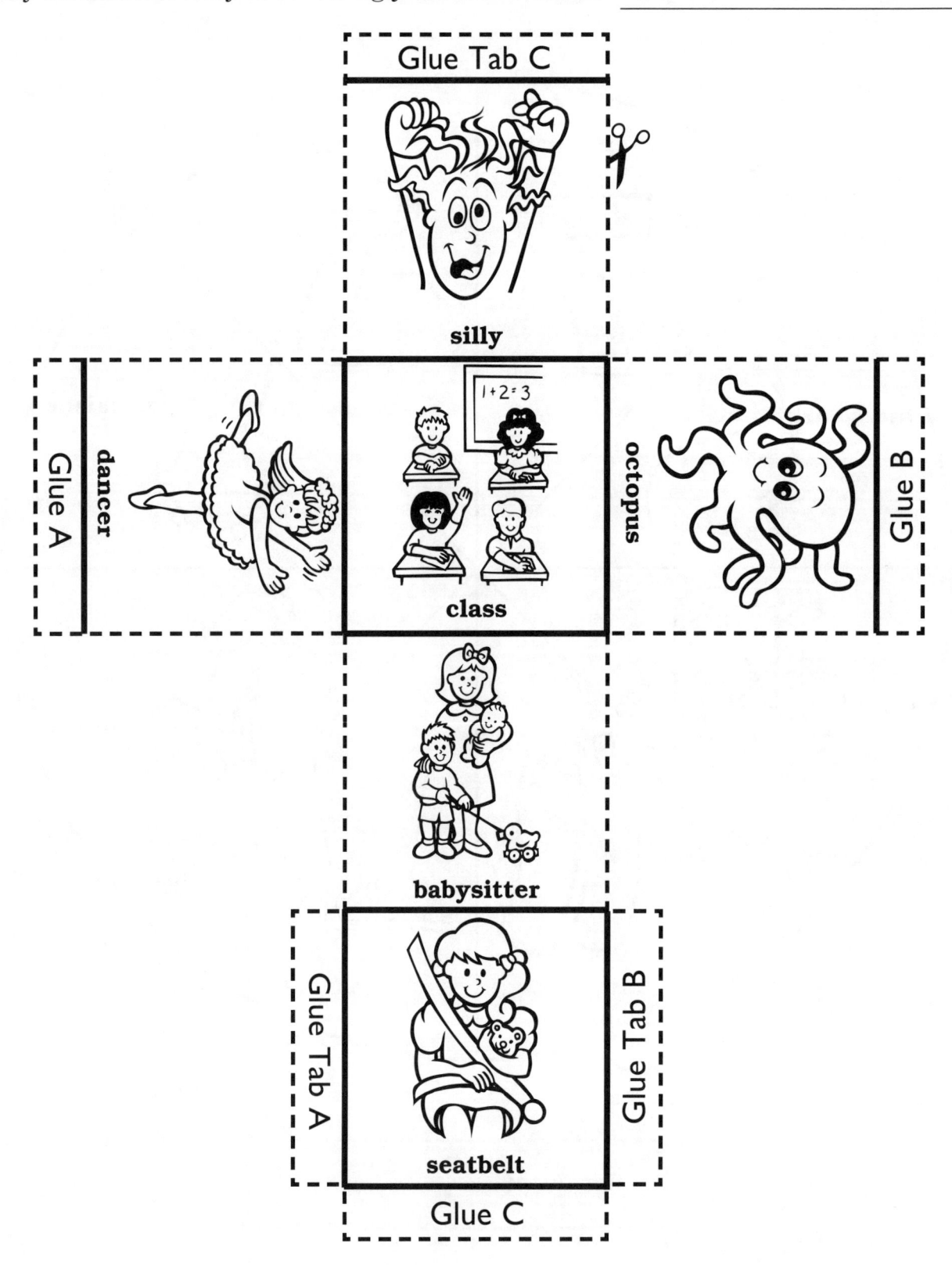

Glue Tab C

silly

Glue A | dancer | class | octopus | Glue B

babysitter

Glue Tab A | seatbelt | Glue Tab B

Glue C

Homework Partner | Date | Speech-Language Pathologist

Combo S Words

Football Mania!

Directions: Read/say aloud the picture–words. Cut out the footballs and place them at the 10 yard line on opposite sides of the field. First player flips a coin and moves 10 yards (heads) or 20 yards (tails). Say the word you land on aloud. Play continues in turn. First player to score a touchdown wins. Next time you play, switch sides.

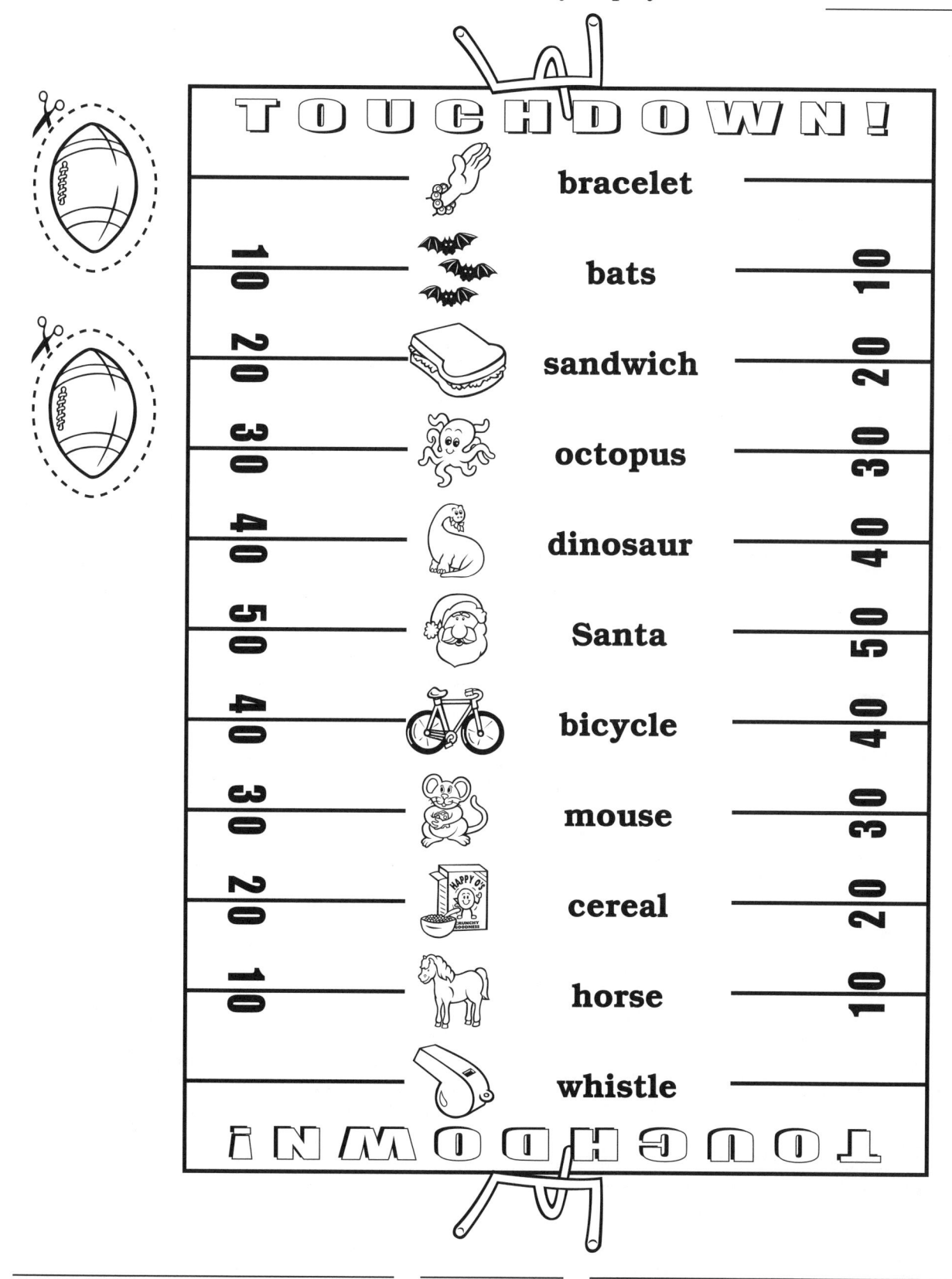

TOUCHDOWN!

- bracelet
- bats
- sandwich
- octopus
- dinosaur
- Santa
- bicycle
- mouse
- cereal
- horse
- whistle

TOUCHDOWN!

Homework Partner | Date | Speech-Language Pathologist

Combo S Words

Unscramble the Words

Directions: Read/say the picture–words on the right. Then, unscramble the words and write the answers in the blanks. Read/say your answers aloud. Fill in the letters from the boxes to make a word at the bottom of the page. Say the word again using your good S sound.

1. **umslce** ___ ___ ___ [1] ___ ___

2. **tpans** ___ [2] ___ ___ ___

3. **nvese** ___ ___ ___ ___ [3]

4. **sldaans** ___ ___ ___ [4] ___ ___ ___

5. **cybciel** ___ ___ ___ ___ ___ [5] ___

6. **resoh** ___ ___ ___ ___ [6]

muscle

sandals

horse

pants

bicycle

7 seven

Clue: What goes on a birthday cake?

[1] [2] [3] [4] [5] [6]

Answers: 1-muscle, 2-pants, 3-seven, 4-sandals, 5-bicycle, 6-horse, Clue-candle

Homework Partner — Date — Speech-Language Pathologist

Combo S Words

S Phrase It

Directions: Assemble the cubes as follows: If you prefer, glue onto construction paper for added durability. Cut along the dotted lines. Fold on solid lines and glue as indicated. To play: Roll both cubes. Read/say the words and pictures together to make up a phrase ("happy dinosaur").

Cube 1 faces: cereal, house, class, bicycle, sandwich, dinosaur

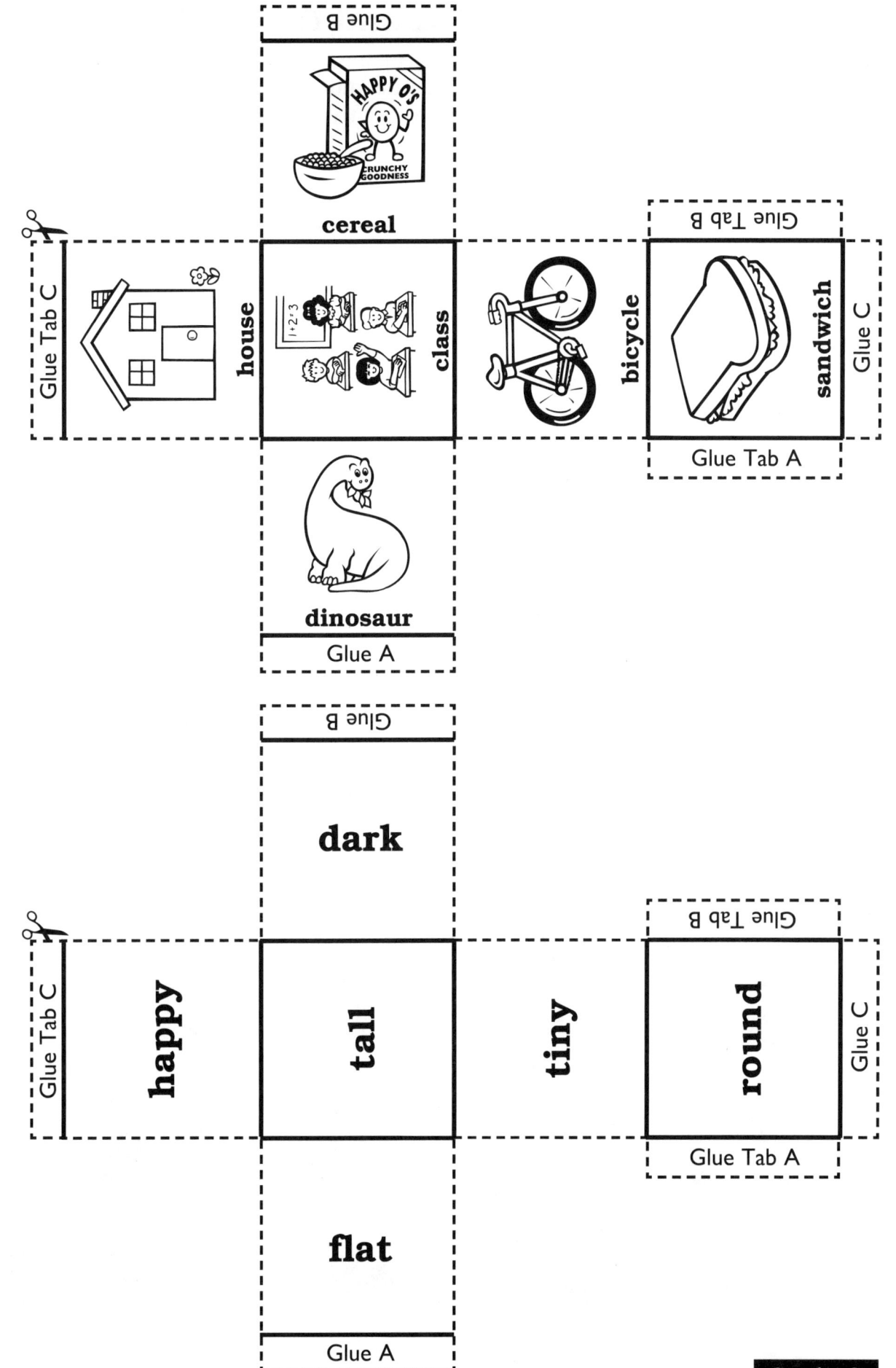

Cube 2 faces: dark, happy, tall, tiny, round, flat

Combo S Phrases

X and O

Directions: Cut out each X and O below. Have each player/partner choose X or O. The first player reads/says the picture phrase aloud and places an X or O on the square. Play continues in turn. The first person to get three in a row wins.

a silly grin	the white house	lucky seven
a green grasshopper	a big muscle	the quick fox
gold necklace	broken sandals	ballet dancer

X X X X X

O O O O O

Homework Partner   Date   Speech-Language Pathologist

Combo S Phrases

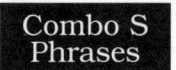

Answer It!

Directions: Read the questions below and choose the phrase that best answers them. Put an X on the correct answers. Read/say the phrases aloud using your good S sound.

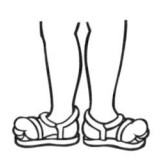

1. What animal do you find at the zoo?
   ____ a) a big dinosaur
   ____ b) a wet seal

2. What jewelry is worn on your neck?
   ____ a) a pretty necklace
   ____ b) a gold bracelet

3. What food can make your mouth cold?
   ____ a) a peanut butter sandwich
   ____ b) an orange popsicle

4. What needs a pedal to make it move?
   ____ a) the long sailboat
   ____ b) the red bicycle

5. What do you wear on your feet?
   ____ a) the brown sandals
   ____ b) the blue pants

Answer key on page 279

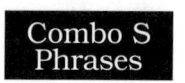

Homework Partner   Date   Speech-Language Pathologist

Combo S Phrases

#BK-290 Webber® Artic Fun Sheets • ©2001 Super Duper® Publications • www.superduperinc.com • 1-800-277-8737

49

Number It Up!

Directions: Read/say aloud the picture–words. Number the words in the Word Bank below from 1-8 in any order you desire. Then, put the words on the line below that match the corresponding numbers ("paper pants"). Read/say the phrases aloud using your good S sound. _____

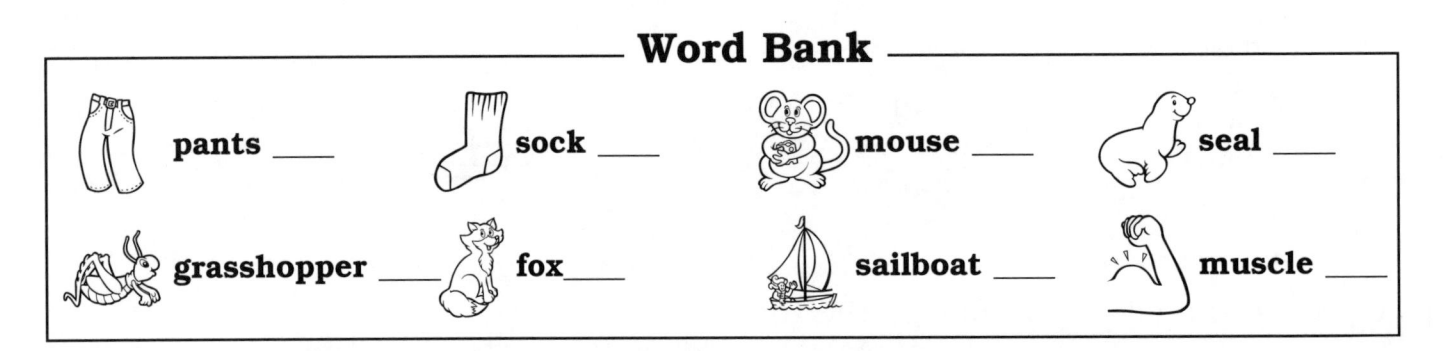

Word Bank

pants ___   sock ___   mouse ___   seal ___

grasshopper ___   fox ___   sailboat ___   muscle ___

1. red _____

2. paper _____

3. wood _____

4. metal _____

5. one _____

6. heavy _____

7. tall _____

8. brown _____

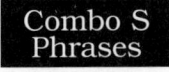

Homework Partner   Date   Speech-Language Pathologist   Combo S Phrases

Sentence Cards

Directions: Read/say the picture–words below. Cut out the cards, keeping the A and the B cards separate. Place the cards face down in two piles. Flip over one A and one B card and make up a silly sentence. Read/say aloud each sentence using your good S sound. _____

A	A	A
purple	new	cold
loud	quiet	friendly

B	B	B
sandals	bicycle	cereal
whistle	octopus	bats

Combo S Sentences

51

Complete It!

Directions: Draw a line from the picture phrase in column A to a phrase in column B. Read/say each complete sentence aloud using your best S sound.

A   **B**

The ham sandwich   has a flat tire.

The charm bracelet   ran into the woods.

My bicycle   took a nap.

The quick fox   had cheese on it.

The tired seal   hid under a chair.

The little mouse   hopped over a flower.

A huge grasshopper   was a birthday gift.

The ballet dancer   took a bow.

Homework Partner   Date   Speech-Language Pathologist

Combo S Sentences

Where Is It?

Directions: Read/say aloud the picture–words below. Then, cut out all the cards below keeping A and B separate. Choose two pictures and make up phrases using "on," "under," or "over" ("The clown stands under the sun"). Use your best S sound.

A clown	A bread	A plant	A frog
A plum	A drum	A triangle	A flower

B whistle	B Santa	B bats	B seven	B octopus
B saw	B purse	B pencil	B babysitter	B sun

Homework Partner · Date · Speech-Language Pathologist

Combo S Sentences

Answer with a Question

Directions: Read each statement below. Then, ask a question about the statement. ("This tool cuts wood. What cuts wood?") Use the pictures as hints. Read/say each question aloud. Each correct question earns one point. The student with the most points wins.

Answer   **Question**

1. This animal lived thousands of years ago.   _____

2. This is how the clown acts.   _____

3. This animal likes to eat cheese.   _____

4. This tool cuts wood.   _____

5. This is something you live in.   _____

6. This is something you wear around your wrist.   _____

7. This is something you eat for breakfast.   _____

8. This is something you see in the sky in the morning. _____

Homework Partner   Date   Speech-Language Pathologist

Combo S Sentences

R Sound

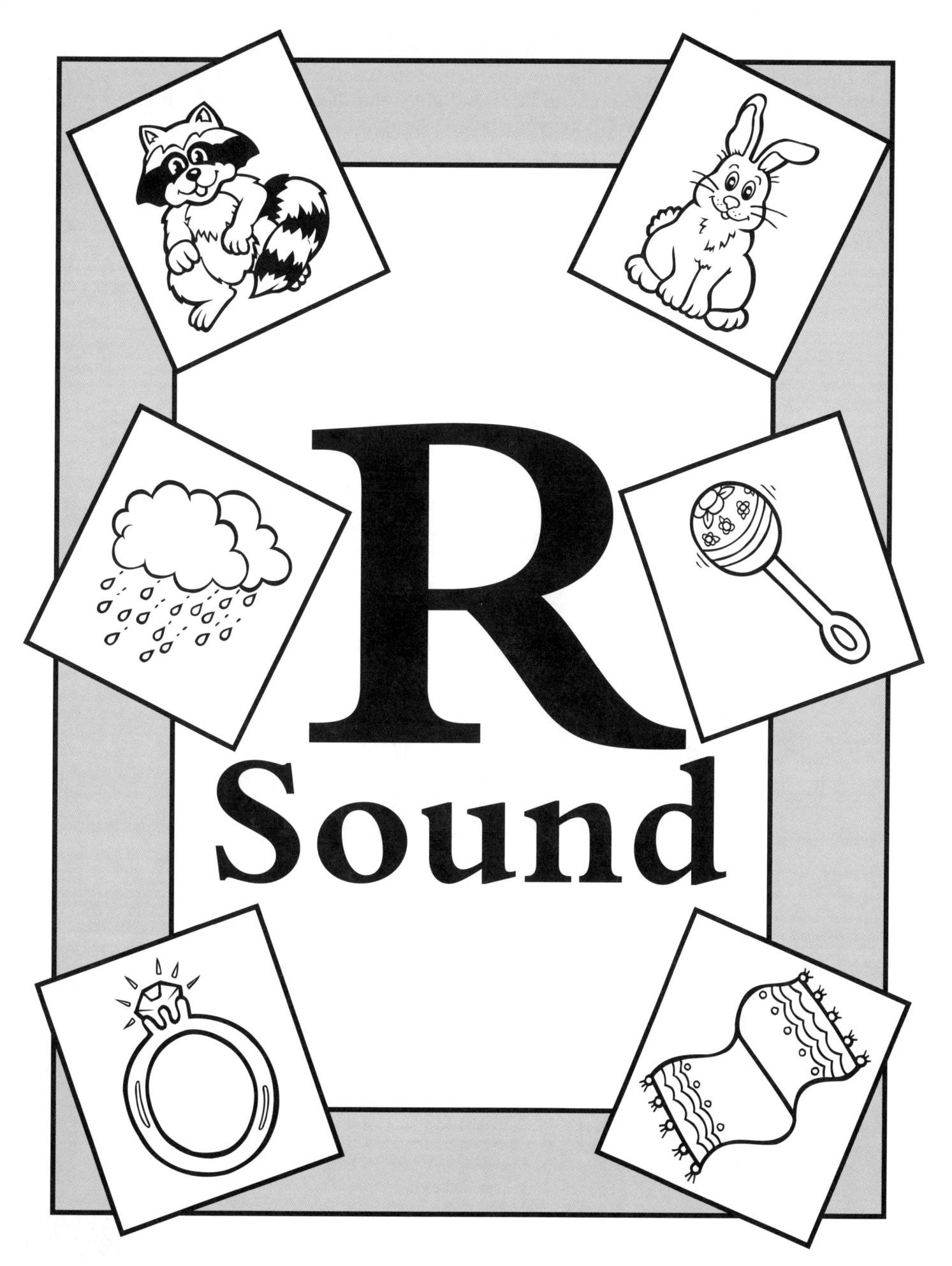

R Cube Roll

Directions: Assemble the cube as follows: Glue onto construction paper for added durability. Cut along the dotted lines. Fold on solid lines and glue as indicated. To play: Roll the cube. Read/say aloud the word you see using your best R sound.

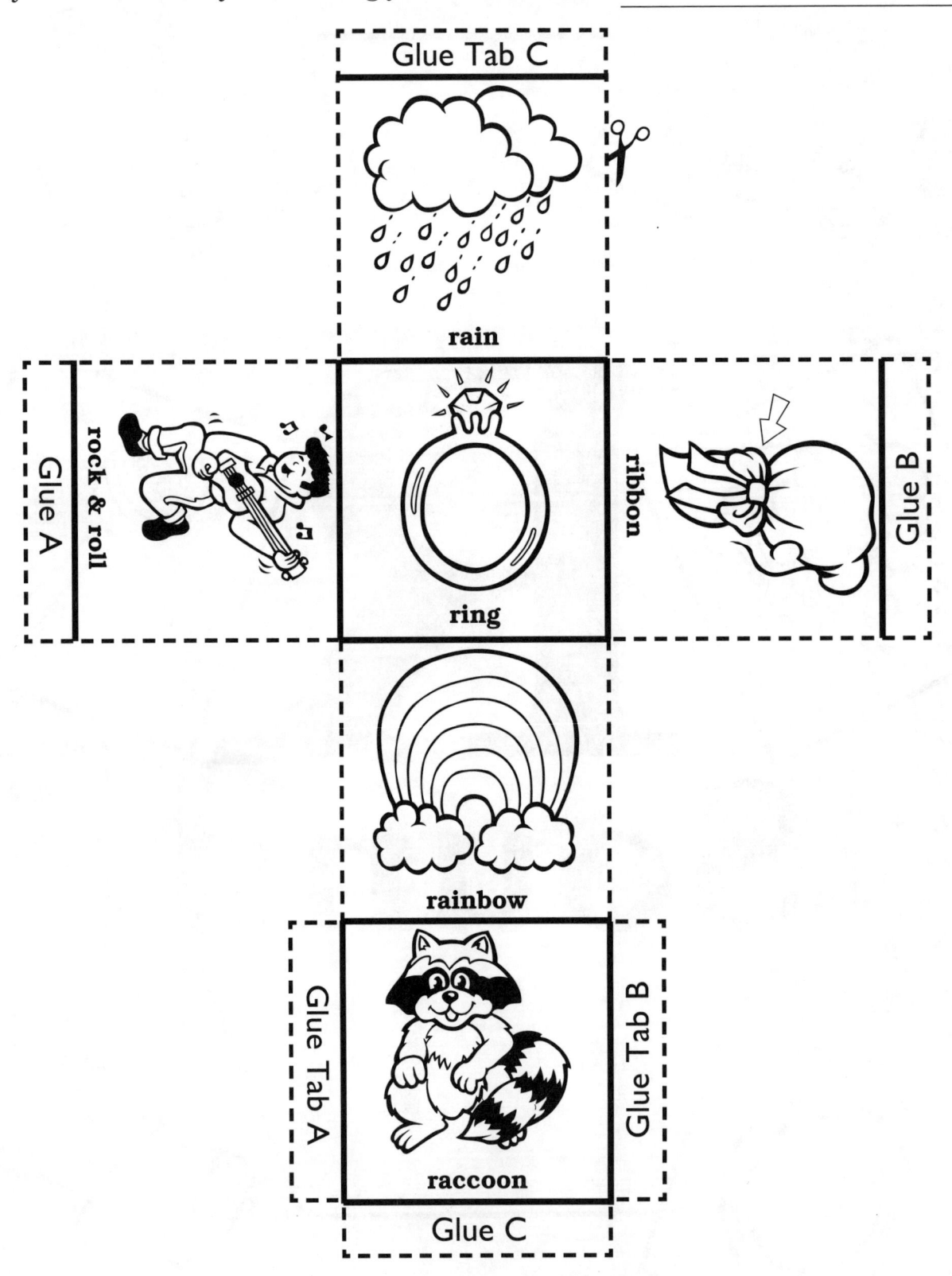

Glue Tab C

rain

rock & roll | Glue A

ring

ribbon | Glue B

rainbow

Glue Tab A | raccoon | Glue Tab B

Glue C

Homework Partner Date Speech-Language Pathologist

Initial R Words

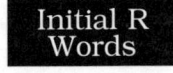

56

3 Games in 1

Directions: Say aloud the picture–words below, using your good R sound.
Then, play one of the following games:
- ☐ Lotto – Caller reads out a word and student repeats the word and covers it with a token/chip.
- ☐ Tic–Tac–Toe – Each time you write an **X** or **O**, say the word you mark over.
- ☐ Memory – Cut out all the cards and place face down. Try to find matching pairs. Say aloud each word you find. Keep all matches. _____

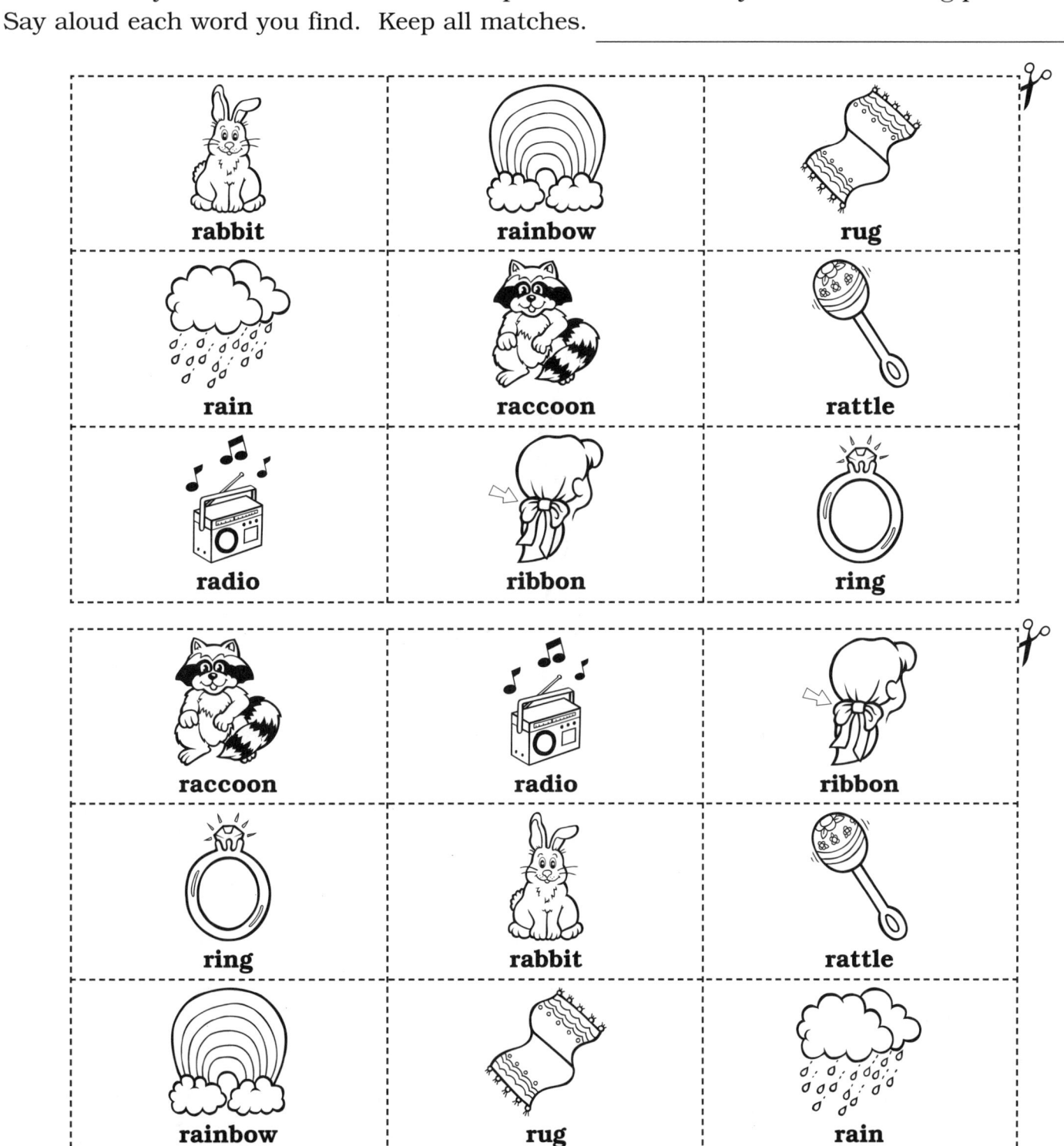

rabbit	rainbow	rug
rain	raccoon	rattle
radio	ribbon	ring
raccoon	radio	ribbon
ring	rabbit	rattle
rainbow	rug	rain

_____ _____ _____ **Initial R Words**
Homework Partner Date Speech-Language Pathologist

57

Flower Power

Directions: Read/say aloud the picture–words. Then, cut out the flower petals. Read/say aloud each picture-word again as you glue/tape or place the petals on the flower.

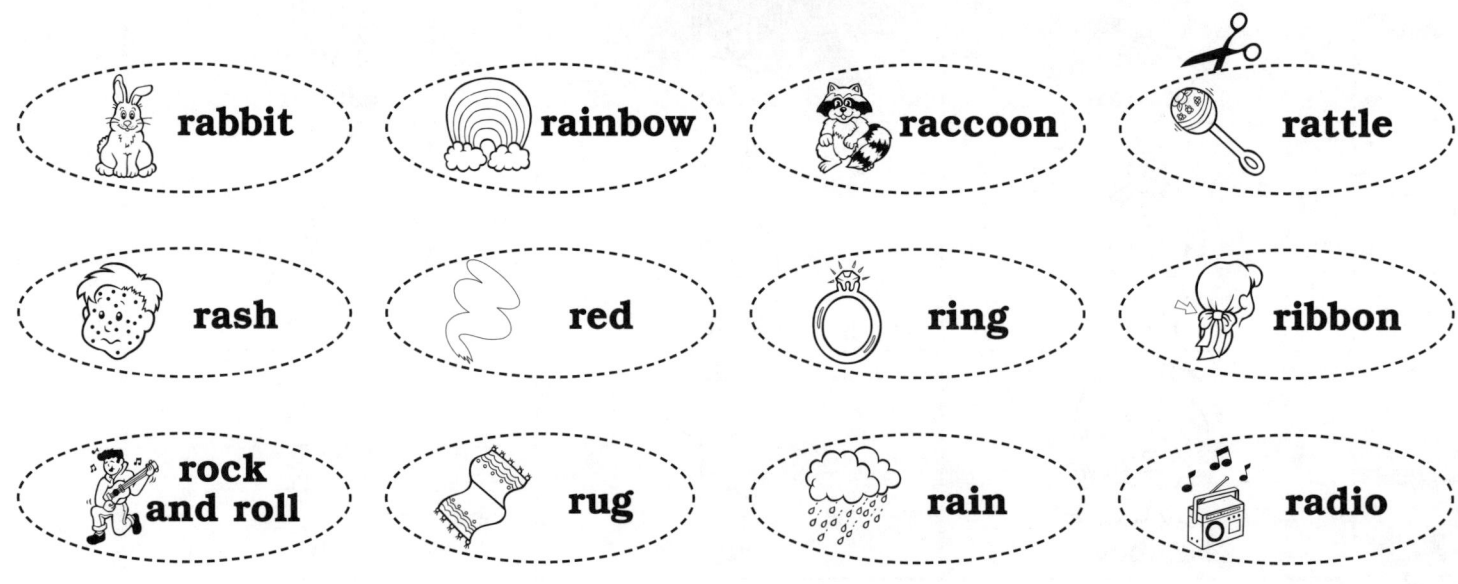

rabbit   rainbow   raccoon   rattle

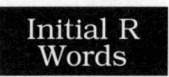

rash   red   ring   ribbon

rock and roll   rug   rain   radio

Homework Partner   Date   Speech-Language Pathologist

Initial R Words

R Spinner Action

Directions: Read/say aloud the picture–words below. If you prefer, glue this page to construction paper for added durability. Cut out the arrow/dial. Use a brad to connect the dial to the circle. Spin the spinner. When you land on a picture, read/say the word aloud, using your best R sound.

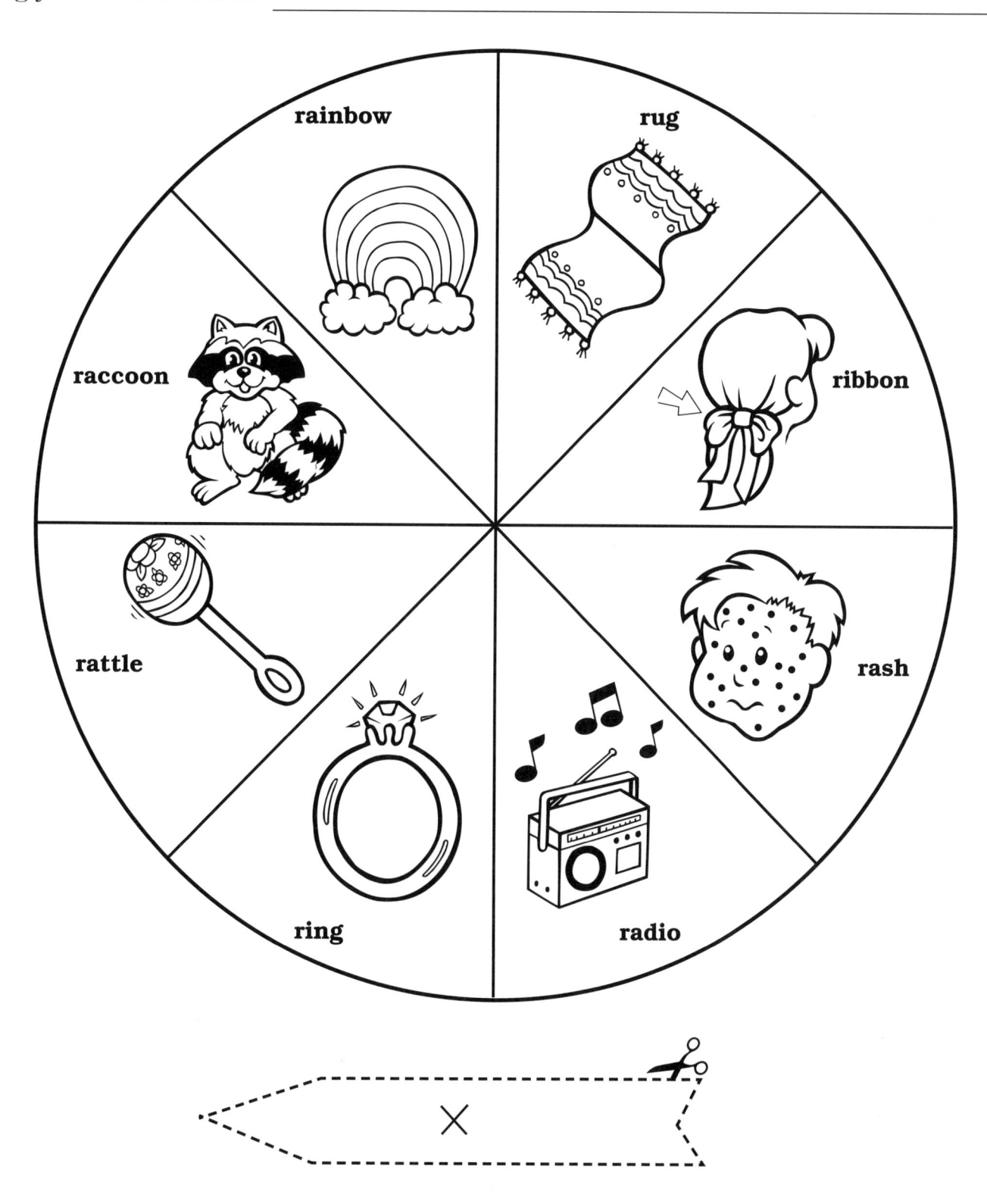

- rainbow
- rug
- ribbon
- rash
- radio
- ring
- rattle
- raccoon

Homework Partner   Date   Speech-Language Pathologist   Initial R Words

Who Said That?

Directions: Read/say each R picture–word aloud. Read the statements in the middle. Then, ask, **"Who said that?"** Answer with the correct word. Then, draw a line from the sentence to the correct picture.

rock & roll

radio

ribbon

ring

"I like to hop."

"I go in your hair."

"I am a kind of music."

"I am a baby's toy."

"I am some jewelry."

"I am itchy."

"Turn me on to hear some tunes."

rattle

rash

rabbit

Homework Partner   Date   Speech-Language Pathologist

Initial R Words

Which Is?

Directions: Read/say the following questions aloud. Then, answer each question using your best R sound.

1. Which is heavier - a **rabbit** or a **balloon**?

2. Which is smaller - a **ring** or a **pool**?

3. Which is noisier - a **leaf** or a **rattle**?

4. Which is lighter - a **ribbon** or a **whale**?

5. Which is worse - a **rash** or **jelly beans**?

6. Which disappears - a **rainbow** or an **apple**?

7. Which is wetter - **rain** or a **lamp**?

8. Which is louder - a **radio** or a **snail**?

Answers: 1. rabbit, 2. ring, 3. rattle, 4. ribbon, 5. rash, 6. rainbow, 7. rain, 8. radio

Homework Partner   Date   Speech-Language Pathologist   Initial R Words

Picture Scenes

Directions: Read/say aloud the picture–words below. Then, fill in the missing word from the sentences in the picture boxes. Say the word aloud again. Use the Word Bank for clues.

Word Bank

radio rain rock & roll

ribbon rabbit rainbow

A _____ hops.

There is a pot of gold at the end of the _____.

He plays _____.

I like the music on the _____.

She has a _____ in her ponytail.

The cloud has a lot of _____ in it.

Homework Partner · Date · Speech-Language Pathologist

Initial R Words

R Cube Roll

Directions: Assemble the cube as follows: Glue onto construction paper for added durability. Cut along the dotted lines. Fold on solid lines and glue as indicated. To play: Roll the cube. Read/say aloud the word you see using your best R sound.

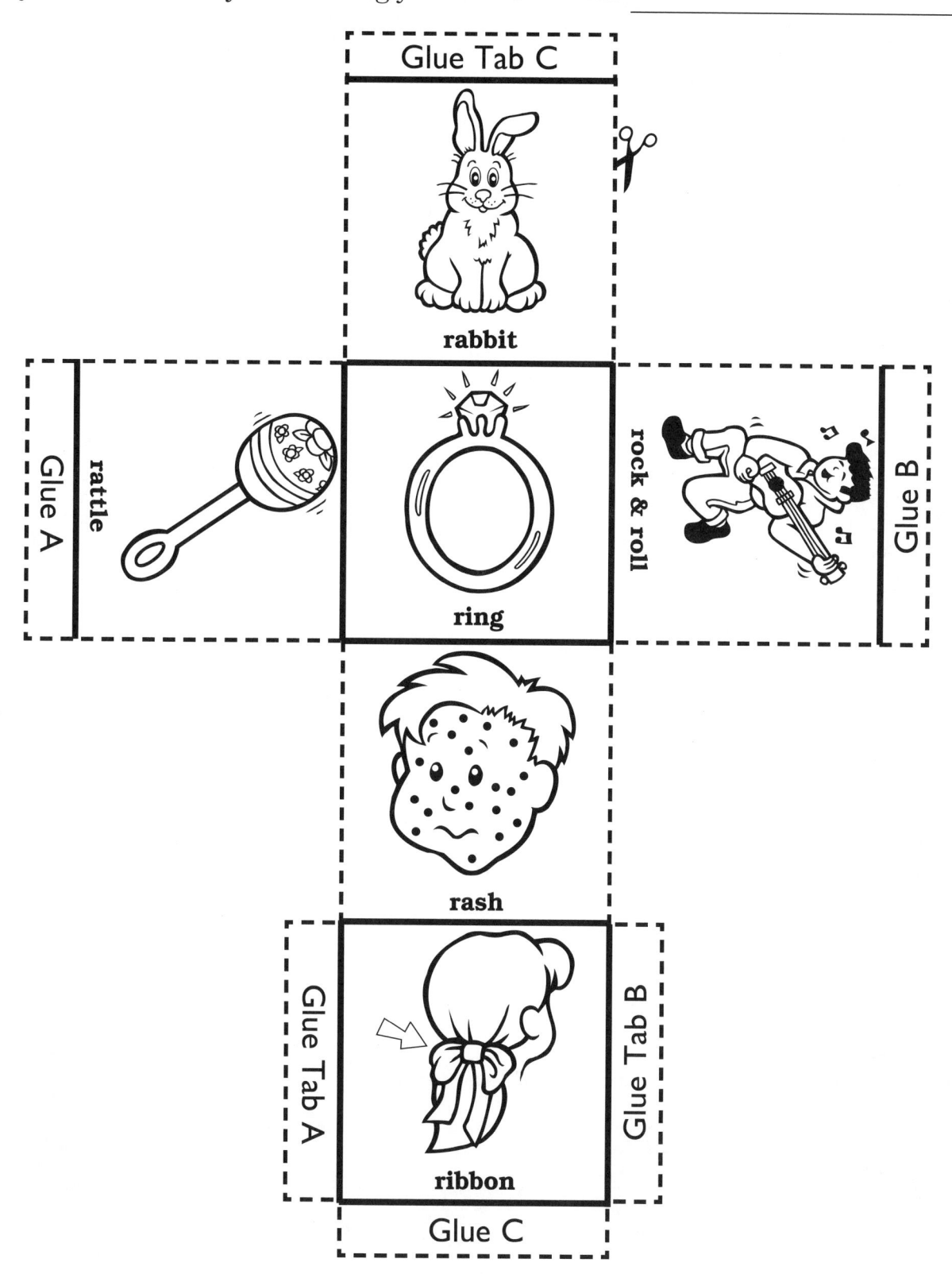

Glue Tab C

rabbit

Glue A | rattle | ring | rock & roll | Glue B

rash

Glue Tab A | ribbon | Glue Tab B

Glue C

Homework Partner   Date   Speech-Language Pathologist

Initial R Words

#BK-290 Webber® Artic Fun Sheets • ©2001 Super Duper® Publications • www.superduperinc.com • 1-800-277-8737

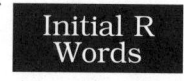

63

Name It!

Directions: Practice saying aloud each R picture–word. Then, read each statement in the middle. Name the item that goes with each statement. Draw a line from a sentence to each correct picture. Say the words again, using your good R sound.

rock & roll

Name something that hops.

rattle

radio

Name a type of music.

rash

Name a baby's toy.

ribbon

Name a piece of jewelry.

rabbit

ring

Name a flower.

rose

Homework Partner　　Date　　Speech-Language Pathologist

Initial R Words

Mirror Image

Directions: Hold this page up to a mirror and read/say the words aloud that appear. Then, write the words correctly on the lines. Use the pictures on the page to help you. Say the words again, using your good R sound.

rabbit _____

rainbow _____

ring _____

rash _____

rock & roll _____

red _____

rug _____

rain _____

raccoon _____

rattle _____

Homework Partner   Date   Speech-Language Pathologist

Initial R Words

65

What's on the Shelf?

Directions: Read/say aloud the picture–words below. Cut out the pictures. Glue/tape or place each picture on the shelf. Each time you put an item on the shelf, say "_____ on the shelf." ("raccoon on the shelf"), using your best R sound.

rabbit	rainbow	ring	rug	raccoon
rattle	radio	ribbon	rain	rock & roll

Homework Partner   Date   Speech-Language Pathologist

Initial R Phrases

Ask and Answer

Directions: Practice saying each R picture–word. Then, read each statement in the middle. Answer with the phrase: "The_____ does!" filling in the correct R word. Then, draw a line from the sentence to the correct picture.

rabbit

What plays music?

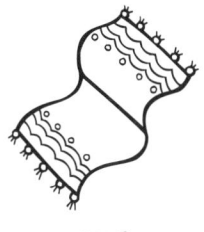

rug

What covers the floor?"

raccoon

What hops?

What has a mask?

radio

rainbow

What goes in a girl's hair?

What is found in the sky?

ribbon

rash

What falls from clouds?

What is itchy?

rain

Homework Partner   Date   Speech-Language Pathologist

Initial R Phrases

How Many?

Directions: Look at the pictures and count the number of items in each box. Write the number on the line. Then, read/say the phrase aloud using your best R sound ("four apples").

1. _____

2. _____

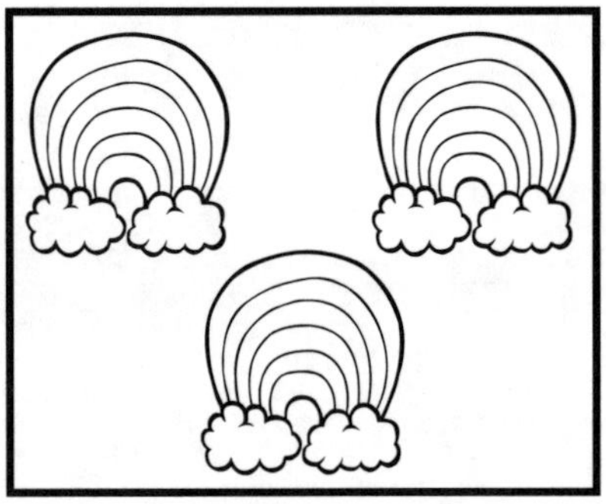

3. _____

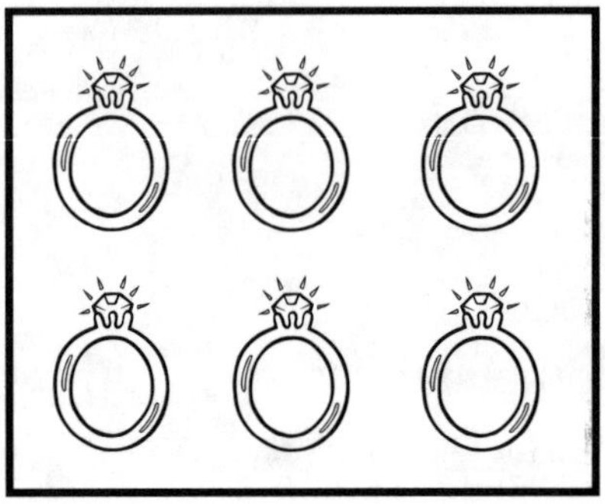

4. _____

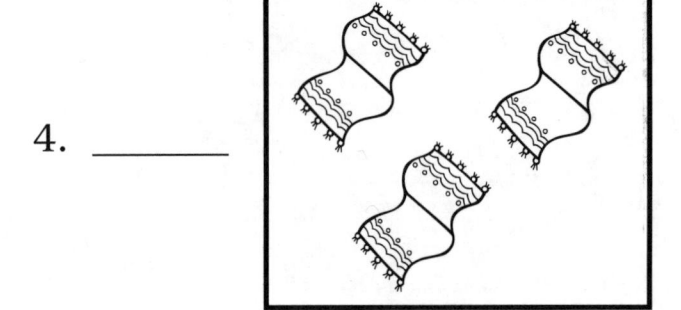

5. _____

6. _____

7. _____

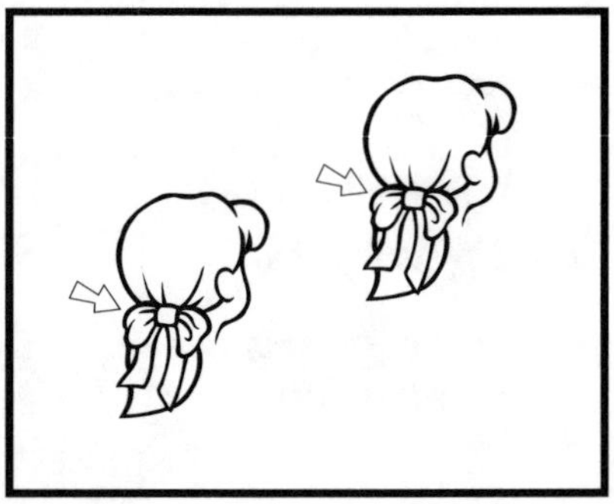

8. _____

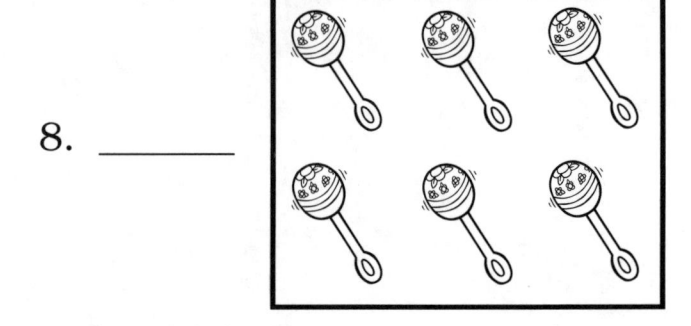

_____   _____   _____   Initial R Phrases
Homework Partner   Date   Speech-Language Pathologist

Sentence Match

Directions: Read/say aloud the picture–words on the right. Then, match the picture to the word it goes with and make up a sentence. Say each sentence aloud using your best R sound.

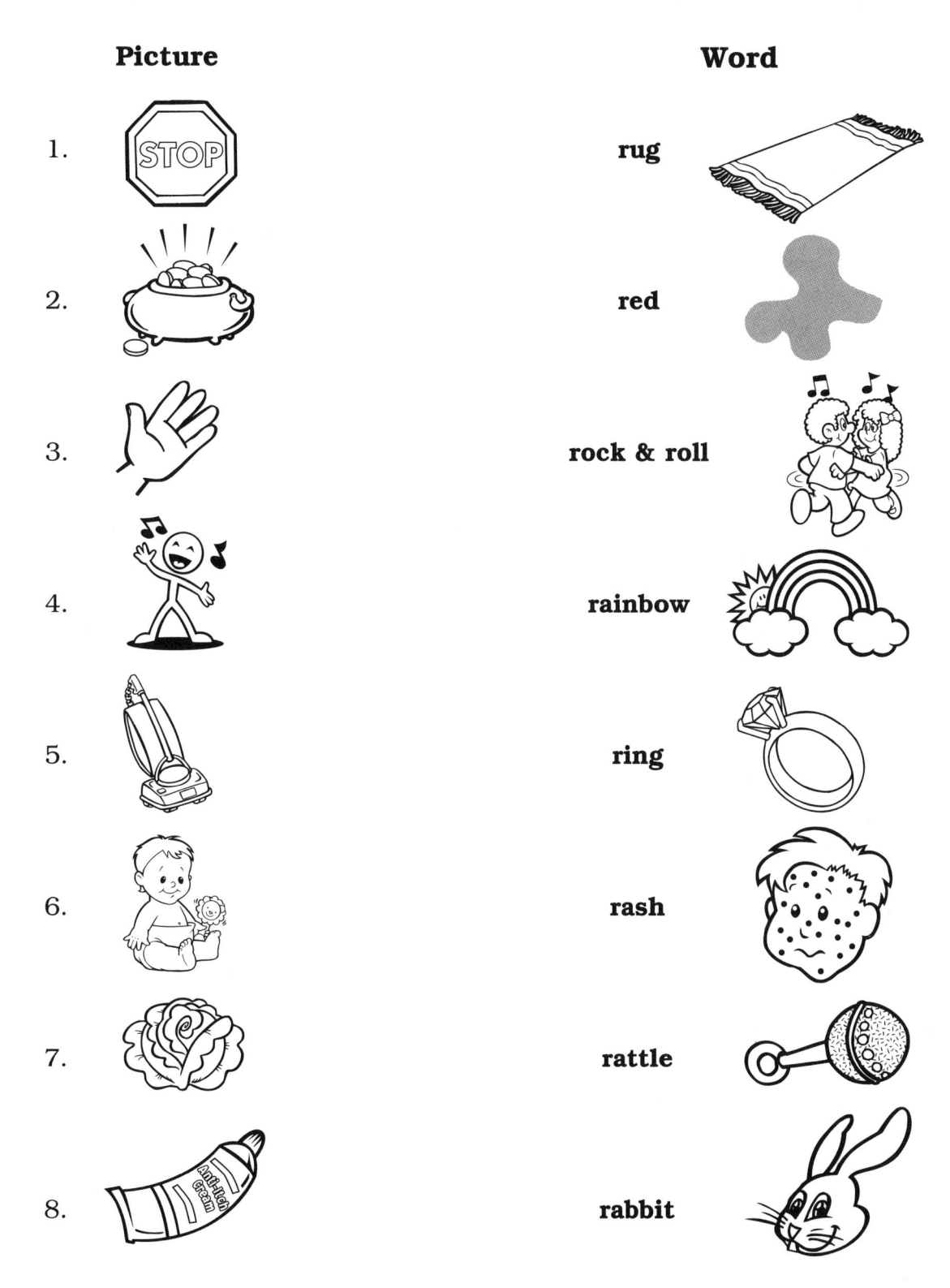

Picture   **Word**

1.   rug
2.   red
3.   rock & roll
4.   rainbow
5.   ring
6.   rash
7.   rattle
8.   rabbit

Answer key: 1-red, 2-rainbow, 3-ring, 4-rock & roll, 5-rug, 6-rattle, 7-rabbit, 8-rash

Homework Partner   Date   Speech-Language Pathologist

Initial R Sentences

#BK-290 Webber® Artic Fun Sheets • ©2001 Super Duper® Publications • www.superduperinc.com • 1-800-277-8737

69

Measure Up

Directions: Cut out the ruler and measure the objects below. Write the length below the picture. Read/say aloud the measurements. ("The doll is two inches long.")

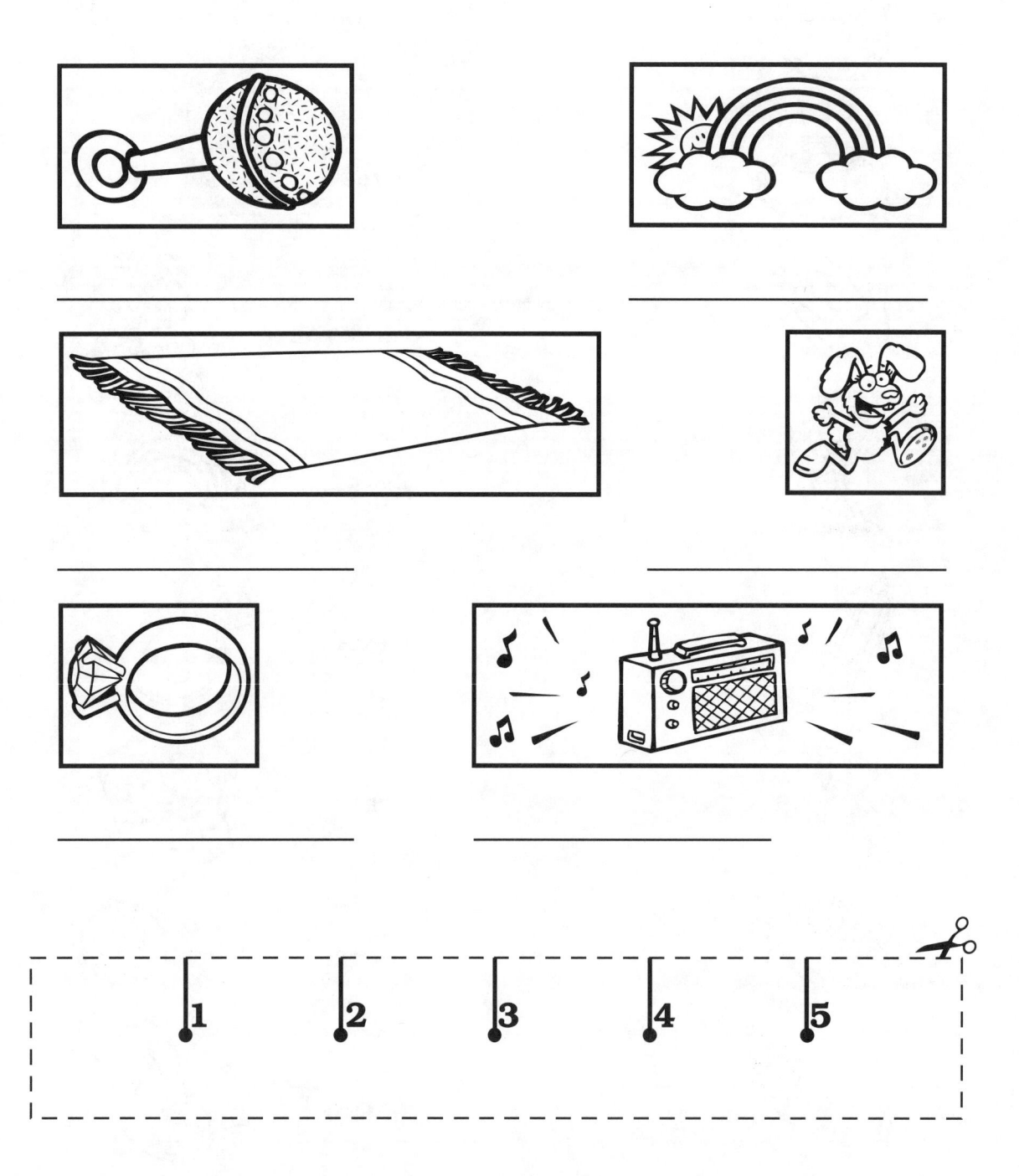

_____ _____

Homework Partner   Date   Speech-Language Pathologist

Initial R Sentences

70   #BK-290 Webber® Artic Fun Sheets • ©2001 Super Duper® Publications • www.superduperinc.com • 1-800-277-8737

Anything Machine

Directions: Tell your partner what each item costs in the vending machine. For example, "The rabbit costs one dollar." Use your best R sound.

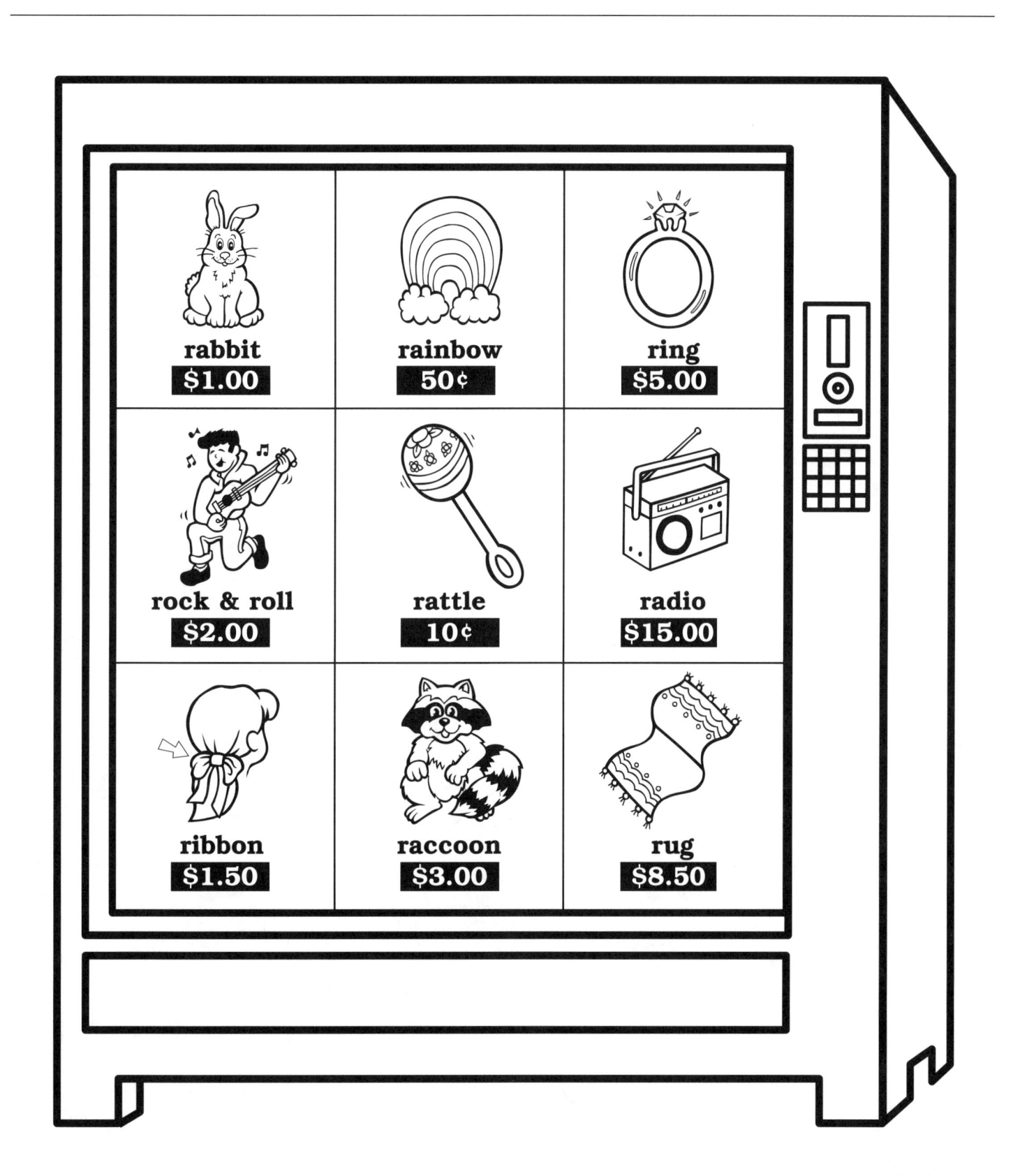

rabbit $1.00	rainbow 50¢	ring $5.00
rock & roll $2.00	rattle 10¢	radio $15.00
ribbon $1.50	raccoon $3.00	rug $8.50

Homework Partner   Date   Speech-Language Pathologist

Initial R Sentences

Things That Go Together

Directions: Match the words on the left to the pictures on the right by writing the correct number in the blank spaces. Read/say your answers aloud using your best R sound ("key/car").

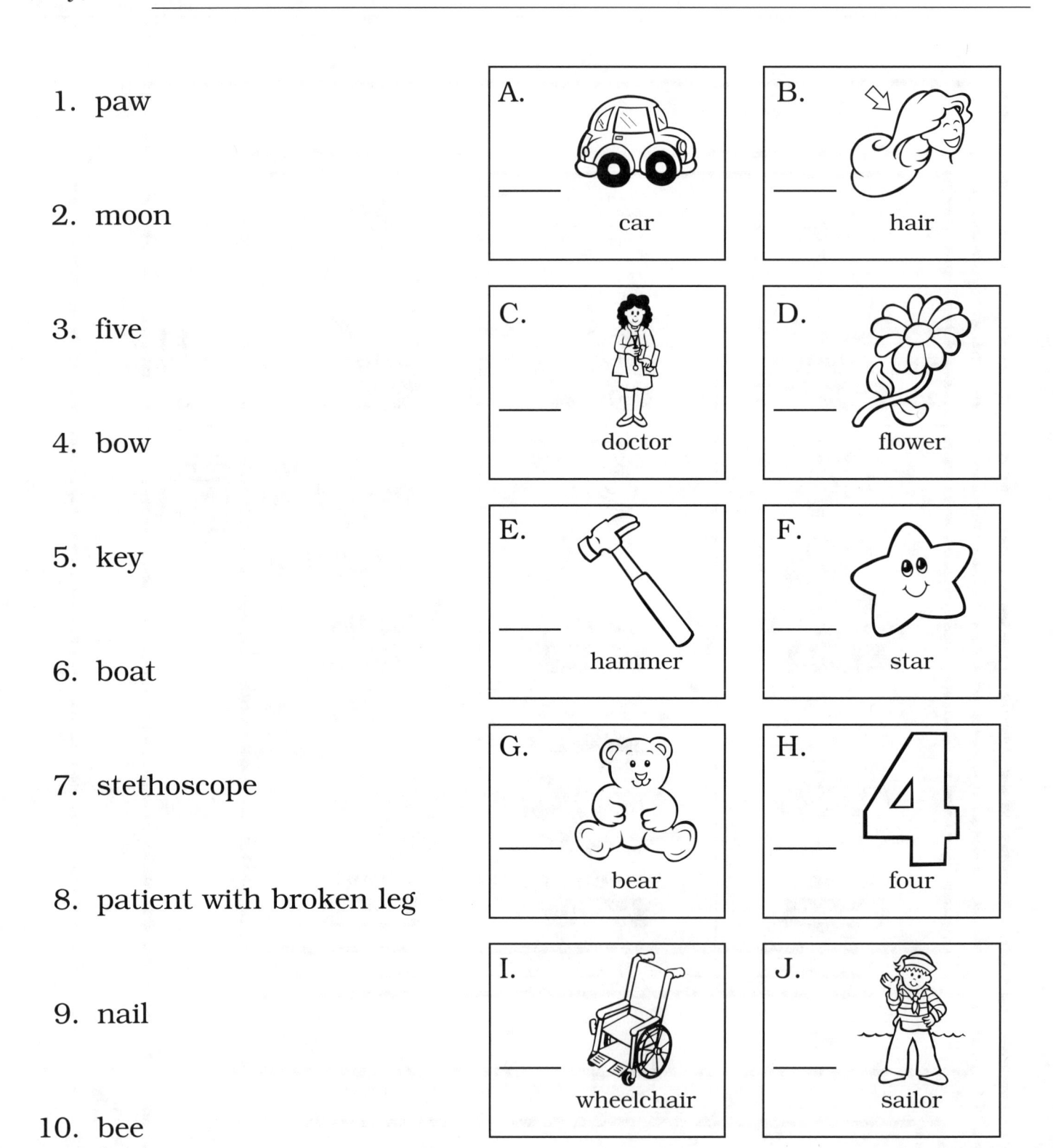

1. paw

2. moon

3. five

4. bow

5. key

6. boat

7. stethoscope

8. patient with broken leg

9. nail

10. bee

A. ___ car
B. ___ hair
C. ___ doctor
D. ___ flower
E. ___ hammer
F. ___ star
G. ___ bear
H. ___ four
I. ___ wheelchair
J. ___ sailor

Answer key on page 279

Homework Partner   Date   Speech-Language Pathologist

Final R Words

72   #BK-290 Webber® Artic Fun Sheets • ©2001 Super Duper® Publications • www.superduperinc.com • 1-800-277-8737

Memory Game

Directions: Read/say aloud each picture–word below. Cut out the pictures. Place all cards face down. Try to match the cards. Say each card as you pick it up, using your good R sound. Keep all matches. Most matches wins!

car	doctor	hammer	bear
wheelchair	hair	flower	star
four	sailor	car	doctor
hammer	bear	wheelchair	hair
flower	star	four	sailor

Homework Partner　　　Date　　　Speech-Language Pathologist

Final R Words

What Doesn't Belong?

Directions: Look at the pictures. Say each word aloud. Circle the item that does not belong. Then, tell why the picture doesn't belong. Use your good R sound. _____

1.	plane	car	balloon	bike
2.	saw	apple	hammer	screwdriver
3.	four	nine	two	B
4.	elephant	whale	bear	lion
5.	socks	rectangle	diamond	star
6.	flower	plant	pencil	clover
7.	doctor	camel	sailor	spaceman
8.	whale	lobster	bulldozer	octopus

Homework Partner Date Speech-Language Pathologist

Final R Words

Name It!

Directions: Practice saying aloud each R word-picture. Then, read each statement in the middle. Name the item that goes with each statement. Draw a line from a sentence to each correct picture. Say the words again, using your good R sound.

bear

wheelchair

star

car

Name something you drive.

Name something that lives in the woods.

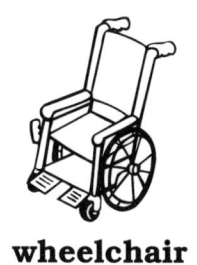

Name something you use to hit nails.

Name something you see at night.

Name something you see in a hospital.

Name something that is cut.

Name something that smells good.

flower

hair

hammer

Homework Partner   Date   Speech-Language Pathologist   Final R Words

75

Search-A-Word

Directions: Read/say the picture–words aloud. Find and circle each word in the Word Search Box. Then, read/say the words again. Use your good R sound. _____

```
P Z W L F Y S R O F C A Z S P
V F L O W E R V N E F N B A R
R M U R Q M H C M B M D S Z E
Z R R I A H C L E E H W T P M
D B U H E C Y D M A B Z A J M
F R I C W S K M W N S K R O A
X D O P B O G M B Z X B N N H
U Z S T D N I G V S K N A M B
U N E P C K I J U R I A H B Y
W H V B K O H F C F L I R I Z
X R E C W V D P B D C O Q B J
U L H A W Q W E E E L Q J L H
V L O H Y Q I A S I A T Y J N
K H W P P T U J A Y B R C Y V
Q X C Y Y D C S B G J I C N Y
```

Answer Key on Page 280

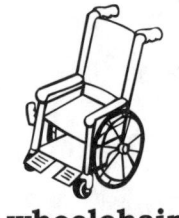

| wheelchair |  star |  hair |  doctor |  sailor |

| hammer |  flower |  bear |  four |  car |

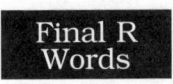

_____ _____ _____ **Final R Words**
Homework Partner   Date   Speech-Language Pathologist

Name an Item in the Category

Directions: Read/say aloud the picture–words below. Then, read each category. Pick an answer from the Word Bank and say your answer aloud. Write the word in the correct space. Some categories may have more than one answer.

Word Bank

| wheelchair | doctor | four | hammer | star |
| hair | flower | car | sailor | bear |

1. Occupation _____

2. Plant _____

3. Transportation _____

4. Tool _____

5. Animal _____

6. Body Part _____

7. Number _____

8. Shape _____

_____ _____ _____   Final R
Homework Partner   Date   Speech-Language Pathologist   Words

Sail Away

Directions: Help Sam the Sailor get to his boat. Cut out the markers. Flip a coin (heads=1, tails=2) to determine how many spaces to move. As you move, read/say each phrase aloud, using your best R sound. First player to reach the finish wins.

START
- the happy sailor
- the number four
- wish upon a star
- smell the flower
- comb my hair
- push the wheelchair
- don't feed the bear
- use the hammer
- our nice babysitter
- wash the car
- call the doctor
- the big bulldozer
- the tiny caterpillar
- the lucky clover
- the happy dancer

FINISH

Homework Partner   Date   Speech-Language Pathologist

Final R Phrases

78   #BK-290 Webber® Artic Fun Sheets • ©2001 Super Duper® Publications • www.superduperinc.com • 1-800-277-8737

Mine or Yours?

Directions: Read/say each picture–word below. Cut out the pictures. At each turn, flip a coin. Heads means the student keeps the picture and says, "My _____" ("My car"). Tails means that the student gives the picture to his partner and says, "Your _____" ("Your car"). Player with the most pictures at the end wins.

car	hammer
sailor	bear
flower	hair
wheelchair	star
four	doctor

_____ _____ _____
Homework Partner   Date   Speech-Language Pathologist

Final R Phrases

X and O

Directions: Cut out each X and O below. Have each player/partner choose X or O. The first player reads/says a picture word aloud and places an X or O on the square. Play continues in turn. The first person to get three in a row wins. _____

hit the hammer	wash hair	plant the flower
push the wheelchair	look at the car	wish upon a star
four, five, six	see the sailor	go to the doctor

X X X X X

O O O O O

_____ _____ _____ **Final R Phrases**
Homework Partner   Date   Speech-Language Pathologist

80 #BK-290 Webber® Artic Fun Sheets • ©2001 Super Duper® Publications • www.superduperinc.com • 1-800-277-8737

Answer with a Question

Directions: Read each statement below. Then, ask a question about the statement. ("This animal eats honey. What eats honey?") Use the pictures as hints. Read/say each question aloud. Each correct question earns one point. The student with the most points wins.

Answer   **Question**

1. This has four tires and a steering wheel.   _____

2. This person keeps you healthy.   _____

3. This person works on a boat.   _____

4. This animal eats honey.   _____

5. This number comes after three.   _____

6. This plant blooms in the spring.   _____

7. This shines in the night sky.   _____

8. You use this to put nails into wood.   _____

_____   _____   _____   **Final R Sentences**
Homework Partner   Date   Speech-Language Pathologist

#BK-290 Webber® Artic Fun Sheets • ©2001 Super Duper® Publications • www.superduperinc.com • 1-800-277-8737   81

Finish the Sentence

Directions: Complete each sentence by telling what you would do. Say the complete sentence aloud, using your best R sound.

1. If I had a pet bear... _____

2. If I wished upon a star... _____

3. If I owned a car... _____

4. If I were a doctor... _____

5. If I were a flower... _____

6. If I had a hammer... _____

7. If I were in a wheelchair... _____

8. If I dyed my hair... _____

Homework Partner   Date   Speech-Language Pathologist

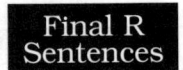

Final R Sentences

One, Two, Three

Directions: Each student gets three turns to roll the die. Each turn represents a phrase to be used in a silly sentence. For example, a student who rolls a two, five, and one will make a sentence with the phrases: "The young boy cuts long hair with a spoon." Read/say each sentence aloud using your good R sound.

	Roll One	Roll Two	Roll Three
1.	The silly sailor	ate chef's salad	with a spoon.
2.	The young boy	bought four balls	and played baseball.
3.	The quiet voice	sat in the field	and wished upon a star.
4.	The yellow flower	danced all day	in the vase.
5.	The old boot	cuts long hair	on Monday.
6.	The metal wheelchair	popped its wheel	on a nail.
7.	The chunky bear	licked a lollipop	by the sea.
8.	The blue hammer	hit the wall	and made a hole.
9.	The young doctor	gave a shot	and went home.
10.	The junky car	fell to pieces	on the hill.

Homework Partner   Date   Speech-Language Pathologist

Final R Sentences

R Cube Roll

Directions: Assemble the cube as follows: Glue onto construction paper for added durability. Cut along the dotted lines. Fold on solid lines and glue as indicated. To play: Roll the cube. Read/say aloud the word you see using your best R sound.

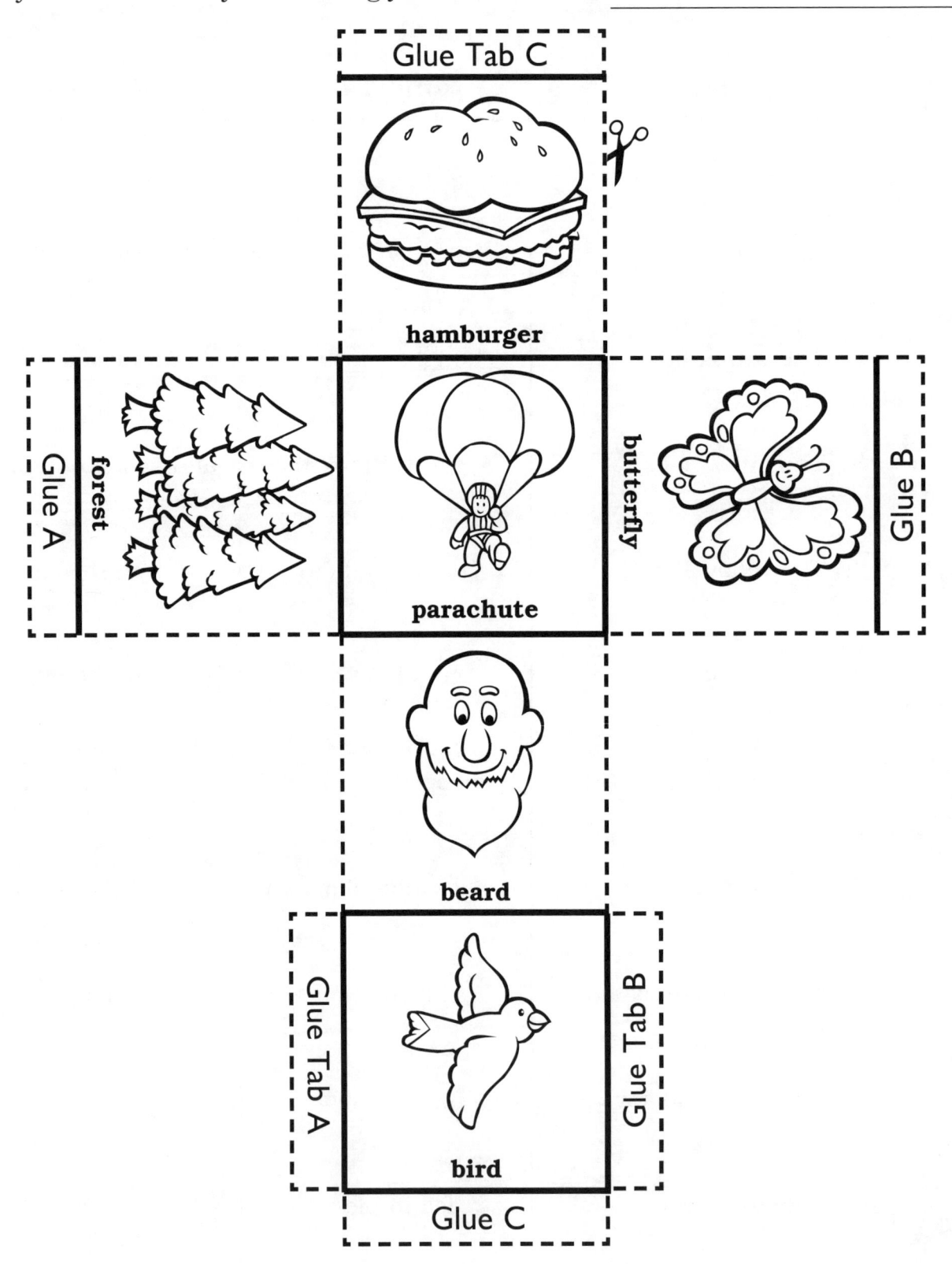

Glue Tab C

hamburger

Glue A | forest | parachute | butterfly | Glue B

beard

Glue Tab A | bird | Glue Tab B

Glue C

Homework Partner | Date | Speech-Language Pathologist

Medial R Words

Name It!

Directions: Practice saying aloud each R picture–word. Then read each statement in the middle. Name the item that goes with each statement. Draw a line from a sentence to each correct picture. Say the words again, using your good R sound.

beard

Name something you eat.

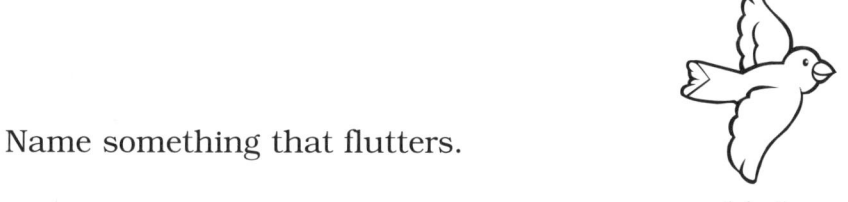

Name something that flutters.

bird

butterfly

Name something that moves slowly.

Name something that you wear on your ears.

earring

turtle

Name something that builds a nest.

Name something you use in skydiving.

parachute

hamburger

Name something a man has on his face.

Homework Partner   Date   Speech-Language Pathologist

Medial R Words

#BK-290 Webber® Artic Fun Sheets • ©2001 Super Duper® Publications • www.superduperinc.com • 1-800-277-8737

Memory Game

Directions: Read/say aloud each picture–word below. Cut out the pictures. Place all cards face down. Try to match the cards. Say each card as you pick it up, using your good R sound. Keep all matches. Most matches wins!

beard	x-ray	butterfly	turtle
parachute	bird	earrings	hamburger
carpet	forest	beard	x-ray
butterfly	turtle	parachute	bird
earrings	hamburger	carpet	forest

_____   _____   _____
Homework Partner   Date   Speech-Language Pathologist

Medial R Words

Unscramble The Words

Directions: Read/say the picture–words on the right. Then, unscramble the words on the left and write the answers in the blanks. Read/say your answers aloud. Fill in the letters from the boxes to make a word at the bottom of the page. Say the word aloud using your good R sound.

1. **uttelr** __ __ __ __ __ __[9]

2. **ambgrhreu** __[6] __[4] __ __ __ __ __ __ __

3. **reigarns** __ __[2] __ __ __ __ __ __

4. **dbri** __ __ __[3] __

5. **ybterutlf** __ __ __[7] __[8] __ __ __ __ __

6. **pteacr** __[5] __ __ __ __[1] __ __

bird

butterfly

carpet

turtle

earrings

hamburger

[1] [2] [3] [4] [5] [6] [7] [8] [9]

Answer key: 1-turtle, 2-hamburger, 3-earrings, 4-bird, 5-butterfly, 6-carpet

Homework Partner   Date   Speech-Language Pathologist   Medial R Words

#BK-290 Webber® Artic Fun Sheets • ©2001 Super Duper® Publications • www.superduperinc.com • 1-800-277-8737

Crazy Crossword

Directions: Read/say the picture–words below. Then, complete the crossword puzzle by reading and answering the clues. Use the pictures to help you. Then, use your best R sound and read/say the R words aloud, as you fill in your answers.

beard

carpet

turtle

x-ray

hamburger

bird

butterfly

forest

Across

1. Another name for woods.
3. An animal with wings.
5. You eat this meat on a bun.
7. This covers the floor.

Down

2. An animal with a shell.
3. Hair on your face.
4. The doctor examines your _____.
6. A caterpillar turns into a _____.

Answers on page 279

Homework Partner   Date   Speech-Language Pathologist

Medial R Words

88   #BK-290 Webber® Artic Fun Sheets • ©2001 Super Duper® Publications • www.superduperinc.com • 1-800-277-8737

A or E?

Directions: Decide which vowel should go in the blank space below, an A or an E? Write "A" or "E" in each space to spell the word correctly. Then read/say aloud each word aloud using your best R sound.

x-r____y

butt____rfly

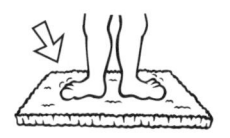

p____rachute

e____rrings

c____rpet

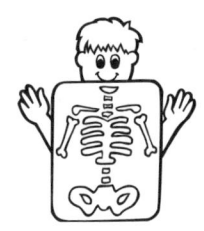

be____rd

for____st

hamburg____r

turtl____

Answers: a, e, a, a, a, a, e, e, e

Homework Partner   Date   Speech-Language Pathologist   **Medial R Words**

Go-Together Match-Ups

Directions: Read/say aloud the picture words on the left. Then find the words that "Go Together." Draw a line from the word in column "A" to the word in column "B" that goes together best. Read/say each phrase aloud ("parachute and plane"). Use your good R sound!

A   **B**

parachute   net

earrings   nest

x-ray   vacuum

butterfly   plane

hamburger   face

carpet   doctor

bird   necklace

beard   ketchup

Homework Partner   Date   Speech-Language Pathologist

Medial R Phrases

R Cube Roll

Directions: Assemble the cubes as follows: If you prefer, glue onto construction paper for added durability. Cut along the dotted lines. Fold on solid lines and glue as indicated. To play: Roll both cubes. Read/say the words and pictures together to make up a phrase ("yummy hamburger").

Glue B

parachute

Glue Tab C | **butterfly** | **turtle** | **forest** | **Glue Tab B** / **carpet** / **Glue C**

Glue Tab A

hamburger

Glue A

Glue B

yummy

Glue Tab C | **happy** | **tall** | **tiny** | **Glue Tab B** / **round** / **Glue C**

Glue Tab A

flat

Glue A

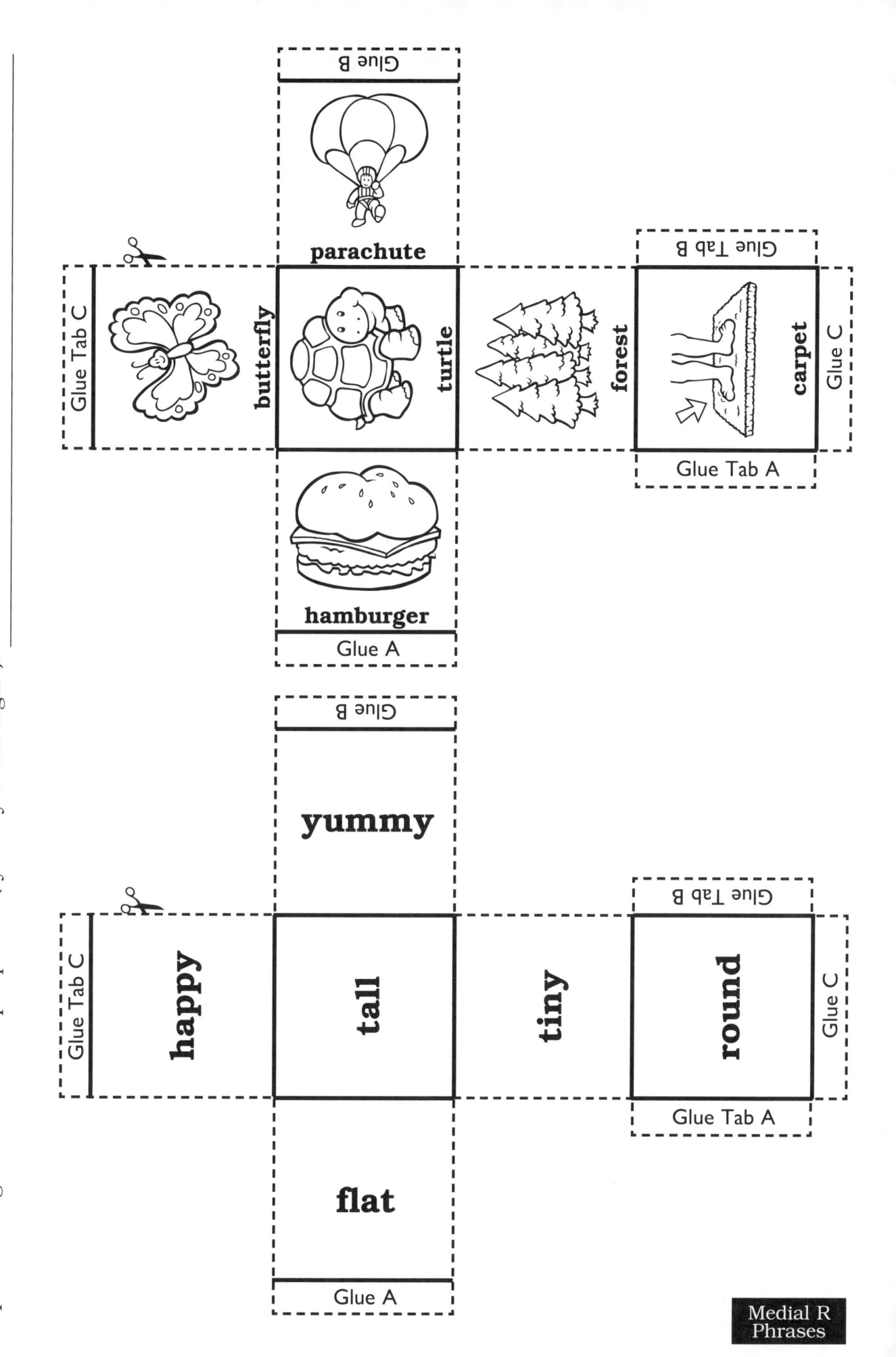

Medial R Phrases

Act It Out!

Directions: Practice each R phrase aloud. Then, cut the squares out and place them face down on a table. The students/helpers take turns picking a card, acting it out, and guessing what the actor is doing. Variations:

1. Pick two cards to act out to have the students use longer phrases ("a slow moving turtle and a long white beard").
2. Homework partner/teacher acts out all cards and student(s) guess the activities.

a pecking/singing bird	a slow moving turtle	a long white beard
a flying butterfly	eating a hamburger	putting on earrings
jump with parachute	fly the magic carpet	check the x-ray

Homework Partner   Date   Speech-Language Pathologist

Medial R Phrases

Crazy Sentence Roll

Directions: Choose a phrase from column A, then roll a die to choose a phrase from column B. Combine the phrases to make a sentence. Read/say each sentence aloud. Use your best R sound.

A

1. I looked up to see...
2. My mom gave me...
3. I walked into...
4. The class listened to...
5. The dog jumped at...
6. I've always wanted...

B

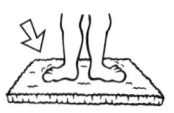

1. a baby bird.
2. a juicy hamburger.
3. a spooky forest.
4. a quiet butterfly.
5. an open parachute.
6. a magic carpet.

Big or Bigger

Directions: Cut out the pictures and arrange them by size on the correct lines. Say the name of each picture using your best R sound. Then, say a sentence aloud to compare the pictures ("This hamburger is big, but this hamburger is bigger.") Use the words under each line to help you compare the objects.

Picture Bank

1. _____   _____
    big   bigger

2. _____   _____
    long   longer

3. _____   _____
    tall   taller

4. _____   _____
    big   bigger

5. _____   _____
    small   smaller

6. _____   _____
    happy   happier

Homework Partner   Date   Speech-Language Pathologist

Medial R Sentences

Finish the Sentence

Directions: Complete each sentence by telling what you would do. Say the complete sentence aloud, using your best R sound.

1. If I saw a bird... _____
_____.

2. If I had a parachute... _____
_____.

3. If I ate a hamburger... _____
_____.

4. If I took an x-ray... _____
_____.

5. If I had a flying carpet... _____
_____.

6. If I caught a butterfly... _____
_____.

7. If I put on earrings... _____
_____.

8. If a turtle could talk... _____
_____.

| Homework Partner | Date | Speech-Language Pathologist | Medial R Sentences |

#BK-290 Webber® Artic Fun Sheets • ©2001 Super Duper® Publications • www.superduperinc.com • 1-800-277-8737

95

Search-A-Word

Directions: Read/say the picture–words aloud. Find and circle each word in the Word Search Box. Then, read/say the words again. Use your good R sound. _____

butterfly

flower

red

sailor

```
R H J K T C R L E P L Q A S R
T A X B U T T E R F L Y A O I
N R C G F T E P R A C I T N N
O S K C L Z Y V A J L C D I G
B L P D O N T E Z O O J E K K
B D Y C W O K F R D X T C J W
I R D C E O N T U R T L E O A
R C P F R V N Z S P G R M E P
W Q F M P Q T I U E X O M V K
S I J R W S I U O Y R A W Y C
E T E Y M Q D O Q L F O E J R
Q D A V A G K X O L S P F W P
I D M R F I R J K J B E J P F
N G L L S E G G Q R K F U E K
H V U O A C N R P P P E O A V
```

Answer Key on Page 280

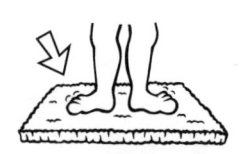

carpet

forest

ribbon

star

ring    **turtle**    **doctor**    **raccoon**

Homework Partner   Date   Speech-Language Pathologist   Combo R Words

96   #BK-290 Webber® Artic Fun Sheets • ©2001 Super Duper® Publications • www.superduperinc.com • 1-800-277-8737

What Am I?

Directions: Read/say aloud each picture–word below. Then, read each clue. Fill in the blank with the appropriate word. Read/say each answer aloud, using your good R sound.

earrings	rain	rattle	doctor	star
bird	rash	rabbit	flower	turtle

1. I am an animal that hops. I am a _____.

2. I am jewelry you put on your ears. I am _____.

3. I am someone who makes you feel better. I am a _____.

4. I am an animal with a hard shell. I am a _____.

5. I am wet and fall from the sky. I am _____.

6. I am a baby's noisy toy. I am a _____.

7. I am an animal with wings and feathers. I am a _____.

8. I shine in the sky at night. I am a _____.

9. I am a colorful plant that comes up from the soil. I am a _____.

10. I am an itchy patch on your skin. I am a _____.

Answer key: 1-rabbit, 2-earrings, 3-doctor, 4-turtle, 5-rain, 6-rattle, 7-bird, 8-star, 9-flower, 10-rash

Homework Partner   Date   Speech-Language Pathologist

Combo R Words

Sentence Completion

Directions: Read/say aloud the picture–words below. Then, cut out the pictures. Find the picture that best completes the sentence and glue/tape or place it under the correct phrase. Read/say the word aloud, using your good R sound.

You wear...	You pick a...	You hear a...	You eat a...	You comb your...
You shave a...	You steer a...	You wish on a...	You bang a...	You shake a...

hamburger | **beard** | **earrings** | **rattle** | **radio**

star | **hammer** | **hair** | **car** | **flower**

Homework Partner — Date — Speech-Language Pathologist

Combo R Words

98 #BK-290 Webber® Artic Fun Sheets • ©2001 Super Duper® Publications • www.superduperinc.com • 1-800-277-8737

X and O

Directions: Cut out each X and O below. Have each player/partner choose X or O. The first player reads/says a picture word aloud and places an X or O on the square. Play continues in turn. The first person to get three in a row wins! _____

x-ray	bear	rattle
rainbow	hamburger	four
wheelchair	carpet	rug

X X X X X

O O O O O

_____ _____ _____ Combo R Words
Homework Partner   Date   Speech-Language Pathologist

Rabbit Roundup

Directions: Cut out the markers. Have the student(s) flip a coin (heads=1, tails=2) to determine how many spaces to move. As they play, the student(s) read/say each word aloud, using their good R sound. First player to reach the finish wins.

START — butterfly — wheelchair — beard — flower — rain — rattle — bear — forest — star — rock & roll — bird — bulldozer — buzzard — carpet — babysitter — FINISH

Homework Partner — Date — Speech-Language Pathologist

Combo R Words

3 Games in 1

Directions: Say aloud the picture–words below, using your good R sound.
Then, play one of the following games:
- ☐ Lotto – Caller reads out a word and student repeats the word and covers it with a token/chip.
- ☐ Tic–Tac–Toe – Each time you write an **X** or **O**, say the word you mark over.
- ☐ Memory – Cut out all the cards and place face down. Try to find matching pairs. Say aloud each word you find. Keep all matches.

raccoon	hammer	hair
parachute	x-ray	radio
earrings	wheelchair	rain
hair	radio	earrings
rain	wheelchair	x-ray
raccoon	hammer	parachute

Homework Partner   Date   Speech-Language Pathologist

Combo R Words

#BK-290 Webber® Artic Fun Sheets • ©2001 Super Duper® Publications • www.superduperinc.com • 1-800-277-8737

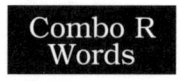

101

R Word Roll

Directions: Assemble the cube as follows: Glue onto construction paper for added durability. Cut along the dotted lines. Fold on solid lines and glue as indicated. To play: Roll both cubes. Read/say the R word aloud, the number of times indicated on the number cube.

- ring
- rash
- earrings
- bird
- hair
- hammer

1, 6, 4, 5, 3, 2

Combo R Words

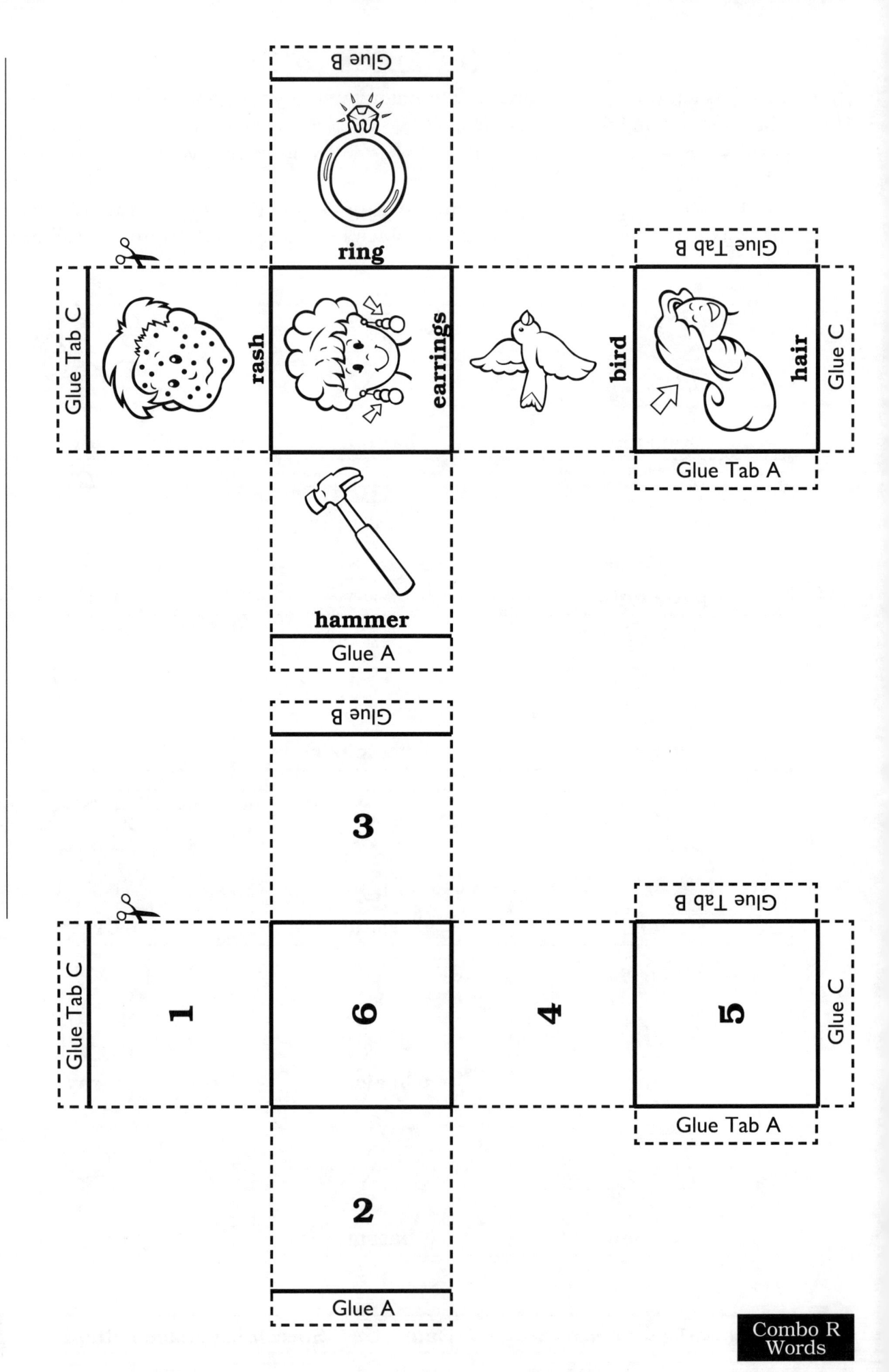

102

Where Do You Find?

Directions: Read/say aloud each phrase from 1–8. Then, pick a place at the bottom of the page where you would find each item. Write the places on the blank lines. Then, read each phrase aloud ("a rash on skin").

1. a rash _____

2. an x-ray _____

3. a beard _____

4. a bird _____

5. a sailor _____

6. a star _____

7. a bear _____

8. a hamburger _____

A. on skin
B. on a chin
C. on a plate
D. in the woods

E. at the hospital
F. in the sky
G. in a nest
H. on a boat

Homework Partner   Date   Speech-Language Pathologist

Combo R Phrases

#BK-290 Webber® Artic Fun Sheets • ©2001 Super Duper® Publications • www.superduperinc.com • 1-800-277-8737

103

Paper Dolls

Directions: Cut out each doll, keeping the girls and the boys separate. Select one girl doll and one boy doll to make a phrase ("a slow car"). Read/say each phrase aloud, using your best R sound.

Boys

- a slow
- pick a
- a beautiful
- a tweeting
- a new

Girls

- flower
- rainbow
- bird
- turtle
- car

Combo R Phrases

Q & A Match Up

Directions: Read the questions and find the answers at the bottom. Write the question number on the line of the matching answer. Then, read/say each answer aloud ("A little turtle"). Use your good R sound!

1 What has many colors?

2 What does a baby play with?

3 What do you jump out of a plane with?

4 What is an animal with a hard shell?

5 What kind of music makes you dance?

6 What is bumpy and itchy?

7 What do you make a wish on?

8 What do you pound a nail with?

9 What takes a picture of your bones?

_____ a little turtle

_____ a heavy parachute

_____ rock & roll

_____ a star

_____ a big hammer

_____ a toy rattle

_____ a rash

_____ an x-ray

_____ a rainbow

Homework Partner   Date   Speech-Language Pathologist

Combo R Phrases

105

#BK-290 Webber® Artic Fun Sheets • ©2001 Super Duper® Publications • www.superduperinc.com • 1-800-277-8737

Act It Out!

Directions: Practice each R phrase aloud. Then, cut the squares out and place them face down on a table. The students/helpers take turns picking a card and acting it out. The others guess what the actor is doing. Variations:

1. Pick two cards to act out to have the students use longer phrases ("hop like a rabbit and eat a hamburger").
2. Homework partner/teacher acts out all cards and student(s) guess the activities.

hop like a rabbit	shake a rattle	eat a hamburger
fly like a bird	comb your hair	put on a ring
hit with a hammer	pick a flower	tie a ribbon

Homework Partner　　　Date　　　Speech-Language Pathologist

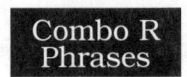

Combo R Phrases

Story Loop

Directions: Read/say aloud each picture–word. Make up a story using all of the pictures in the circle. You can start anywhere in the circle and go in either direction, but you must always end where you started to complete the loop. Say your story aloud, using your good R sound.

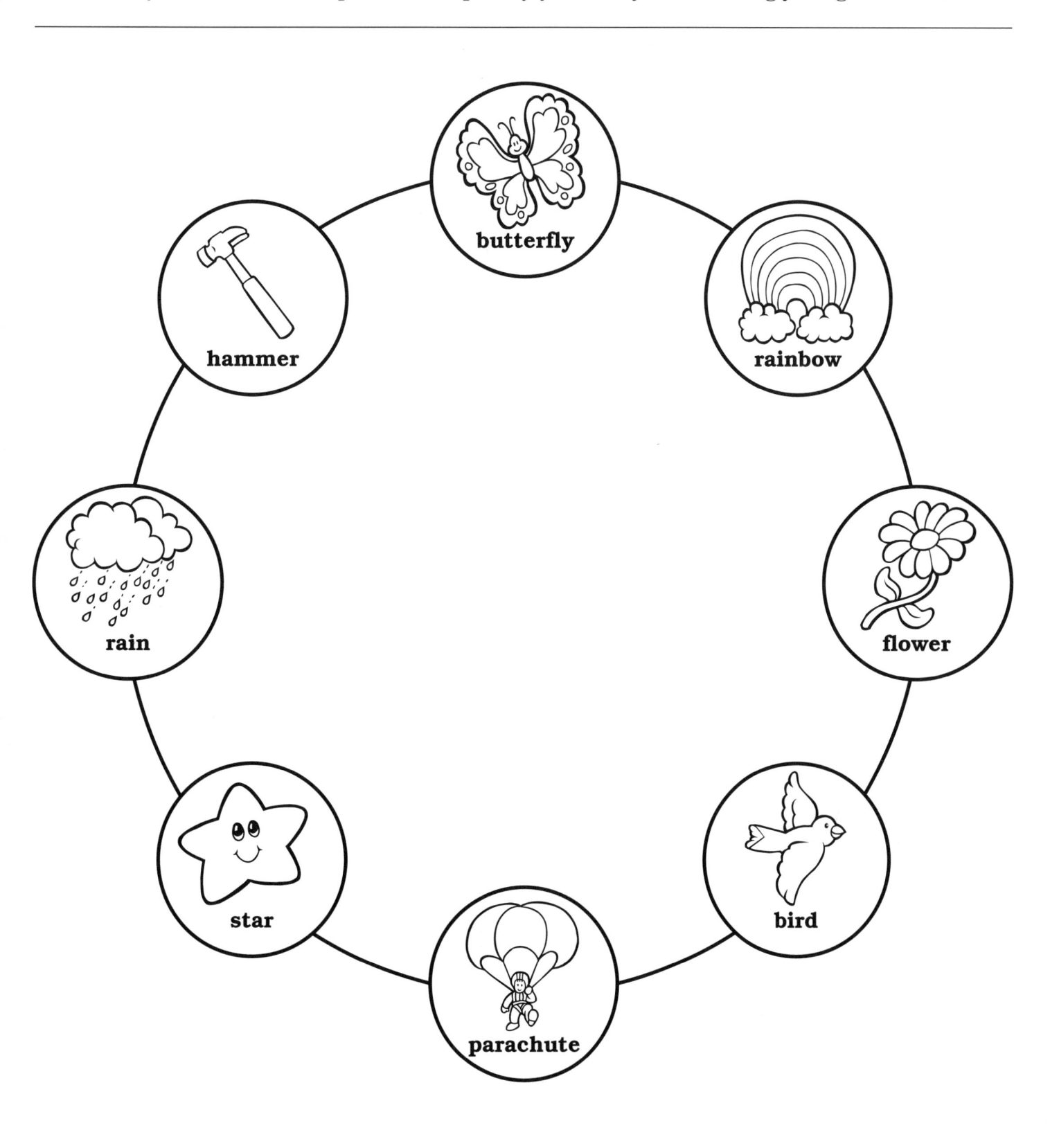

- butterfly
- rainbow
- flower
- bird
- parachute
- star
- rain
- hammer

Homework Partner   Date   Speech-Language Pathologist

Combo R Sentences

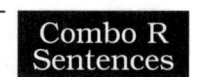

107

Number It Up!

Directions: Read/say aloud the picture–words. Number the words in the Word Bank below from 1-8 in any order you desire. Then, put the words on the lines below that match the corresponding numbers ("lost in the ring"). Read/say the sentences aloud using your good R sound. _____

Word Bank

rug ____   four ____   butterfly ____   raccoon ____

forest ____   ring ____   flower ____   turtle ____

1. Lost in the _____.

2. He is only _____.

3. Put on a _____.

4. A very slow _____.

5. I see a _____.

6. Pick a nice _____.

7. Lay down a _____.

8. Don't touch the _____.

_____   _____   _____
Homework Partner   Date   Speech-Language Pathologist

Combo R Sentences

108   #BK-290 Webber® Artic Fun Sheets • ©2001 Super Duper® Publications • www.superduperinc.com • 1-800-277-8737

What Do You Think?

Directions: Read the sentences and circle the correct answers. Then, read/say the correct sentence aloud. Remember to use your good R sound.

1. Rain **is/isn't** wet.

2. A doctor **does/doesn't** make you feel better.

3. You **do/don't** eat a carpet.

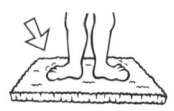

4. A raccoon **is/isn't** a vehicle.

5. A forest **has/doesn't have** animals in it.

6. A woman **does/doesn't** have a beard.

7. A hammer **is/isn't** a tool.

8. A rash **is/isn't** itchy.

9. A flower **can/can't** be picked.

10. A star **does/doesn't** shine.

Homework Partner   Date   Speech-Language Pathologist

Combo R Sentences

Scrambled Sentences

Directions: Try to unscramble each sentence. Write it on the line below the egg. Then read/say the sentence aloud. Remember to use your good R sound.

1. The baby has a rattle.

2. Do you hear a bird singing?

3. Wish upon a star.

4. Don't go out in the rain.

5. I like your new earrings.

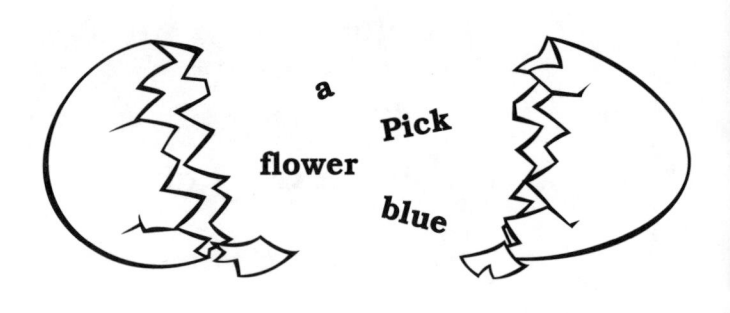

6. Pick a blue flower.

L Sound

Leaf It Up

Directions: Read/say the word on each leaf _____ times aloud. Cut out the leaves. Then, glue/tape or place the leaves on the tree while you say the L words again. _____

leaf lobster ladder lap lemon

lips lion log lamp leopard

Homework Partner   Date   Speech-Language Pathologist

Initial L Words

Iggy Inchworm

Directions: Read/say aloud each picture–word below. Then, each player rolls a die and advances that number of spaces, reading/saying each word aloud as he/she moves. The first player to land on Iggy's head wins! Use your best L sound.

lizard
legs
laundry
leaf
lap
lemon
lion
lamp
leopard
ladder
log
lips
lobster
START

Homework Partner Date Speech-Language Pathologist

Initial L Words

3 Games in 1

Directions: Say aloud the picture–words below, using your good L sound.
Then, play one of the following games:

- ☐ Lotto – Caller reads out a word and student repeats the word and covers it with a token/chip.
- ☐ Tic–Tac–Toe – Each time you write an **X** or **O**, say the word you mark over.
- ☐ Memory – Cut out all the cards and place face down. Try to find matching pairs. Say aloud each word you find. Keep all matches.

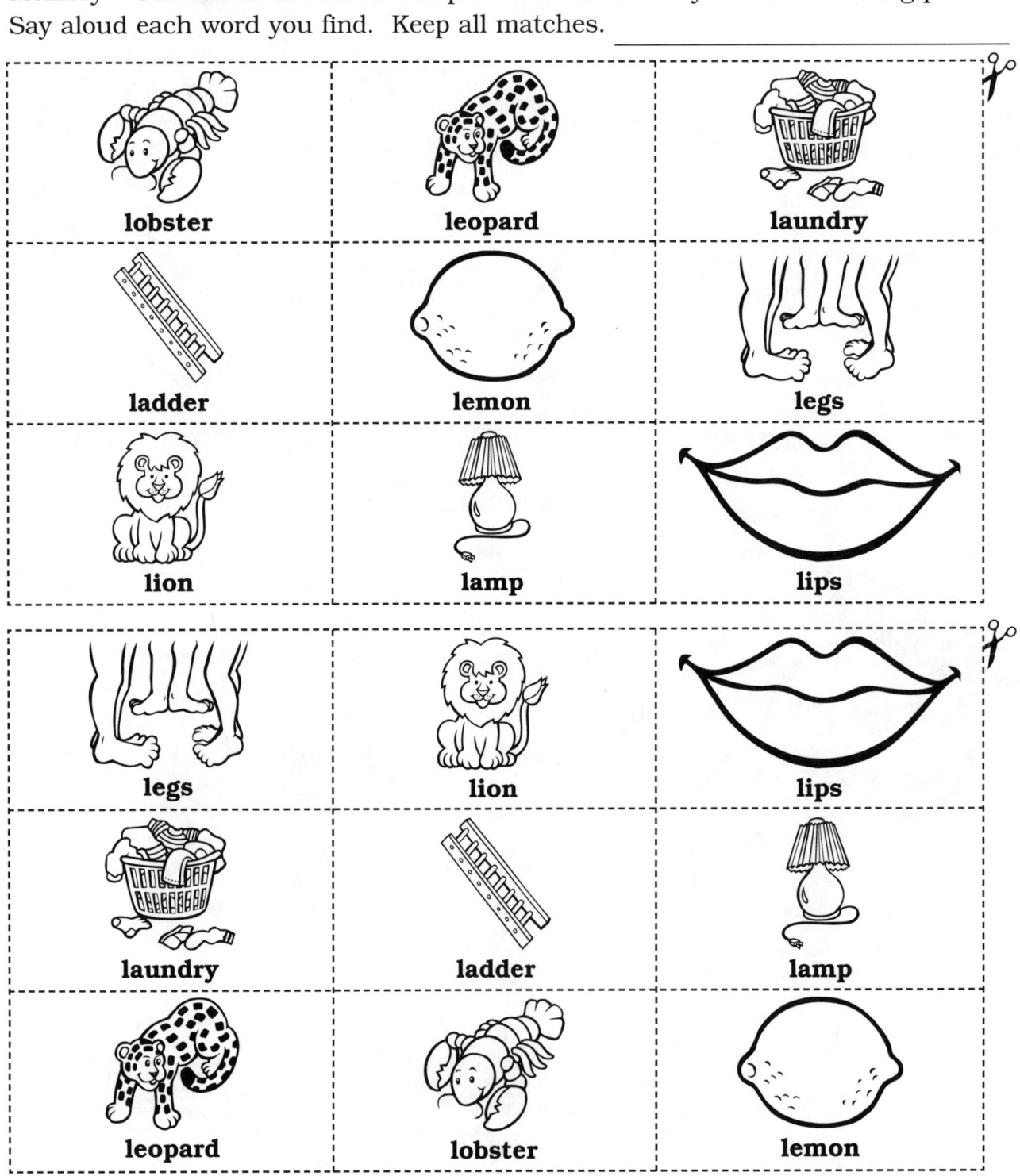

lobster	leopard	laundry
ladder	lemon	legs
lion	lamp	lips
legs	lion	lips
laundry	ladder	lamp
leopard	lobster	lemon

Homework Partner   Date   Speech-Language Pathologist

Initial L Words

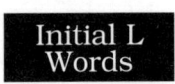

114

Spinner Action

Directions: Read/say aloud each picture–word below. If you prefer, glue this page to construction paper for added durability. Cut out the arrow/dial. Use a brad to connect the dial to the circle. Spin the spinner. When you land on a picture, read/say the word aloud, using your best L sound.

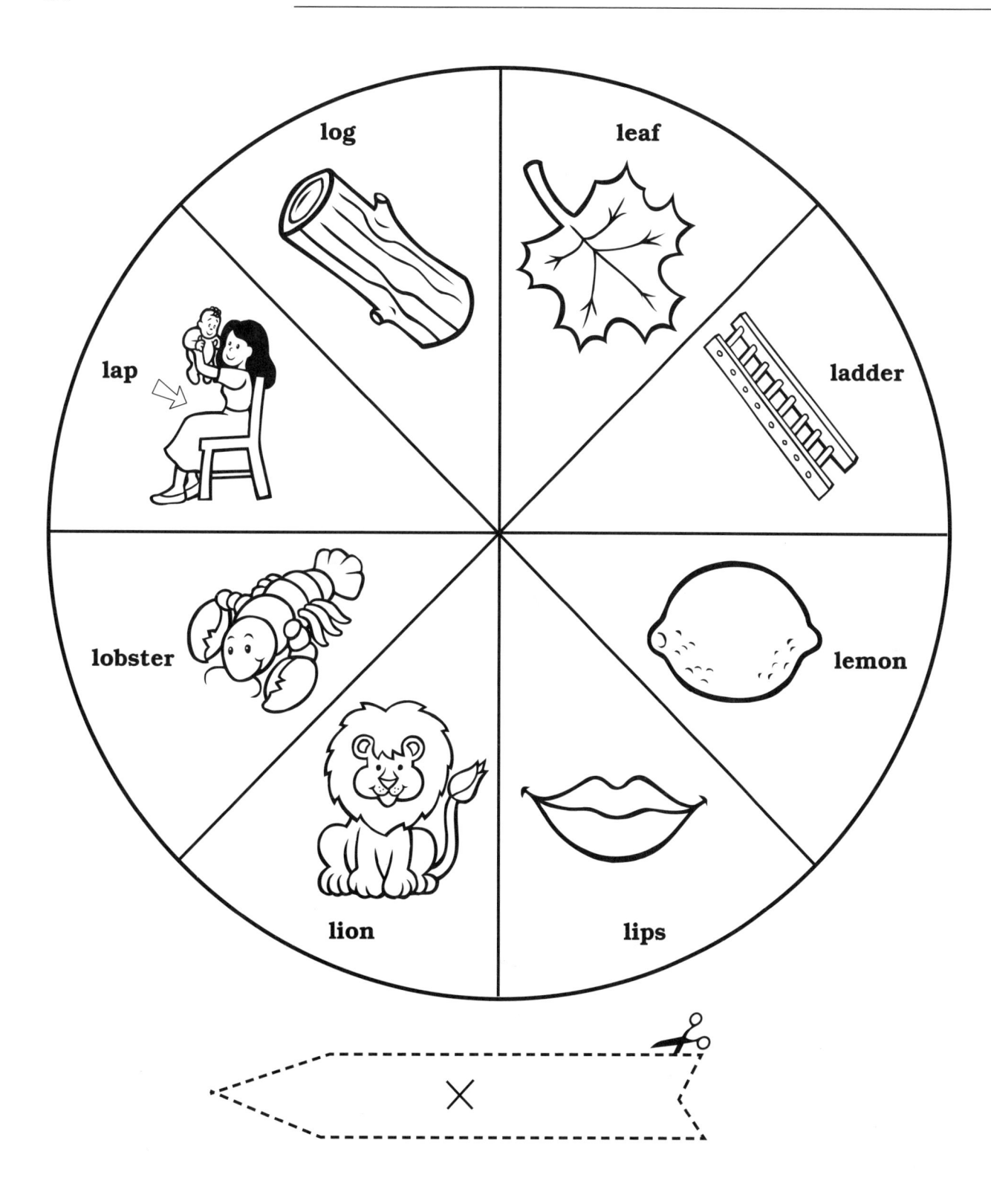

- log
- leaf
- ladder
- lemon
- lips
- lion
- lobster
- lap

Homework Partner   Date   Speech-Language Pathologist

Initial L Words

#BK-290 Webber® Artic Fun Sheets • ©2001 Super Duper® Publications • www.superduperinc.com • 1-800-277-8737

115

Sound Sorter

Directions: Read/say each picture–word aloud. Listen to the first sound in each word. Cross out the picture and/or pictures that do not start with the L sound. Then, read/say aloud the words that begin with the L sound.

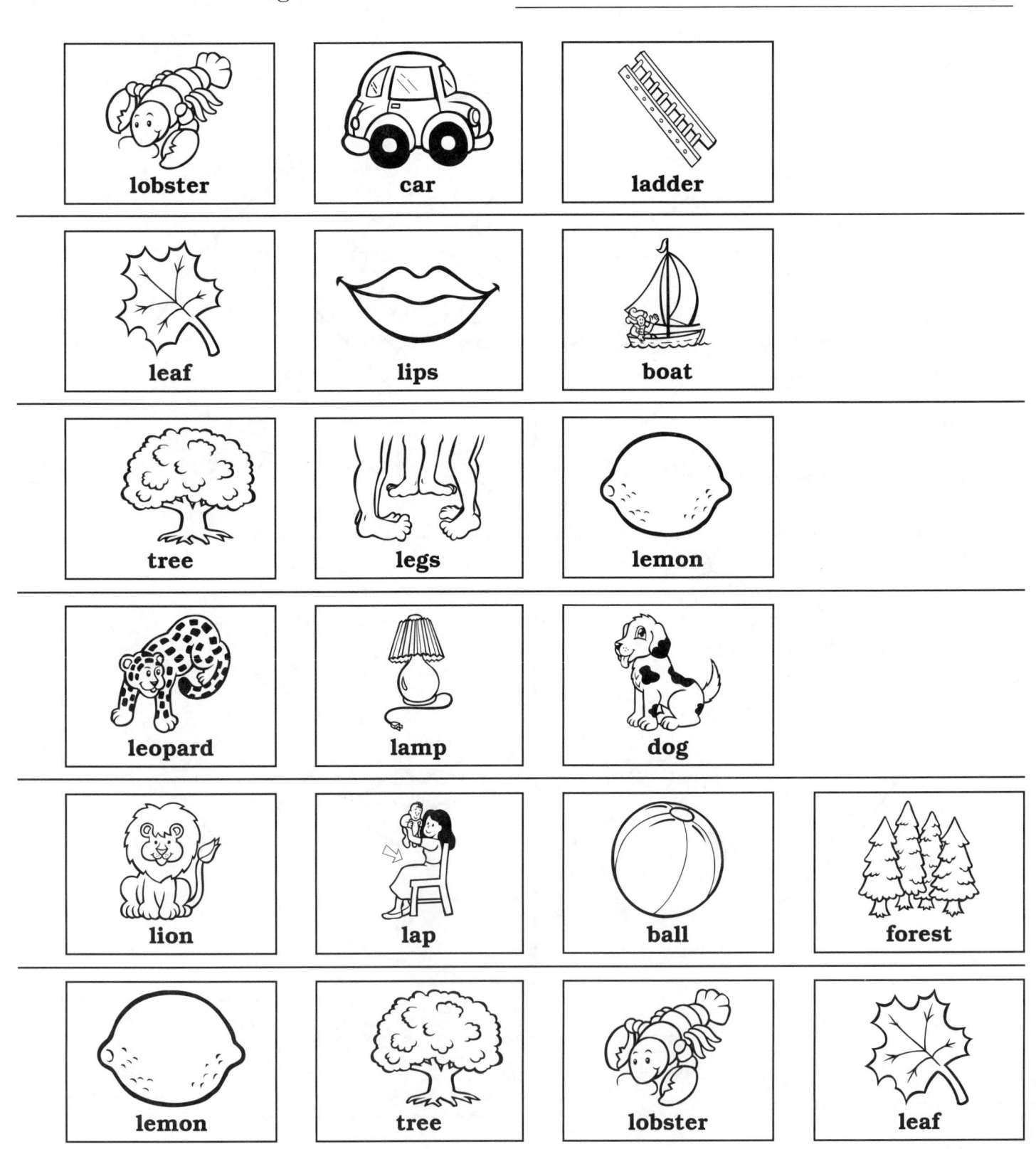

lobster	car	ladder	
leaf	lips	boat	
tree	legs	lemon	
leopard	lamp	dog	
lion	lap	ball	forest
lemon	tree	lobster	leaf

Homework Partner   Date   Speech-Language Pathologist

Initial L Words

Secret Word

Directions: Read/say aloud each picture–word below. Write the answers from the Word Bank in the blank spaces. The letters in the square will spell out a secret word. Say aloud the secret word, using your good L sound.

Word Bank

lion   lamp   lobster   lap
laundry   legs   ladder

Secret Word

Answer key: 1-lobster, 2-legs, 3-lion, 4-lamp, 5-lap, 6-laundry, 7-ladder Bonus-leopard

Homework Partner   Date   Speech-Language Pathologist

Initial L Words

#BK-290 Webber® Artic Fun Sheets • ©2001 Super Duper® Publications • www.superduperinc.com • 1-800-277-8737

What Am I?

Directions: Read/say aloud each picture–word below. Then, read each question. Fill in the blank with the appropriate word. Read/say each answer aloud, using your good L sound.

 leopard	 lamp	 lemon	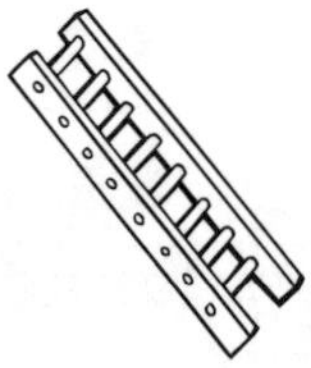 ladder
 lap	 lion	 lobster	 leaf

1. I live in the ocean. I am a _____.

2. I am a big cat with spots. I am a _____.

3. I am a sour fruit. I am a _____.

4. Turn me on to see. I am a _____.

5. Firemen use me to get to high windows. I am a _____.

6. I am made when you sit down. I am a _____.

7. I am found on a tree. I am a _____.

8. I am a big cat with a mane. I am a _____.

Answers: 1-lobster, 2-leopard, 3-lemon, 4-lamp, 5-ladder, 6-lap, 7-leaf, 8-lion

_____   _____   _____   **Initial L Words**
Homework Partner   Date   Speech-Language Pathologist

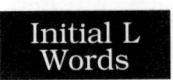

Category Match

Directions: Read/say each picture–word aloud. Then, choose the correct category from the choices below. Write the letter of the answer in the space provided. _____

1. **legs**

2. **lobster**

3. **laundry**

4. **leopard**

5. **lips**

6. **lamp**

7. **lion**

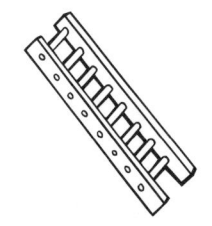

8. **ladder**

9. **lap**

A	B	C
Animals	Things At Home	Body Parts

Answer key: 1-C, 2-A, 3-B, 4-A, 5-C, 6-B, 7-A, 8-B, 9-C

Homework Partner   Date   Speech-Language Pathologist

Initial L Words

119

Leaping Lilypads

Directions: Read/say aloud each picture–phrase below. Then, cut out the markers. Flip a coin to determine how many spaces to move (heads = 2, tails = 1). As you move around the pad, say each phrase on the lily pads aloud. The first student to finish wins! _____

START

a brave lion

two legs

on my lap

a green leaf

a sour lemon

up the ladder

do the laundry

frog on a log

a broken lamp

a big leopard

FINISH

Homework Partner   Date   Speech-Language Pathologist

Initial L Phrases

120   #BK-290 Webber® Artic Fun Sheets • ©2001 Super Duper® Publications • www.superduperinc.com • 1-800-277-8737

Where Do You Find?

Directions: Read/say aloud each phrase from 1–12. Then, pick a place at the bottom of the page where you would find each item. Write the places on the blank lines. Then, read each phrase aloud ("a lobster at the zoo"). _____

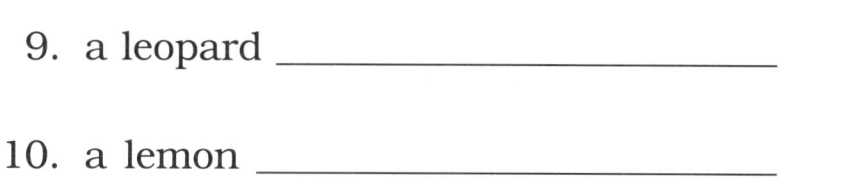

1. a lobster _____
2. a lion _____ 
3. a leaf _____ 
4. a lamp _____ 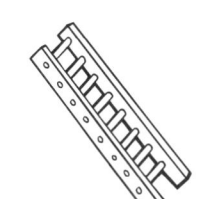
5. a lap _____ 
6. the laundry _____  
7. two lips _____ 
8. a ladder _____ 
9. a leopard _____ 
10. a lemon _____ 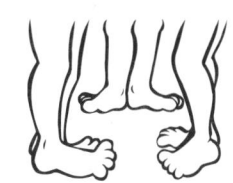
11. legs _____ 
12. a log _____ 

A. in the house
B. at the zoo
C. on a person
D. in the ocean
E. in the woods

Homework Partner   Date   Speech-Language Pathologist

Initial L Phrases

#BK-290 Webber® Artic Fun Sheets • ©2001 Super Duper® Publications • www.superduperinc.com • 1-800-277-8737

121

X and O

Directions: Cut out each X and O below. Have each player/partner choose X or O. The first player reads/says a picture–phrase aloud and places an X or O on the square. Play continues in turn. The first person to get three in a row wins. _____

cut the lemon	do the laundry	catch a lobster
a spotted leopard	two skinny legs	a pretty leaf
a short ladder	a bright lamp	a log home

X X X X X

O O O O O

_____ _____ _____

Homework Partner   Date   Speech-Language Pathologist

Initial L Phrases

Balloon Platoon

Directions: Match each balloon with the correct clown by drawing a line to it. Then, read/say the complete sentence aloud, using your best L sound. ("A red lobster comes from the ocean.")

Clown (left)	Balloon	Balloon	Clown (right)
needs to be washed.	A red lobster	The lamp	comes from the ocean.
ate meat for supper.	The lemon wedge	A furry lion	to get on the roof.
woke me this morning.	The green leaf	The dirty laundry	tastes sour.
grew on the oak tree.	He goes up the ladder	My aching legs	is on the desk.

Homework Partner   Date   Speech-Language Pathologist

Initial L Sentences

#BK-290 Webber® Artic Fun Sheets • ©2001 Super Duper® Publications • www.superduperinc.com • 1-800-277-8737

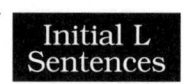

123

Laugh Lines

Directions: Cut out the phrases at the bottom of the page. Turn them face down. Choose a phrase from 1-8 and read it. Then, pick a card from the pile to complete the sentence. Read/say the complete sentences aloud using your best L sound. _____

1. The red **lobster** _____

2. A hungry **lion** _____

3. Mother's **lap** _____

4. The heavy **log** _____

5. My dirty **laundry** _____

6. The **leaf** _____

7. The spotted **leopard** _____

8. The brown **ladder** _____

ran away.	is smooth and soft.	swam in the ocean.	ate berries.
made a big crash.	needs to be washed.	is very fast.	scared the boy.

Homework Partner   Date   Speech-Language Pathologist   Initial L Sentences

124   #BK-290 Webber® Artic Fun Sheets • ©2001 Super Duper® Publications • www.superduperinc.com • 1-800-277-8737

Scrambled Sentences

Directions: Try to unscramble each sentence. Write it on the line below the egg. Then read/say the sentence aloud. Use your good L sound.

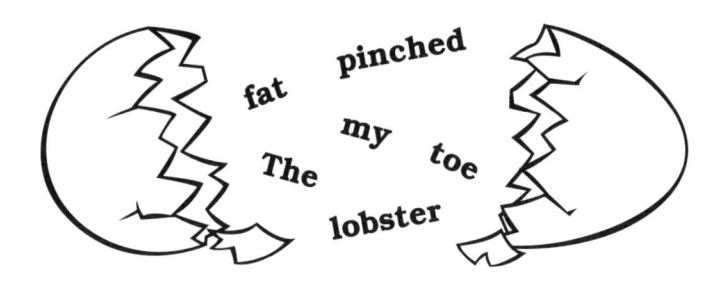

1. The fat lobster pinched my toe.

2. The lion fed her mother cubs. *(scrambled words: The her fed mother lion cubs)*

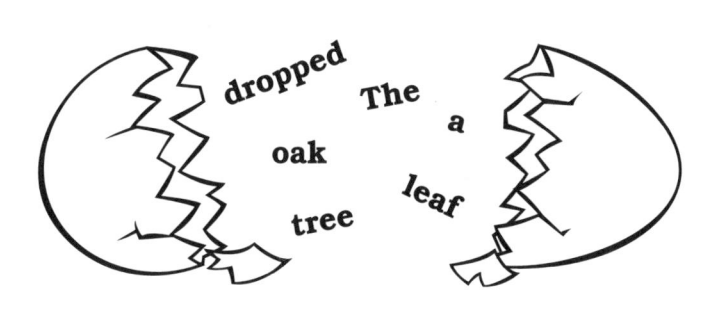

3. The runner's legs hurt after the race.

4. The oak tree dropped a leaf.

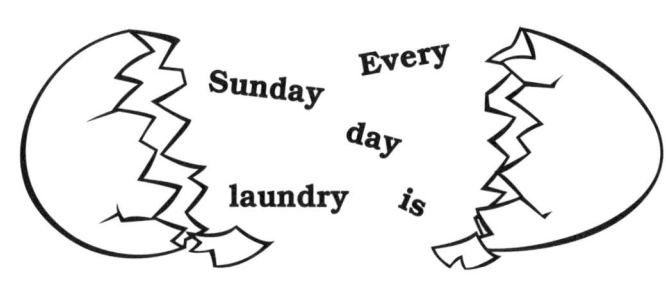

5. The baby sits in daddy's lap.

6. Every Sunday is laundry day.

7. He knocked over the lamp.

8. May I have lemon in my tea?

Homework Partner — Date — Speech-Language Pathologist

Initial L Sentences

Word Game

Directions: Read/say aloud the picture–words below. Then, cut out the markers. Flip a coin (heads=1, tails=2) to determine how many spaces to move. As you move, read/say each word aloud, using your good L sound. First player to reach the finish wins. _____

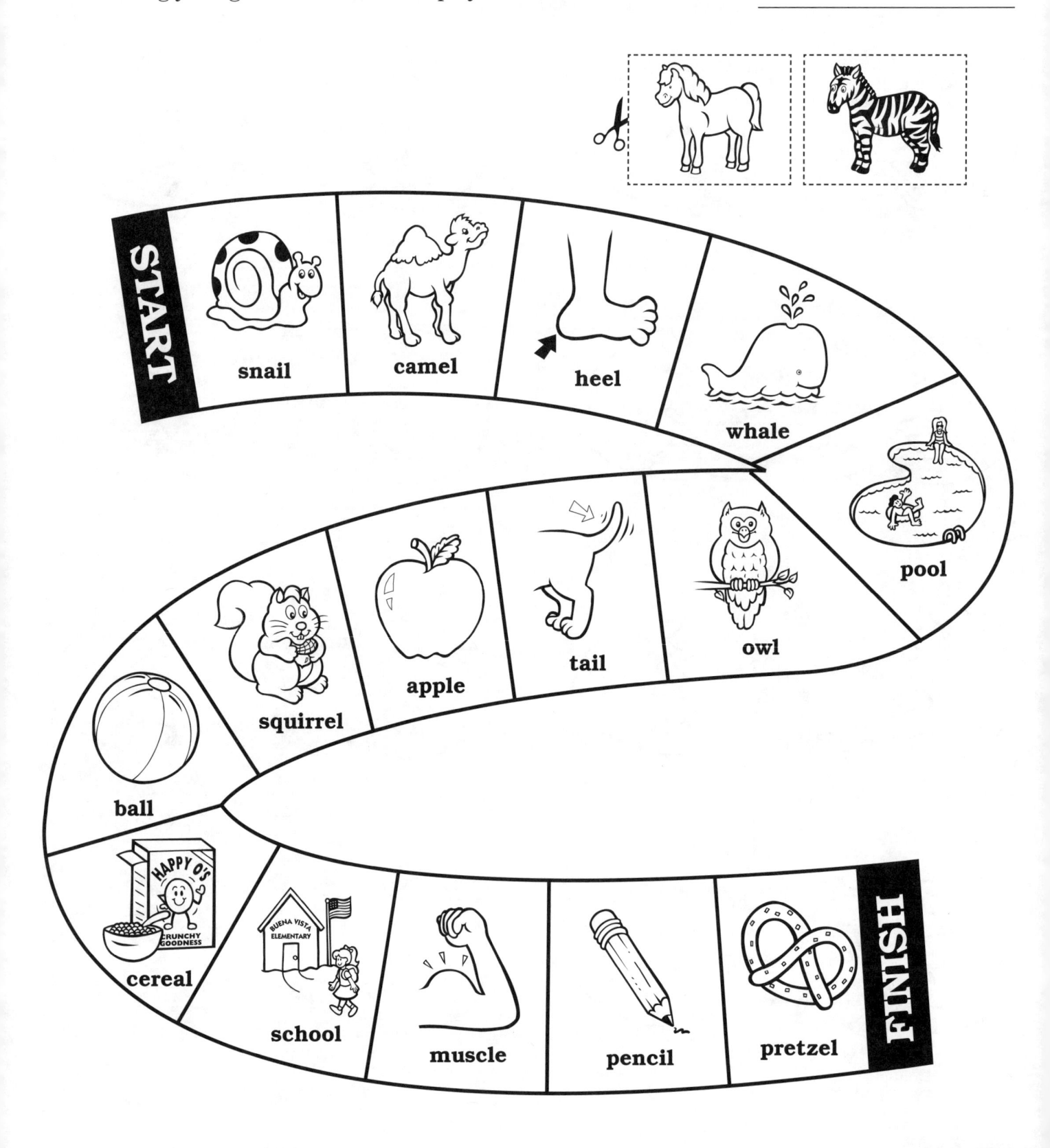

START

- snail
- camel
- heel
- whale
- pool
- owl
- tail
- apple
- squirrel
- ball
- cereal
- school
- muscle
- pencil
- pretzel

FINISH

Homework Partner   Date   Speech-Language Pathologist

Final L Words

126   #BK-290 Webber® Artic Fun Sheets • ©2001 Super Duper® Publications • www.superduperinc.com • 1-800-277-8737

Kick It!

Directions: Copy this page twice and cut out the soccer balls. Give each student a net. First player flips a coin. If heads, he/she picks up one ball, if tails, he/she picks up two balls. Player says aloud the word(s) on the ball(s) and "scores" a goal by placing the ball(s) in the other player's net. Play continues in turn. Most goals wins.

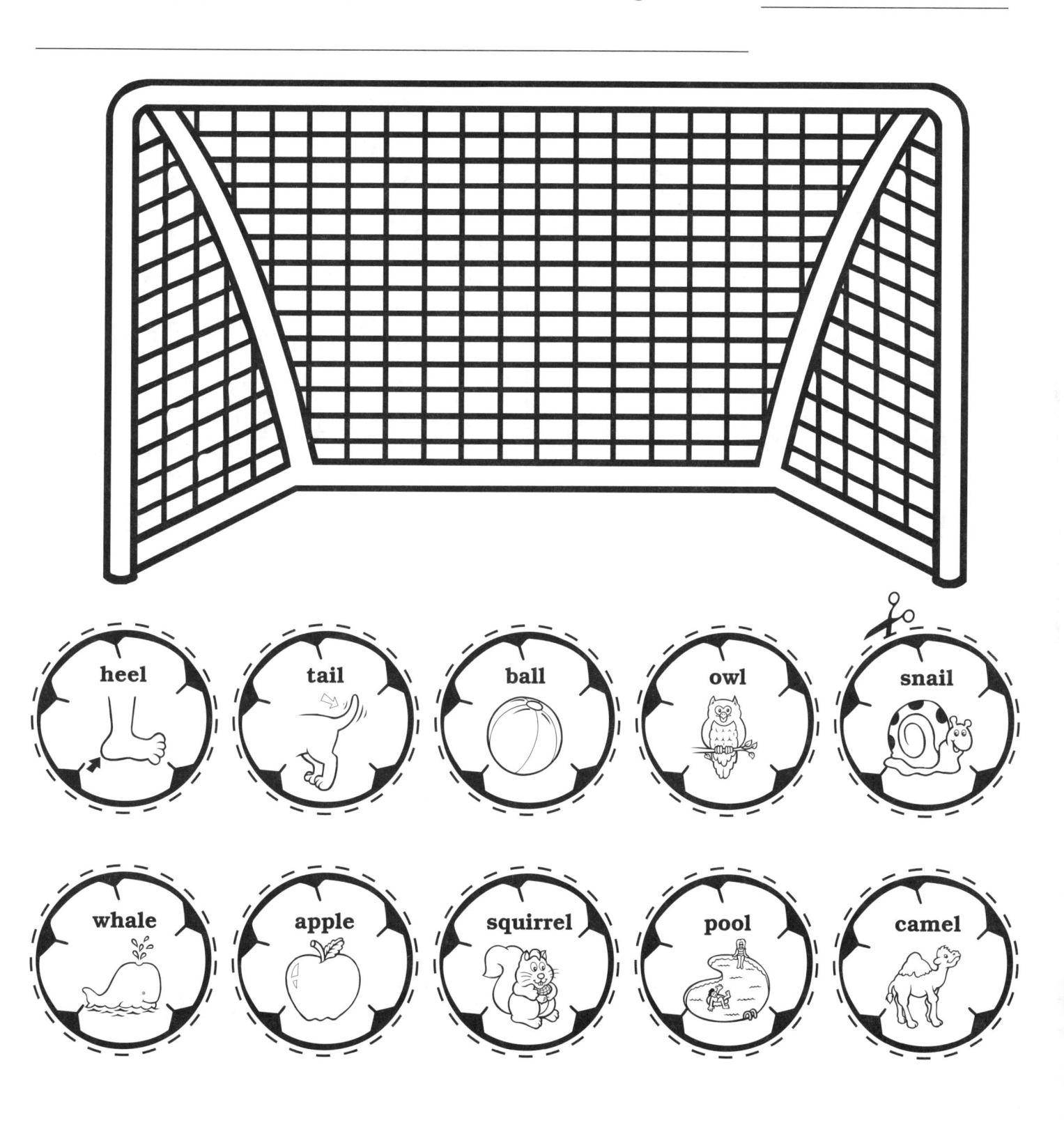

- heel
- tail
- ball
- owl
- snail
- whale
- apple
- squirrel
- pool
- camel

Homework Partner Date Speech-Language Pathologist

Final L Words

Spinner Action

Directions: Read/say aloud the picture–words below. If you prefer, glue this page to construction paper for added durability. Cut out the arrow/dial. Use a brad to connect the dial to the circle. Spin the spinner. When you land on a picture, read/say the word aloud, using your best L sound.

snail camel squirrel heel owl ball apple pool

Homework Partner   Date   Speech-Language Pathologist

Final L Words

128

L Cube Roll

Directions: Assemble the cube as follows: Glue onto construction paper for added durability. Cut along the dotted lines. Fold on solid lines and glue as indicated. To play: Roll the cube. Read/say aloud the word you see using your best L sound.

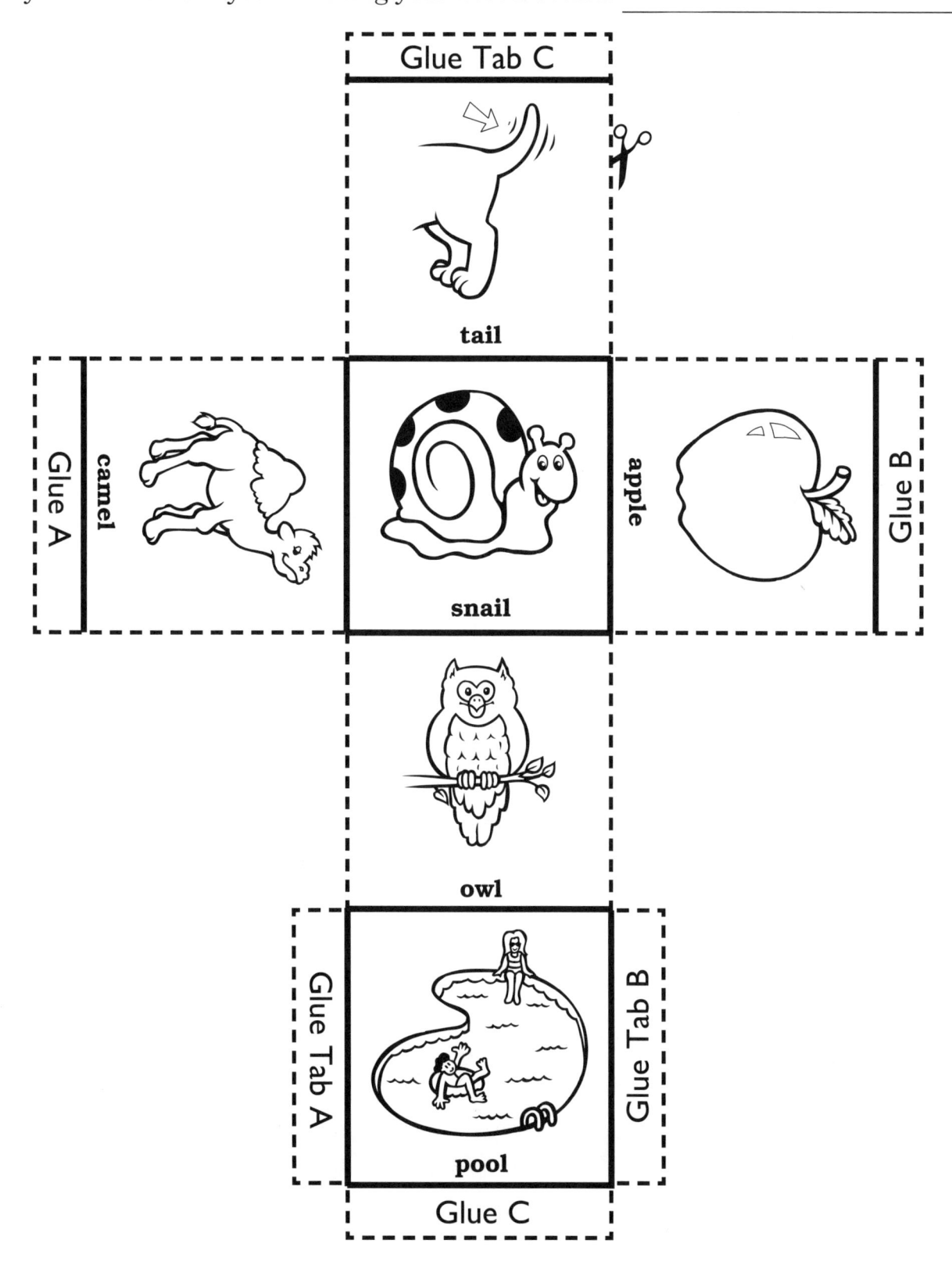

Glue Tab C

tail

Glue A | camel | snail | apple | Glue B

owl

Glue Tab A | pool | Glue Tab B

Glue C

Homework Partner Date Speech-Language Pathologist Final L Words

3 Games in 1

Directions: Say aloud the picture–words below, using your good L sound.
Then, play one of the following games:

- ☐ Lotto – Caller reads out a word and student repeats the word and covers it with a token/chip.
- ☐ Tic–Tac–Toe – Each time you write an **X** or **O**, say the word you mark over.
- ☐ Memory – Cut out all the cards and place face down. Try to find matching pairs. Say aloud each word you find. Keep all matches.

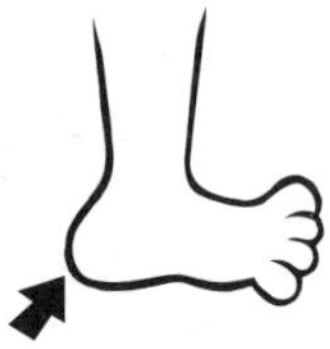 heel	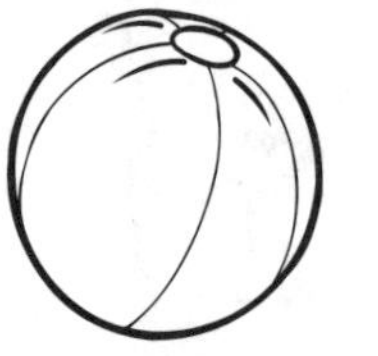 ball	 owl
 apple	 squirrel	 pool
 whale	 camel	 tail
 owl	 pool	 camel
 tail	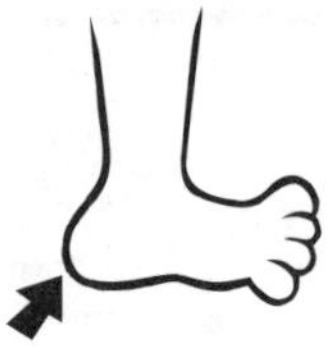 heel	 ball
 squirrel	 apple	 whale

Homework Partner   Date   Speech-Language Pathologist   **Final L Words**

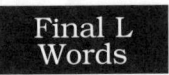

130   #BK-290 Webber® Artic Fun Sheets • ©2001 Super Duper® Publications • www.superduperinc.com • 1-800-277-8737

Finger Hopscotch

Directions: Read/say aloud the picture–words below. Then, slide a penny across the hopscotch board. Hop your finger to the square it lands on. Read/say the name of the picture–word again, practicing your good L sound. Play again until you have landed on all the words.

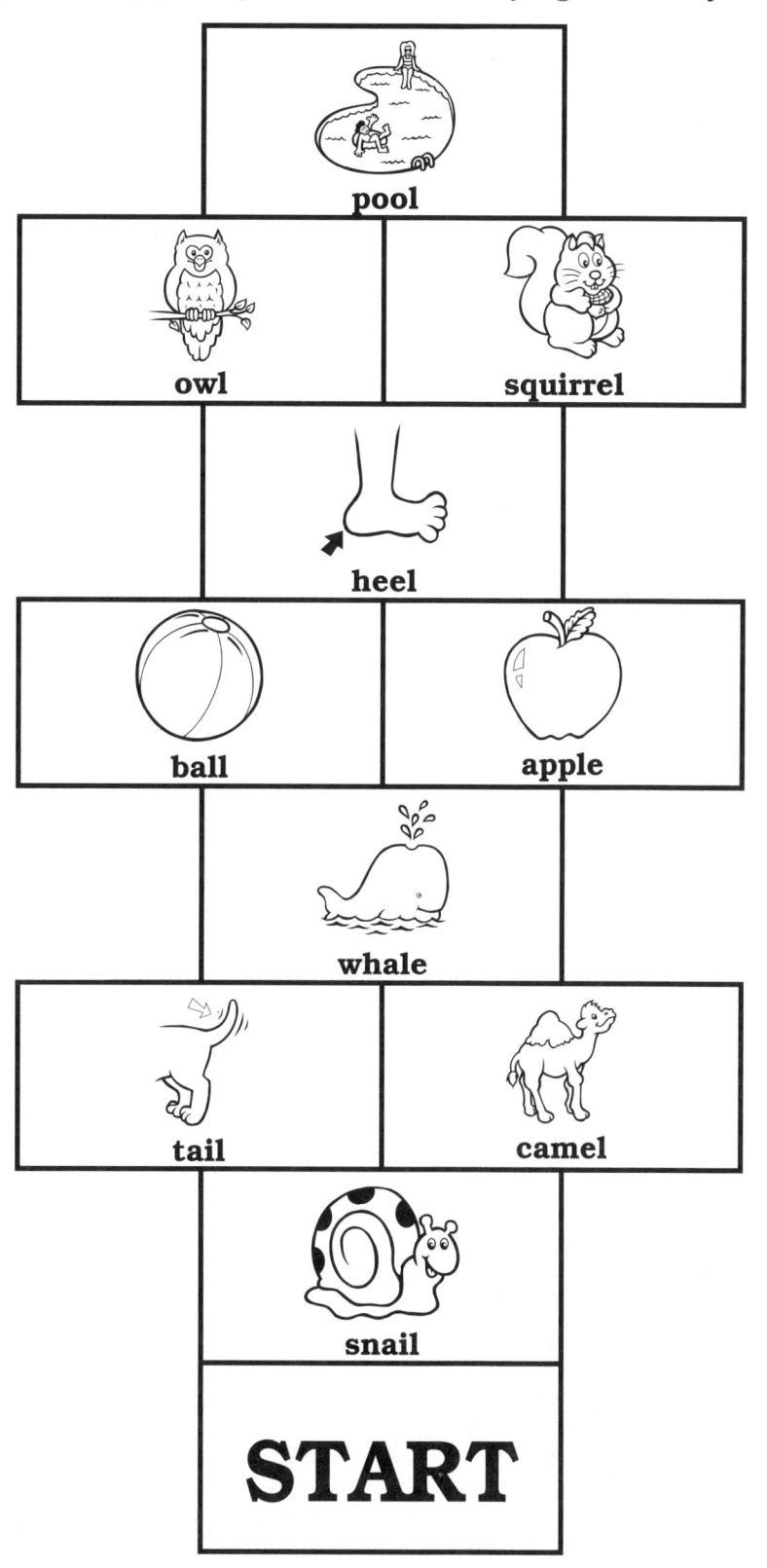

pool

owl | squirrel

heel

ball | apple

whale

tail | camel

snail

START

Homework Partner | Date | Speech-Language Pathologist | Final L Words

131

Pig Pile

Directions: Read/say aloud the phrases below. Then, cut out the pigs, and place them face down. Flip over a pig and read/say the phrase aloud. As you play, put the pigs on top of each other, making a "pig pile."

- swim in the pool
- a tiny snail
- a red apple
- the whale spouted
- the dog's tail
- the owl hooted
- a hungry camel
- my heel hurts

Homework Partner   Date   Speech-Language Pathologist

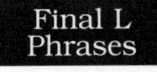

Final L Phrases

Ask and Answer

Directions: Practice saying each L picture–word. Then, read each statement in the middle. Answer with the phrase: "The_____ does!" filling in the correct L word. Then, draw a line from the sentence to the correct picture.

apple

What wags?

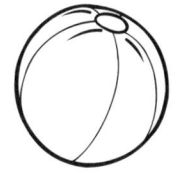

ball

What says, "whoo?"

whale

What crunches?

squirrel

What eats nuts?

snail

What bounces?

What creeps?

tail

camel

What drinks water?

What swims in water?

owl

Homework Partner — Date — Speech-Language Pathologist

Final L Phrases

Letter Shuffle

Directions: Read/say aloud the picture–words. Then, unscramble the letters in parenthesis to complete each phrase. Write the word in the blank space. Read/say each phrase aloud, using your best L sound.

whale

heel

1. a furry _____ (ailt)

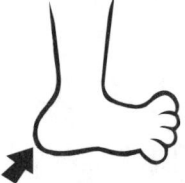

2. _____ to toe (eleh)

3. bounce the _____ (lalb)

4. Snooky the _____ (asiln)

tail

apple

5. a barn _____ (low)

6. the spout of a _____ (ewalh)

7. a _____ in the desert (cmlea)

camel

ball

8. the swimming _____ (oolp)

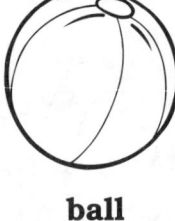

9. a nutty _____ (rreilqsu)

10. the crunchy _____ (epalp)

snail

owl

pool

squirrel

Homework Partner   Date   Speech-Language Pathologist

Final L Phrases

134 #BK-290 Webber® Artic Fun Sheets • ©2001 Super Duper® Publications • www.superduperinc.com • 1-800-277-8737

Pick a Toy

Directions: Finish the phrase, "I will catch a(n) ____," with a toy from the machine below. Read/say the completed sentence aloud using your best L sound.

"I will catch a(n) _____."

camel   apple   owl   squirrel

ball   heel   tail   whale

Homework Partner   Date   Speech-Language Pathologist

Final L Sentences

#BK-290 Webber® Artic Fun Sheets • ©2001 Super Duper® Publications • www.superduperinc.com • 1-800-277-8737

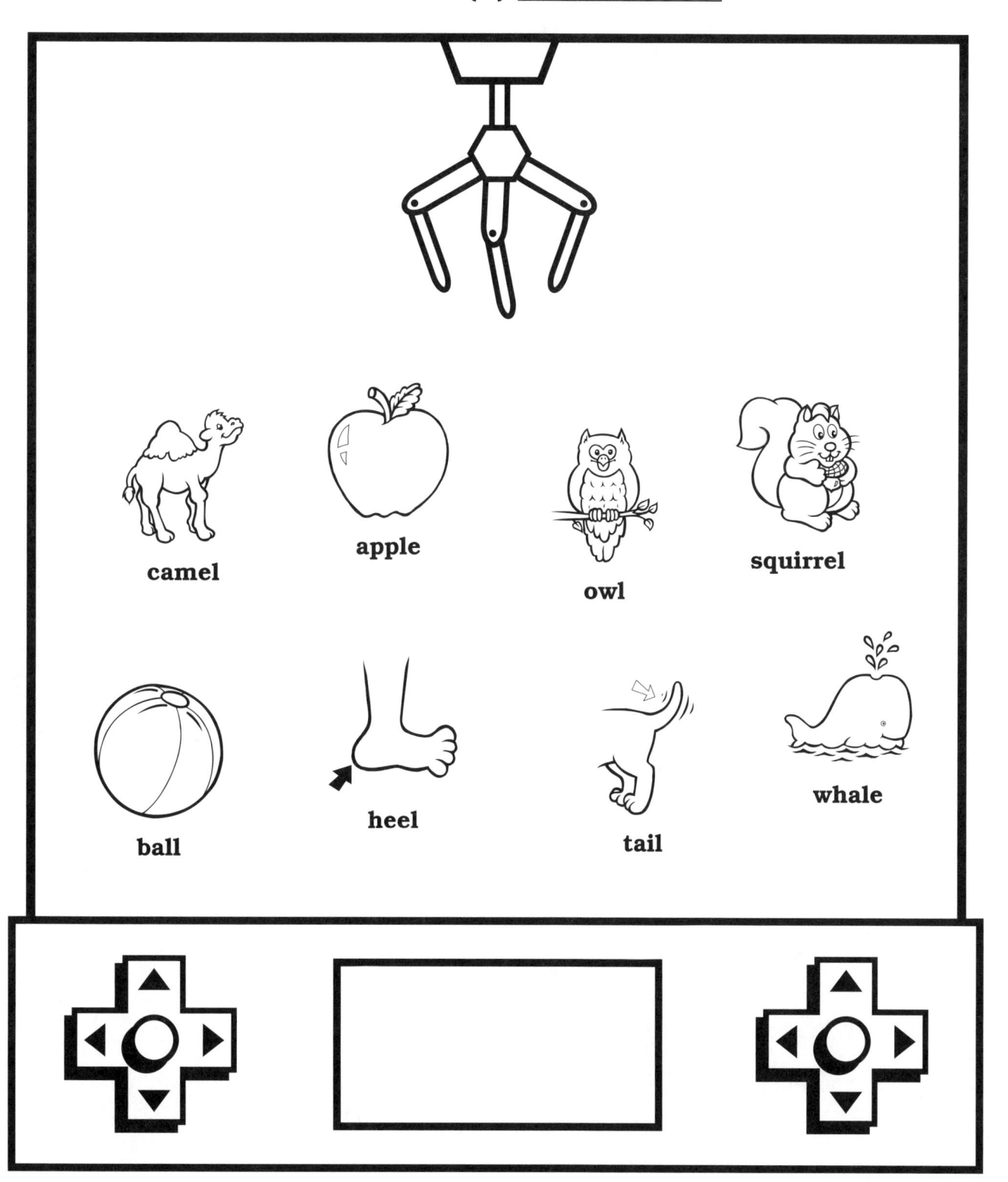

135

Fill 'er Up

Directions: Read/say aloud the picture–words. Fill up each sentence with a word from the Word Bank. Read/say each sentence aloud, using your best L sound.

Word Bank

- whale
- ball
- tail
- apple
- heel
- squirrel
- pool
- owl

1. Jump in the _____.

2. My dog's _____ is wagging.

3. The _____ is crunchy and juicy.

4. The gray _____ ran up the tree.

5. The _____ hunts food at night.

6. The great _____ swam to the shore.

7. The round _____ bounced high.

8. I hurt my _____ yesterday.

Answers: 1-pool, 2-tail, 3-apple, 4-squirrel, 5-owl, 6-whale, 7-ball, 8-heel

Homework Partner Date Speech-Language Pathologist

Final L Sentences

136 #BK-290 Webber® Artic Fun Sheets • ©2001 Super Duper® Publications • www.superduperinc.com • 1-800-277-8737

Scrambled Sentences

Directions: Try to unscramble each sentence. Write it on the line below the egg. Then read/say the sentence aloud, using your best L sound. _____

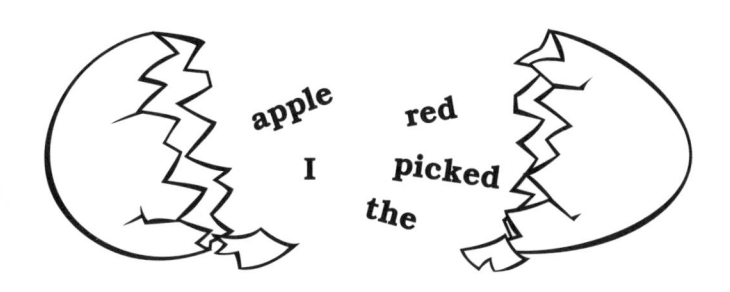

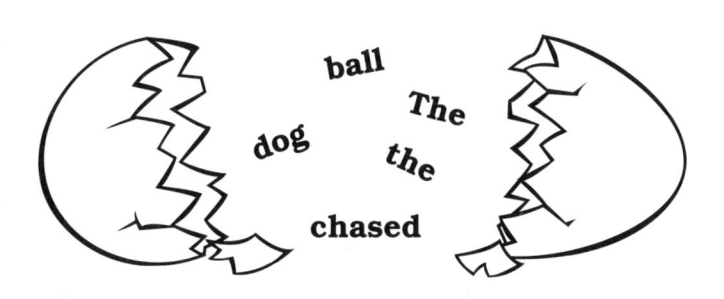

1. _____. (camel two humps The has)

2. _____. (My hurt cat tail its)

3. _____. (apple red I picked the)

4. _____. (sleeps day the owl in The)

5. _____. (ball The dog the chased)

6. _____. (ocean a whale He in saw the)

Answer key page 279

Homework Partner   Date   Speech-Language Pathologist

Final L Sentences

#BK-290 Webber® Artic Fun Sheets • ©2001 Super Duper® Publications • www.superduperinc.com • 1-800-277-8737

137

Sentence Completion

Directions: Read/say aloud the picture–words below. Then, cut out the pictures. Find the picture that best completes the sentence and glue/tape or place it under the correct phrase. Read/say the sentences aloud, using your good L sound.

You pick...	You make a sandwich with...	You pop a...	You drive a...	You bend your...
You catch a...	You bat your...	At the circus you see an...	You see a big beak on a...	You eat...

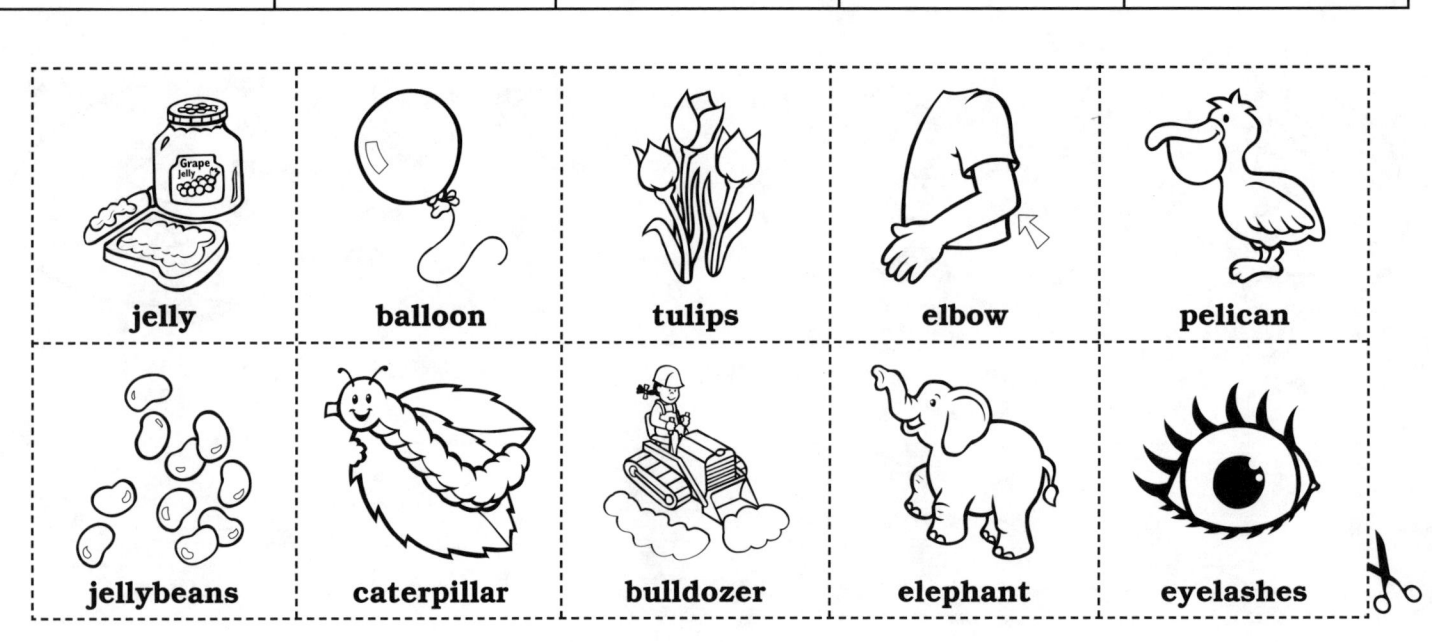

jelly   **balloon**   **tulips**   **elbow**   **pelican**

jellybeans   **caterpillar**   **bulldozer**   **elephant**   **eyelashes**

Homework Partner   Date   Speech-Language Pathologist   Medial L Words

Word in a Word

Directions: Read/say aloud the words on the left. Then, find smaller words inside the words you read that answer the statements on the right. ("**Jellybeans:** We had **beans** for dinner.") Read the sentence and answer aloud using your best L sound.

A   B

1. **jellybeans**   I am small and green. ___ ___ ___ ___

2. **caterpillar** You take me to feel better. ___ ___ ___ ___

3. **balloon**   You can kick this. ___ ___ ___ ___

4. **tulips**   You use these to kiss. ___ ___ ___ ___

5. **pelican**   You can drink soda out of me. ___ ___ ___

6. **elbow**   Girls wear me in their hair. ___ ___ ___

7. **bulldozer**   I am a large animal with horns. ___ ___ ___ ___

8. **eyelashes**   You use me to see. ___ ___ ___

Answers: 1-bean, 2-pill, 3-ball, 4-lips, 5-can, 6-bow, 7-bull, 8-eye

Homework Partner   Date   Speech-Language Pathologist   **Medial L Words**

Which Is?

Directions: Read/say the following questions aloud. Then, answer each question using your best L sound.

1. Which is smaller - a **pelican** or an **elephant**?

2. Which is bigger - an **elephant** or **tulips**?

3. Which is tinier - a **caterpillar** or a **pelican**?

4. Which is faster - a **pelican** or a **bulldozer**?

5. Which is heavier - an **elephant** or a **caterpillar**?

6. Which is lighter - a **balloon** or a **bulldozer**?

7. Which is harder - an **elbow** or **eyelash**?

8. Which is softer - **jellybeans** or **jelly**?

Answers: 1-pelican, 2-bulldozer, 3-caterpillar, 4-pelican, 5-elephant, 6-balloon, 7-elbow, 8-jelly.

Homework Partner   Date   Speech-Language Pathologist

Medial L Words

Categories

Directions: Read/say each word aloud. Then, choose the correct category from the choices below. Write the letter of the answer in the space provided.

1. **jellybeans** ____

2. **pelican** ____

3. **tulips** ____

4. **bulldozer** ____

5. **eyelashes** ____

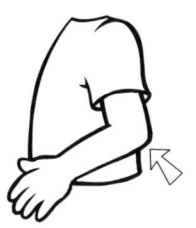

6. **elbow** ____

7. **caterpillar** ____

8. **elephant** ____

9. **jelly** ____

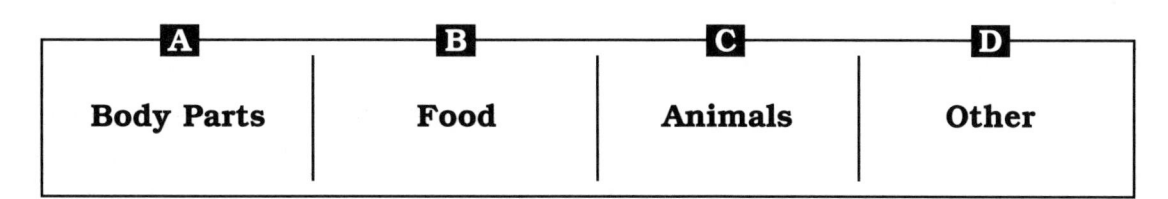

A	B	C	D
Body Parts	Food	Animals	Other

Answers: 1-B, 2-C, 3-D, 4-D, 5-A, 6-A, 7-C, 8-C, 9-B

Homework Partner _____ Date _____ Speech-Language Pathologist _____

Medial L Words

Who Said That?

Directions: Practice saying each L picture-word aloud. Read the statement in the middle. then, ask, **"Who said that?"** Answer with the correct word. Then, draw a line from the sentence to the correct picture.

pelican

"I grow in the garden."

jelly

"I'm fruity, chewy, and sweet."

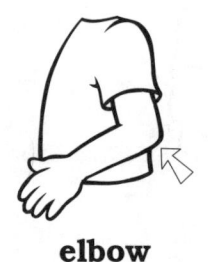

elbow

"I push up dirt and trees."

elephant

"I want to wade in water and eat fish."

tulips

"Feed me peanuts at the zoo."

jellybeans

"Put me on bread with peanut butter."

balloon

"When you hit me, it's <u>not</u> funny."

"I have air in me and go to birthday parties."

bulldozer

Homework Partner — Date — Speech-Language Pathologist

Medial L Words

Check it Out!

Directions: Read/say aloud the picture-words. Choose a word from the Word Bank and write it in the correct alphabetical space. Read/say the L word again, using your best L sound.

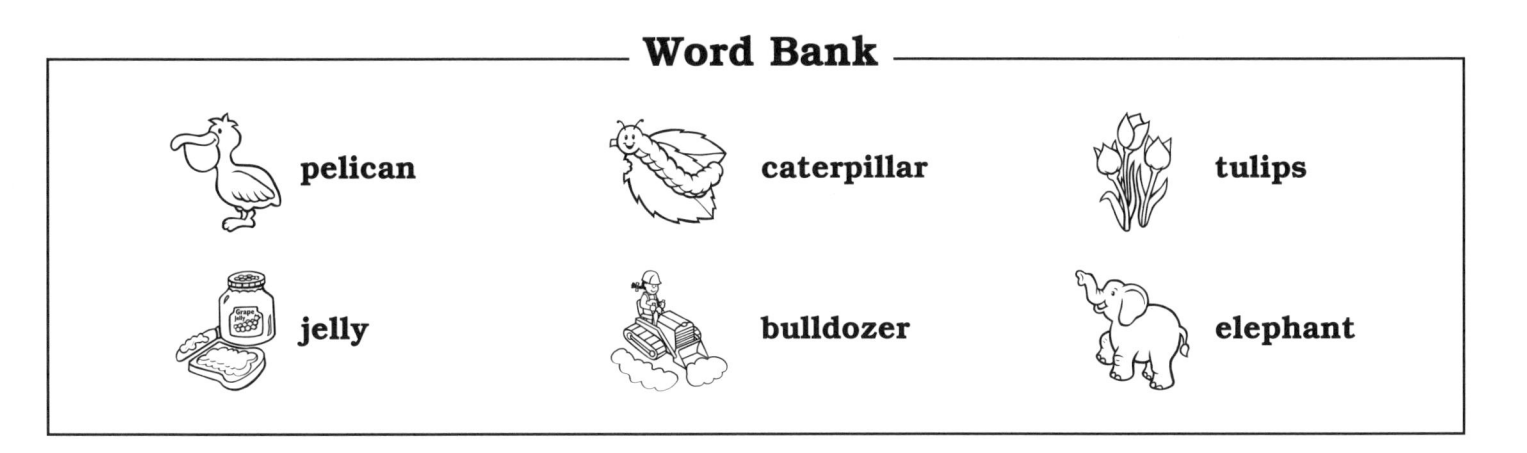

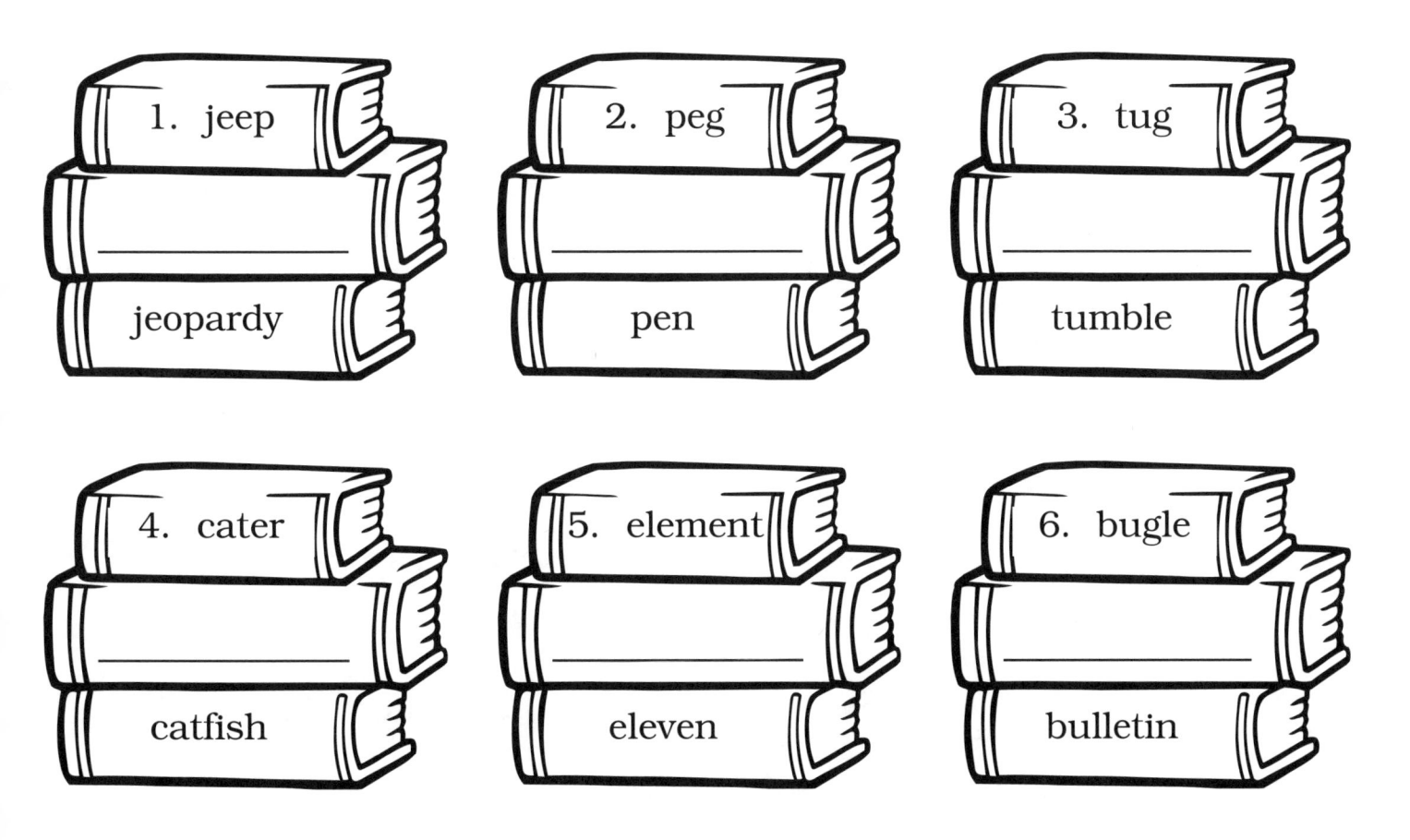

Word Bank

- pelican
- caterpillar
- tulips
- jelly
- bulldozer
- elephant

1. jeep
   _____
   jeopardy

2. peg
   _____
   pen

3. tug
   _____
   tumble

4. cater
   _____
   catfish

5. element
   _____
   eleven

6. bugle
   _____
   bulletin

Answer key: 1-jelly, 2-pelican, 3-tulips, 4-caterpillar, 5-elephant, 6-bulldozer.

Homework Partner   Date   Speech-Language Pathologist

Medial L Words

Crazy Phrase

Directions: Read/say aloud the picture–words on the right. Then, draw a line from the describing word in column "A" to a picture–word in column "B." Read/say each phrase aloud ("bending elbow"). Make the phrases as silly as you want.

A   **B**

bending   balloon

hungry   pelican

gigantic   elephant

big   elbow

noisy   bulldozer

sweet   jellybeans

puffy   eyelashes

soft   caterpillar

pretty   tulips

Homework Partner   Date   Speech-Language Pathologist

Medial L Phrases

Fix It! Phrases

Directions: Each phrase below has an incorrect letter in it. Fix each phrase by using/circling the correct letter on the right side of the book. Read/say aloud each correct phrase, using your good L sound.

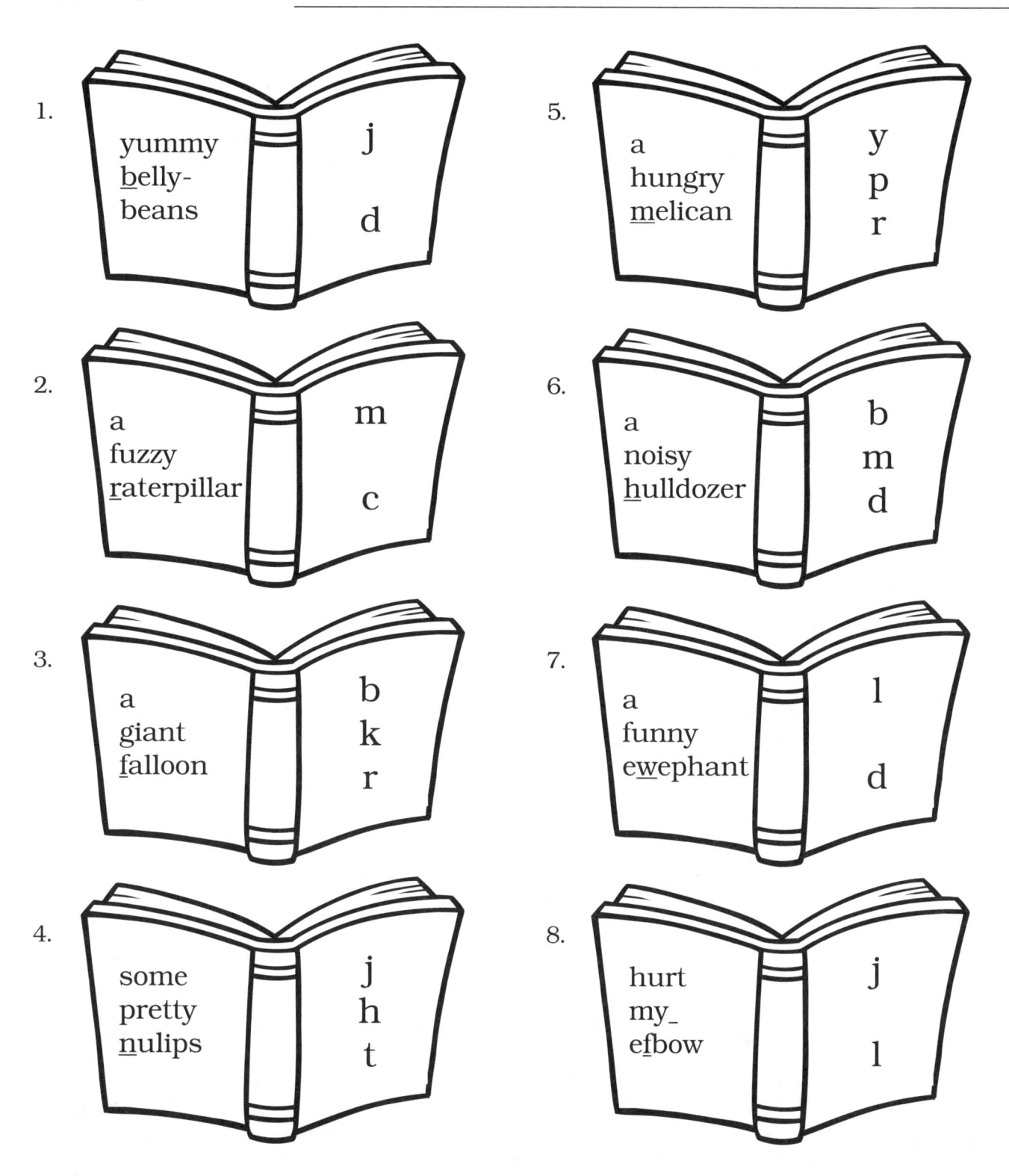

1. yummy <u>b</u>elly-beans — j / d

2. a fuzzy <u>r</u>aterpillar — m / c

3. a giant <u>f</u>alloon — b / k / r

4. some pretty <u>n</u>ulips — j / h / t

5. a hungry <u>m</u>elican — y / p / r

6. a noisy <u>h</u>ulldozer — b / m / d

7. a funny e<u>w</u>ephant — l / d

8. hurt my e<u>f</u>bow — j / l

Answer key: 1-j, 2-c, 3-b, 4-t, 5-p, 6-b, 7-l, 8-l

Homework Partner   Date   Speech-Language Pathologist

Medial L Phrases

145

"L" Soup

Directions: Cut out the phrases below. Pick up each phrase and place it on the matching picture in the soup bowl. Read/say each phrase aloud as you place it on the picture.

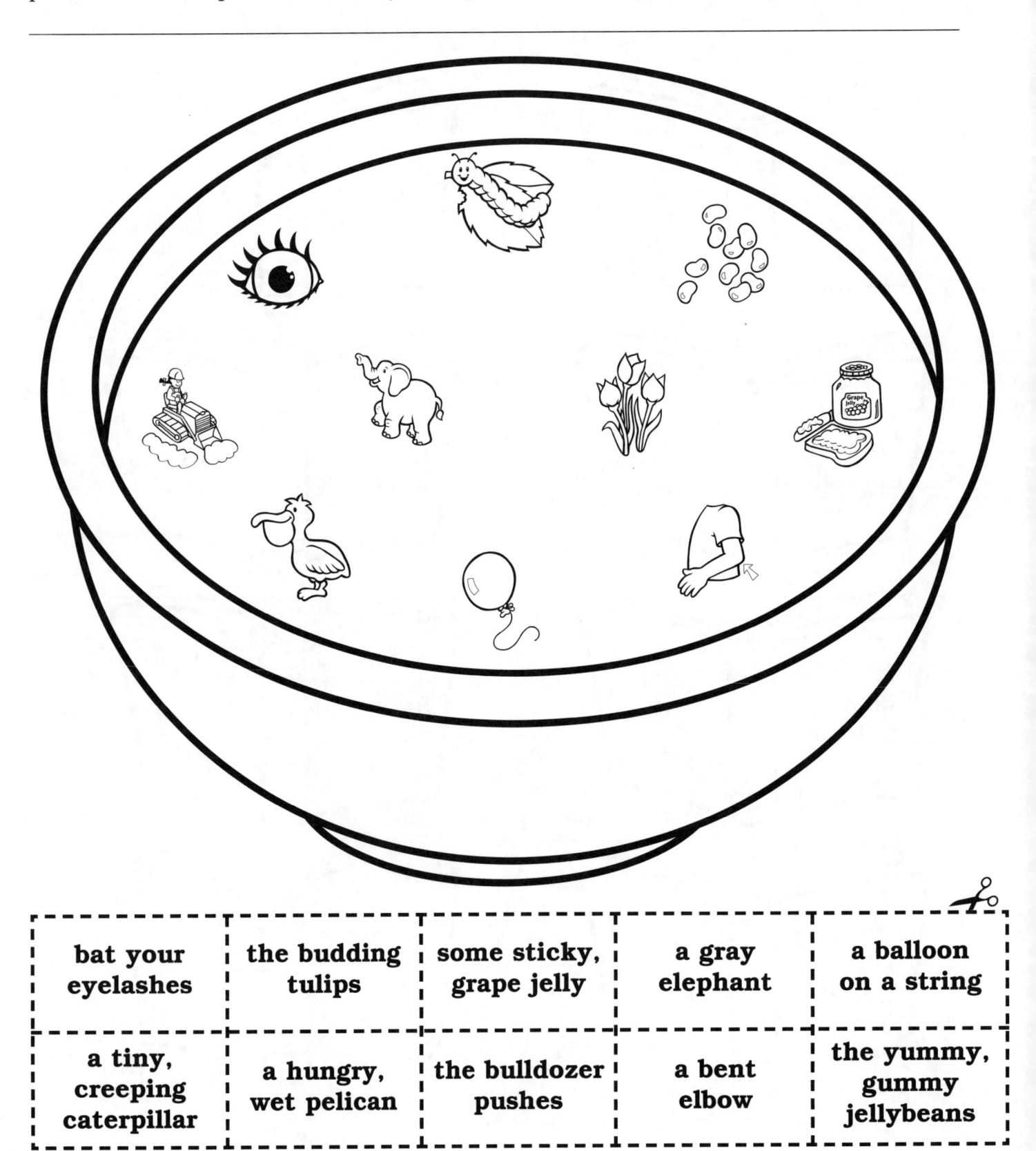

bat your eyelashes	the budding tulips	some sticky, grape jelly	a gray elephant	a balloon on a string
a tiny, creeping caterpillar	a hungry, wet pelican	the bulldozer pushes	a bent elbow	the yummy, gummy jellybeans

Homework Partner   Date   Speech-Language Pathologist

Medial L Phrases

Which One Fits?

Directions: Read/say each picture-word on the right. Then, complete each sentence by circling the correct answer. Read/say each sentence aloud using your best L sound.

1. I found _____ in my Easter basket.   **jellybeans**   **tulips**

2. I hurt my _____ playing soccer.   **eyelash**   **elbow**

3. The _____ climbed up the tree.   **elephant**   **caterpillar**

4. The farmer used a _____ to move the hay.   **bulldozer**   **pelican**

5. I got a _____ at the circus.   **elephant**   **balloon**

6. _____ are growing in my garden.   **tulips**   **jellybeans**

7. I put mascara on my _____.   **eyelashes**   **elbow**

8. I want a peanut butter and _____ sandwich.   **jelly**   **pelican**

Answer key: 1-jellybeans, 2-elbow, 3-caterpillar, 4-bulldozer, 5-balloon, 6-tulips, 7-eyelashes, 8-jelly

Homework Partner   Date   Speech-Language Pathologist   **Medial L Sentences**

True/False

Directions: Read the sentences below. Decide which ending makes the sentence true or false. Then, put a **T** for true and **F** for false on the line next to the correct answer. Read/say each true sentence aloud, using your good L sound.

1. The balloon will...
   _____ A. go up to the sky.
   _____ B. grow in the ground.

2. The big bulldozer...
   _____ A. carries tigers to the zoo.
   _____ B. moves dirt around.

3. The pelican...
   _____ A. creeps in the grass.
   _____ B. catches fish from the ocean.

4. The tulips...
   _____ A. grow in a garden.
   _____ B. grow in the water.

5. The elbow...
   _____ A. makes your knee bend.
   _____ B. makes your arm bend.

Answer key: 1. A) T, B) F; 2. A) F, B) T; 3. A) F, B) T; 4. A) T, B) F; 5. A) F, B) T

Homework Partner   Date   Speech-Language Pathologist

Medial L Sentences

Scoop-A-Sentence

Directions: Cut out the ice cream cone and scoops of ice cream. Read/say aloud each phrase on the scoops. Make a treat by putting an A scoop over a B scoop and placing them in the cone. Read/say the sentences aloud.

A

- A. Open the jellybeans
- A. Don't poke your elbow
- A. Smell the tulips
- A. Put some jelly
- A. Make a water balloon
- A. The elephant stomps
- A. Drive the bulldozer
- A. Watch the pelican

B

- B. in my ribs.
- B. and put them in a bowl.
- B. on the water.
- B. in a vase.
- B. around the circus tent.
- B. on the construction site.
- B. on the toast.
- B. in the yard.

Homework Partner   Date   Speech-Language Pathologist

Medial L Sentences

Number It Up!

Directions: Read/say aloud the picture–words. Number the words in the Word Bank below from 1-8 in any order you desire. Then, fill in the words on the lines that match the numbers. Read/say the sentences aloud using your good L sound.

Word Bank

caterpillar ____   balloon ____   elbow ____   eyelashes ____

tulips ____   bulldozer ____   jelly ____   elephant ____

1. I put mascara on my _____.

2. The _____ went up in the air.

3. She picked the pretty _____.

4. I fed the _____ a peanut.

5. I hurt my _____.

6. The _____ is noisy.

7. I want a _____ sandwich.

8. The _____ is in the cocoon.

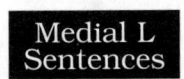

Homework Partner   Date   Speech-Language Pathologist

Medial L Sentences

Fire and Ice

Directions: Have your partner pick a picture on this page, but tell him/her not to tell you what it is. Then, try to figure out which picture your partner chose by asking questions. ("Lobster?") If the picture you chose is close to target, your partner should say, "You are hot." If it is far away from the target, he/she should say, "You are cold." Keep trying until you guess your partner's picture. Then, switch places.

lobster	**ball**	**caterpillar**	**lamp**
elbow	**ladder**	**laundry**	**camel**
apple	**bulldozer**	**tulips**	**log**

Homework Partner   Date   Speech-Language Pathologist

Combo L Words

Secret Word

Directions: Read/say aloud each picture–word below. Write the answers from the Word Bank in the blank spaces. The letters in the square will spell out a secret word. Use the Bonus Clue to help you. Say aloud the secret word, using your good L sound.

Word Bank

lamp   owl   leaf   elbow
tulips   pool   ladder   jellybeans

1. I grow in the ground. __ __ __ __ __ __
                             8

2. I hoot. __ __ __
                1

3. Turn me on to see. __ __ __ __
                          9

4. These are small candies. __ __ __ __ __ __ __ __ __ __
                                5   3

5. Jump in for a quick swim. __ __ __ __
                                   2

6. I am the part of your arm that bends. __ __ __ __ __

7. Crawl up my rungs. __ __ __ __ __ __
                          4   6

8. I grow on a tree. __ __ __ __
                             7

Secret Word ☐ ☐ ☐ ☐ ☐ ☐ ☐ ☐ ☐ !
             1 2 3 4 5 6 7 8 9

Answer: wonderful!

Homework Partner   Date   Speech-Language Pathologist   Combo L Words

152   #BK-290 Webber® Artic Fun Sheets • ©2001 Super Duper® Publications • www.superduperinc.com • 1-800-277-8737

What Is It?

Directions: Read the questions. Then, circle the correct answer to each question. Read/say each answer aloud, using your best L sound.

1. What has wings and a large beak?	pelican	dancer
2. What can pop?	saw	balloon
3. What tastes sour?	lemon	sandwich
4. What can we eat?	apple	seven
5. What do firemen use?	fox	ladder
6. What do we put on a sandwich?	bats	jelly
7. What can we kick?	ball	sun
8. What do we wash?	laundry	dinosaur

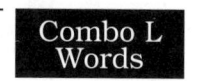

Homework Partner   Date   Speech-Language Pathologist

Combo L Words

Finger Hopscotch

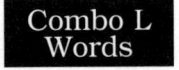

Directions: Read/say aloud the picture–words below. Then, slide a penny across the hopscotch board. Hop your finger to the square it lands on. Read/say the name of the picture–word again, practicing your good L sound. Play again until you have landed on all the words.

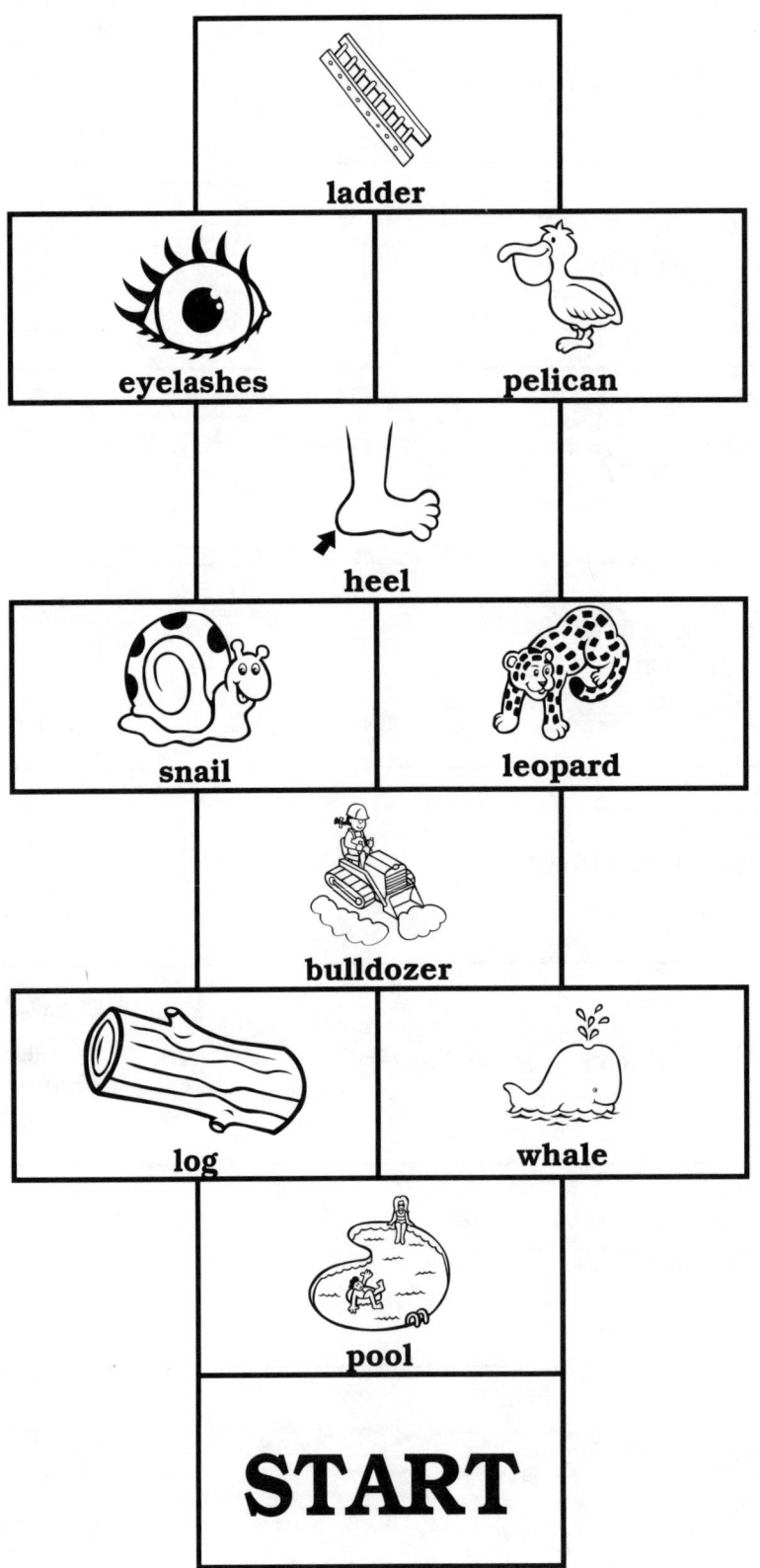

ladder

eyelashes | pelican

heel

snail | leopard

bulldozer

log | whale

pool

START

Homework Partner | Date | Speech-Language Pathologist

Combo L Words

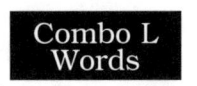

Analogies

Directions: Read/say aloud the picture-words below. Then, read each analogy and choose an answer from the Word Bank. Read/say your answer aloud using your best L sound.

1. Smell is to nose as walk is to _____.

2. Sweet is to sugar as sour is to _____.

3. Leg is to knee as arm is to _____.

4. Spaghetti is to meatball as peanut butter is to _____.

5. Pig is to snout as _____ is to trunk.

6. Fast is to rabbit as slow is to _____.

7. Grape is to vine as _____ is to tree.

8. Fish is to water as _____ is to desert.

Word Bank

elephant   lemon   snail   elbow
jelly   apple   legs   camel

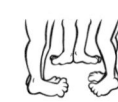

Scrambled Words

Directions: Read/say aloud the picture–words on the right. Then, unscramble the words below and write the answers in the blanks. Use the pictures to help you. Read/say your answers aloud using your best L sound.

1. **mlace** ___ ___ ___ ___ ___

2. **bwloe** ___ ___ ___ ___ ___

3. **fael** ___ ___ ___ ___

4. **ropelad** ___ ___ ___ ___ ___ ___ ___

5. **ehle** ___ ___ ___ ___

6. **tilspu** ___ ___ ___ ___ ___ ___

7. **qlusrrie** ___ ___ ___ ___ ___ ___ ___ ___

8. **apnliec** ___ ___ ___ ___ ___ ___ ___

9. **lpma** ___ ___ ___ ___

heel

elbow

leaf

leopard

tulips   lamp   pelican   squirrel   camel

Answer key: 1-camel, 2-elbow, 3-leaf, 4-leopard, 5-heel, 6-tulips, 7-squirrel, 8-pelican, 9-lamp

Homework Partner   Date   Speech-Language Pathologist

Combo L Words

156   #BK-290 Webber® Artic Fun Sheets • ©2001 Super Duper® Publications • www.superduperinc.com • 1-800-277-8737

Color Phrase

Directions: Color each picture a different color. Then, make up a phrase combining the color with the object in the picture ("a pink apple"). Say each phrase aloud, using your good L sound.

Homework Partner   Date   Speech-Language Pathologist

Combo L Phrases

Phrase Race

Directions: Read/say aloud the picture–words below. Then, cut out the markers. Flip a coin (heads=1, tails=2) to determine how many spaces to move. As you move, read/say each phrase aloud, using your good L sound. First player to reach the finish wins.

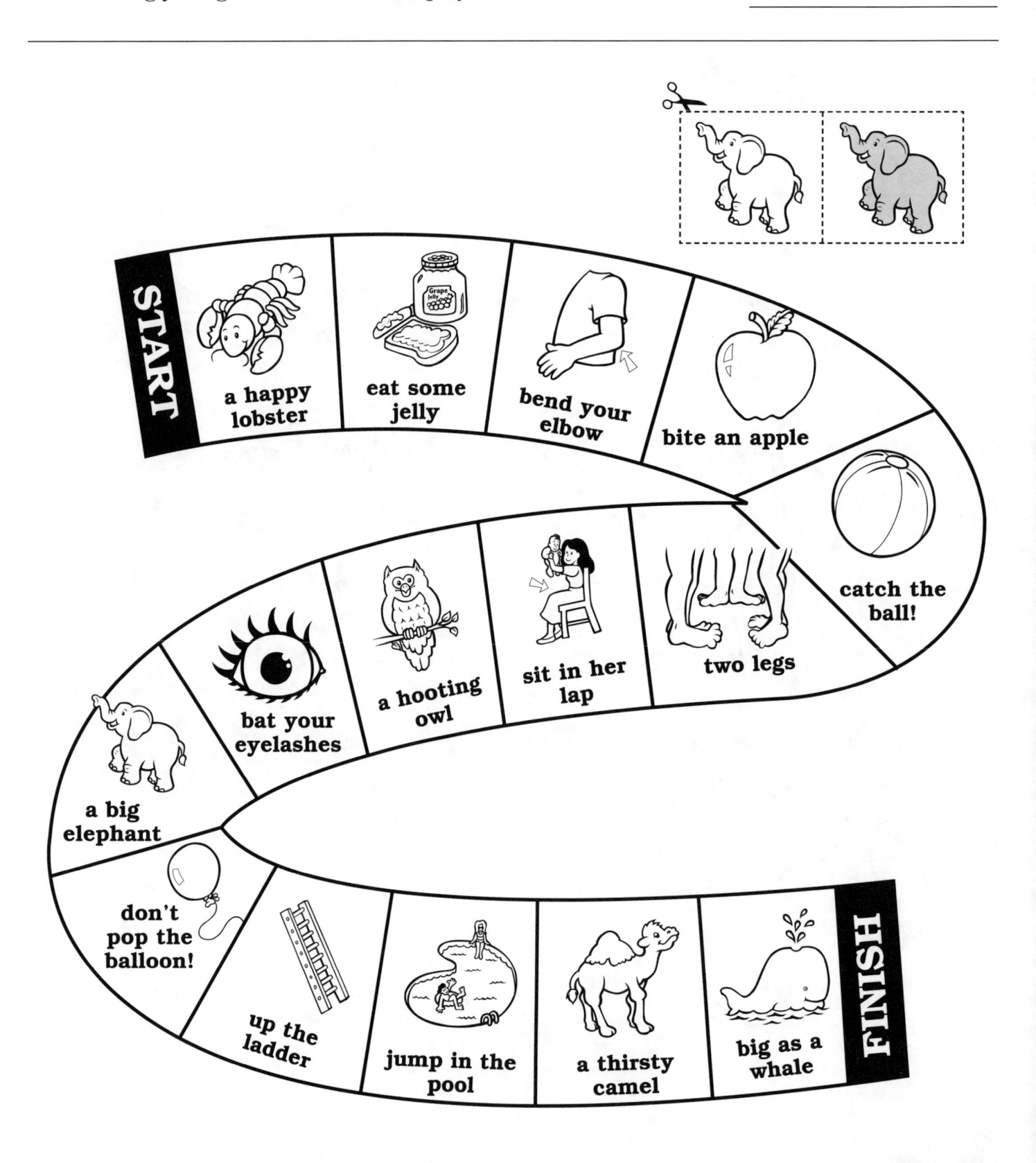

START
- a happy lobster
- eat some jelly
- bend your elbow
- bite an apple
- catch the ball!
- two legs
- sit in her lap
- a hooting owl
- bat your eyelashes
- a big elephant
- don't pop the balloon!
- up the ladder
- jump in the pool
- a thirsty camel
- big as a whale

FINISH

Homework Partner   Date   Speech-Language Pathologist

Combo L Phrases

158

L Phrase It

Directions: Assemble the cube as follows: If you prefer, glue onto construction paper for added durability. Cut along the dotted lines. Fold on solid lines and glue as indicated. To play: Roll both cubes. Read/say the word and picture together aloud to make up a phrase ("hungry squirrel"). Remember to use your good L sound.

Glue B

lamp

Glue Tab C | laundry | pelican | snail | jellybeans | Glue Tab B
Glue C

Glue Tab A

squirrel

Glue A

Glue B

yummy

Glue Tab C | hungry | dirty | bright | tired | Glue Tab B
Glue C

Glue Tab A

quiet

Glue A

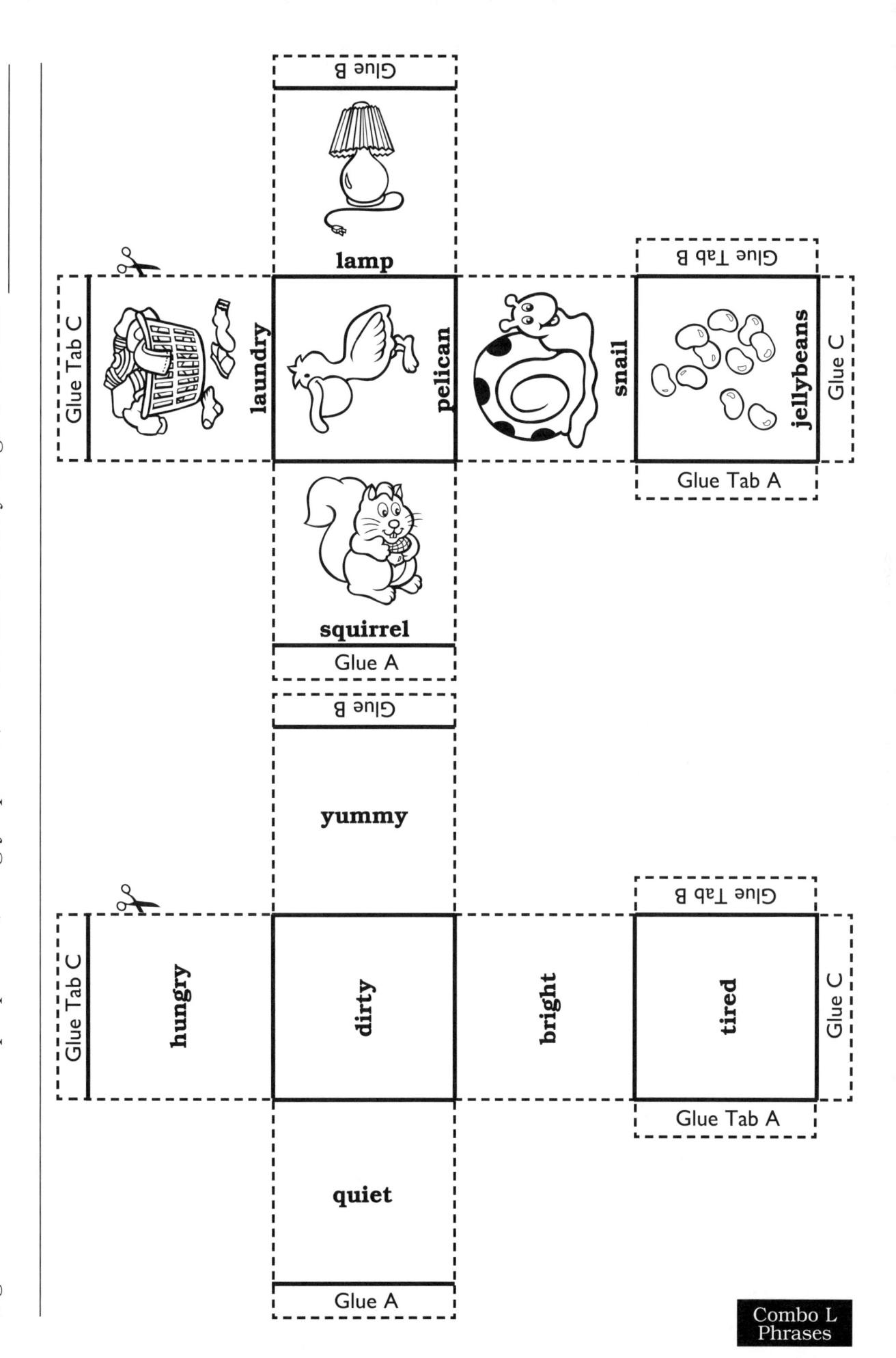

Combo L Phrases

Q & A Match Up

Directions: Read the questions and find the answers at the bottom. Write the question number on the line of the matching answer. Then, read/say each answer aloud ("thick eyelashes"). Use your good L sound!

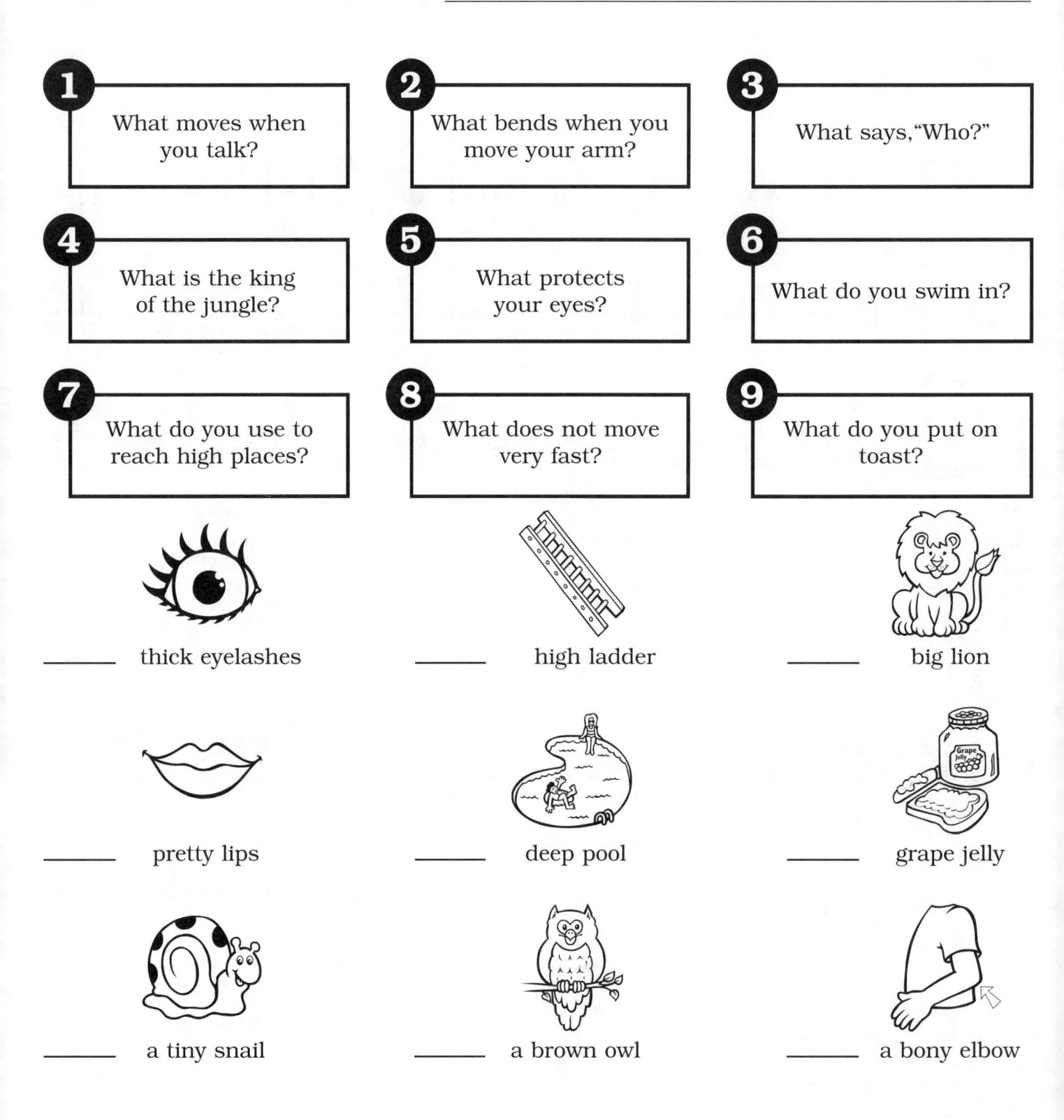

1 What moves when you talk?

2 What bends when you move your arm?

3 What says, "Who?"

4 What is the king of the jungle?

5 What protects your eyes?

6 What do you swim in?

7 What do you use to reach high places?

8 What does not move very fast?

9 What do you put on toast?

_____ thick eyelashes

_____ high ladder

_____ big lion

_____ pretty lips

_____ deep pool

_____ grape jelly

_____ a tiny snail

_____ a brown owl

_____ a bony elbow

Homework Partner   Date   Speech-Language Pathologist

Combo L Phrases

Fill It Up!

Directions: Read/say aloud the picture–words below. Then, read each sentence and put the correct word in each blank space. Read/say the sentences aloud using your good L sound.

Word Bank

- lion
- balloon
- leopard
- tulips
- lemon
- whale
- heel
- caterpillar

1. A _____ is in the tree.
2. The _____ is hungry.
3. Don't pop the _____.
4. We picked the _____.
5. We saw a big _____.
6. I hurt my _____.
7. A _____ is roaring.
8. I ate a sour _____.

Homework Partner   Date   Speech-Language Pathologist

Combo L Sentences

Finish the Sentence

Directions: Complete each sentence by telling what you would do. Say the complete sentence aloud, using your best L sound.

1. If I had a pet leopard... _____
_____.

2. If I picked some tulips... _____
_____.

3. If I had a tail... _____
_____.

4. If I could drive a bulldozer... _____
_____.

5. If my house was a log... _____
_____.

6. If I was a snail... _____
_____.

7. If I ate 1,000 jellybeans... _____
_____.

8. If I rode a camel... _____
_____.

Homework Partner   Date   Speech-Language Pathologist

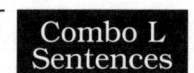

Combo L Sentences

Make It Fit!!

Directions: Circle the words that best finish the sentences below. Then, read/say the sentences aloud, using your best L sound.

1. The boy went up the   **whale**   **ladder**   **tulips**   .

2. I hurt my   **elbow**   **squirrel**   **lamp**   .

3. I need to do the   **bulldozer**   **owl**   **laundry**   .

4. Swim in the   **pelican**   **pool**   **lemon**   .

5. I popped my red   **balloon**   **lap**   **whale**   .

6. "Hoot-Hoot" said the   **leopard**   **elbow**   **owl**   .

7. I took a bite of the   **leaf**   **apple**   **caterpillar**   .

Homework Partner   Date   Speech-Language Pathologist

Combo L Sentences

#BK-290 Webber® Artic Fun Sheets • ©2001 Super Duper® Publications • www.superduperinc.com • 1-800-277-8737

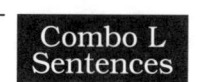

Scrambled Sentences

Directions: Try to unscramble each sentence. Write it on the line below the egg. Then read/say the sentence aloud, using your good L sound.

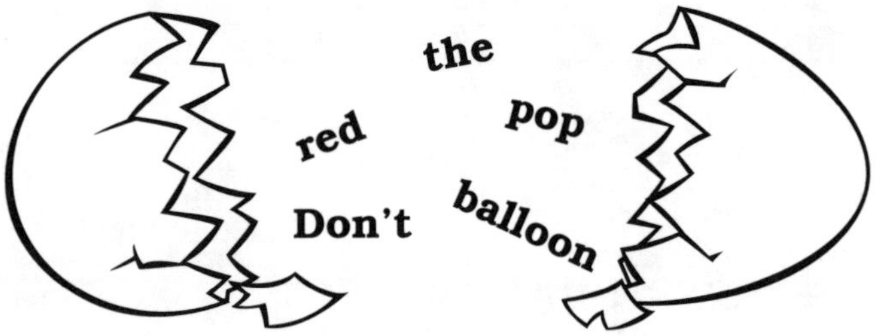

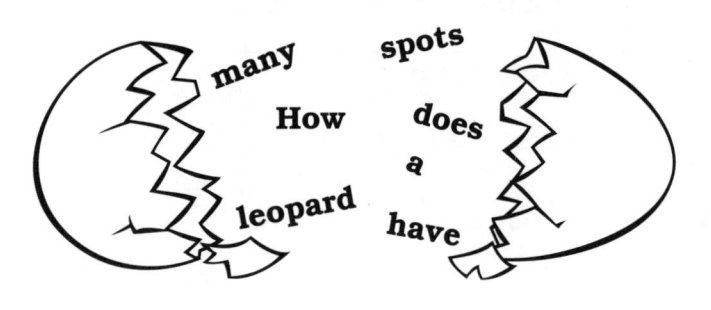

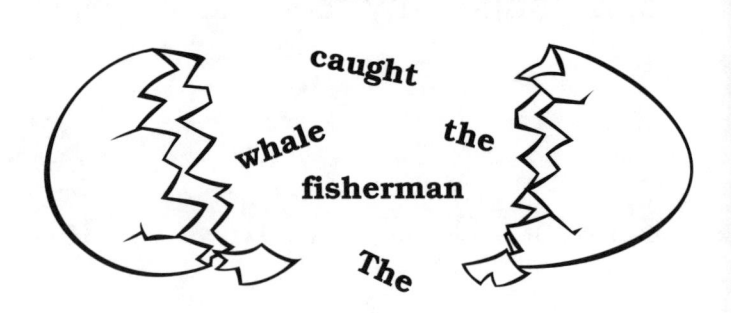

1. I ate jellybeans at Easter.

2. She hit her heel on the chair.

3. The baby sat on Santa's lap.

4. Don't pop the red balloon.

5. How many spots does a leopard have?

6. The fisherman caught the whale.

Z Sound

3 Games in 1

Directions: Say aloud the picture-words below, using your good Z sound.
Then, play one of the following games:

☐ Lotto – Caller reads out a word and student repeats the word and covers it with a token/chip.

☐ Tic-Tac-Toe – Each time you write an **X** or **O**, say the word you mark over.

☐ Memory – Cut out all the cards and place face down. Try to find matching pairs. Say aloud each word you find. Keep all matches.

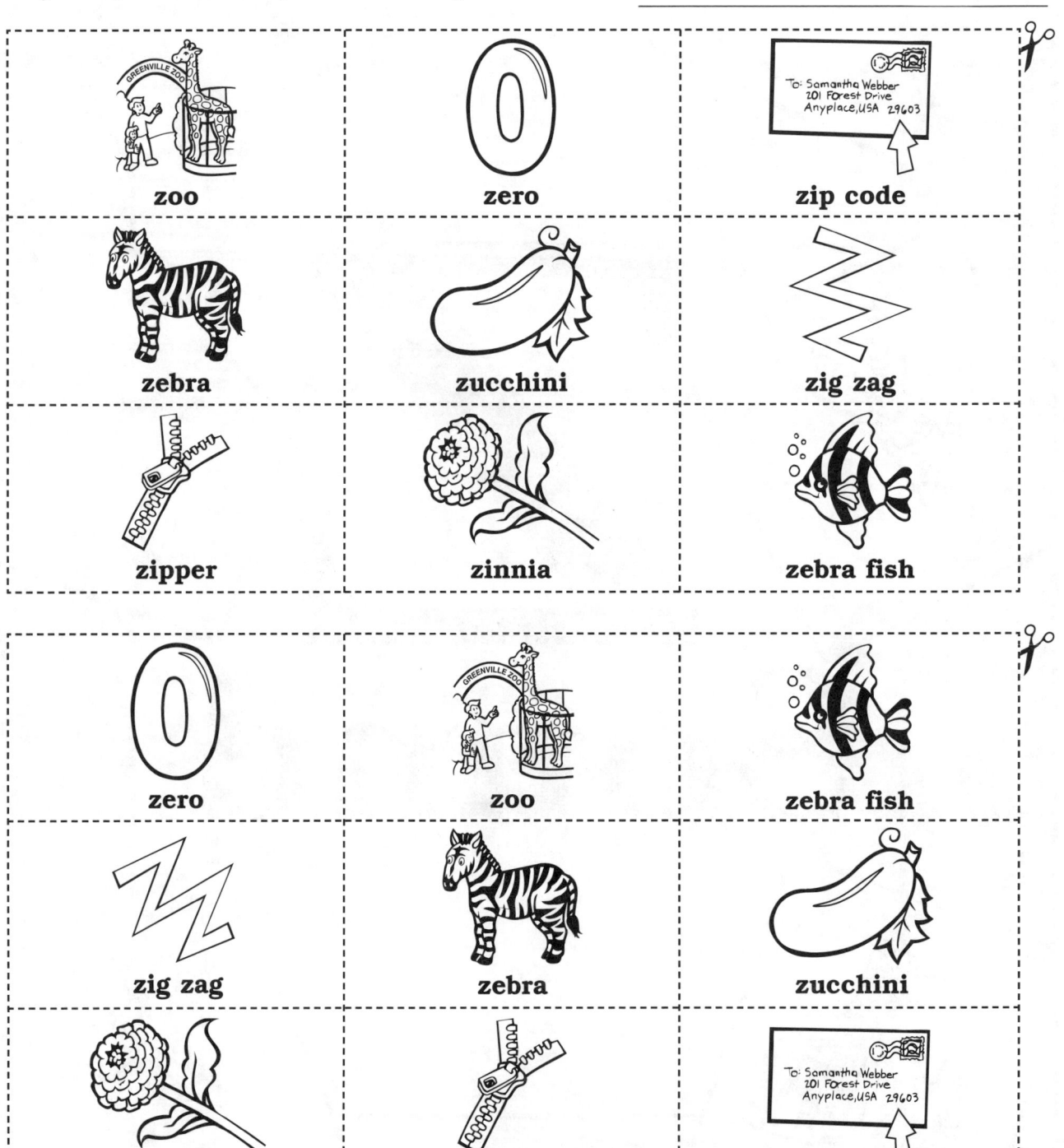

zoo	zero	zip code
zebra	**zucchini**	**zig zag**
zipper	**zinnia**	**zebra fish**

zero	zoo	zebra fish
zig zag	**zebra**	**zucchini**
zinnia	**zipper**	**zip code**

Homework Partner   Date   Speech-Language Pathologist   Initial Z Words

166   #BK-290 Webber® Artic Fun Sheets • ©2001 Super Duper® Publications • www.superduperinc.com • 1-800-277-8737

Z Cube Roll

Directions: Assemble the cube as follows: Glue onto construction paper for added durability. Cut along the dotted lines. Fold on solid lines and glue as indicated. To play: Roll the cube. Read/say aloud the word you see using your best Z sound.

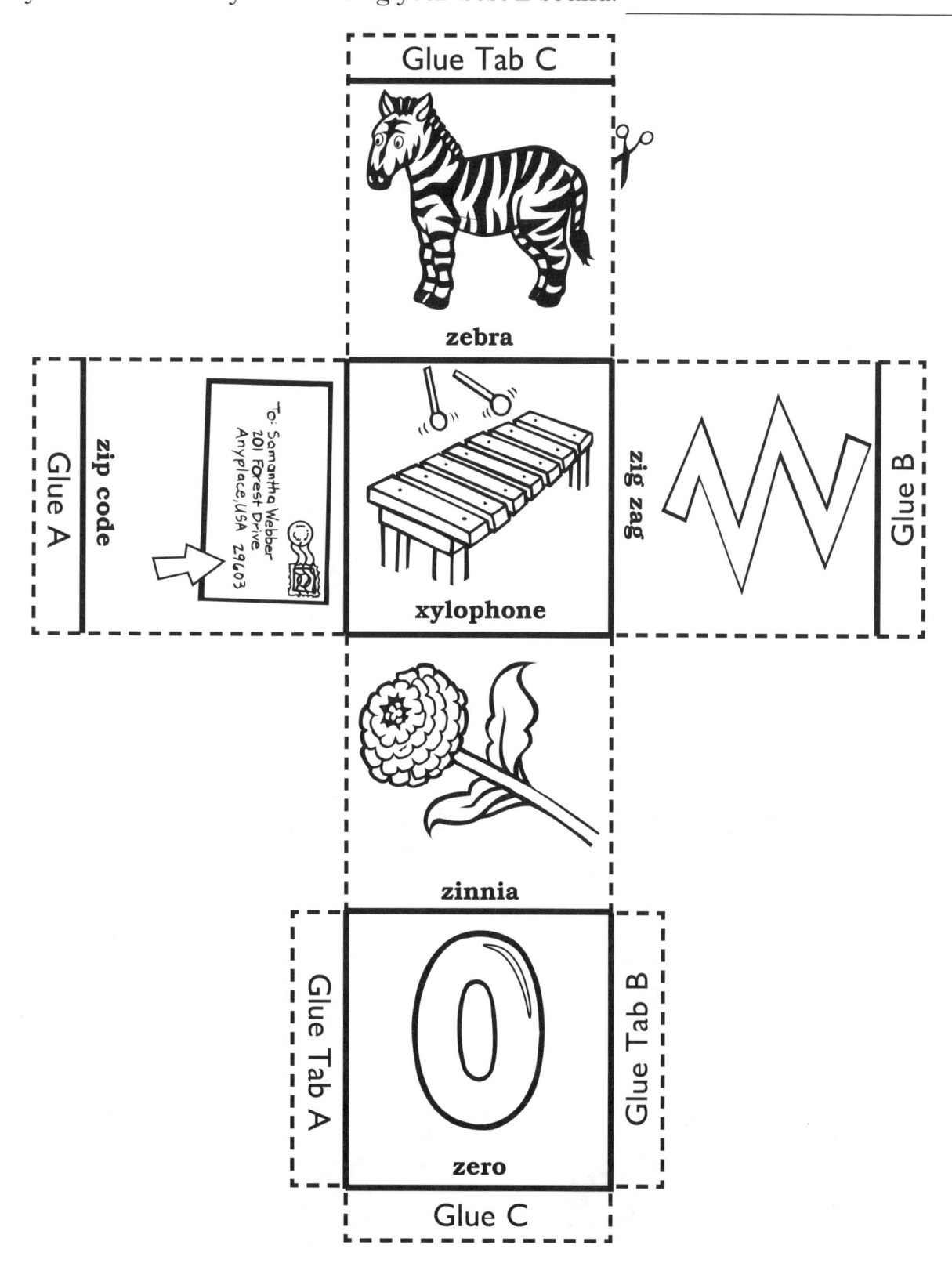

Glue Tab C

zebra

Glue A | zip code | xylophone | zig zag | Glue B

zinnia

Glue Tab A | zero | Glue Tab B

Glue C

Homework Partner | Date | Speech-Language Pathologist

Initial Z Words

167

#BK-290 Webber® Artic Fun Sheets • ©2001 Super Duper® Publications • www.superduperinc.com • 1-800-277-8737

Make a Zebra

Directions: Read/say aloud the Z words below. Then, cut out the stripes at the bottom. As you read/say each word again, glue/tape or place them on the zebra. _____

zebra

zinnia

zucchini

zebra fish

zipper

zip code

zoo

zero

_____ _____ _____ Initial Z Words
Homework Partner Date Speech-Language Pathologist

168 #BK-290 Webber® Artic Fun Sheets • ©2001 Super Duper® Publications • www.superduperinc.com • 1-800-277-8737

Under the Sea

Directions: Read/say aloud the words below. Then, cut out the fish. Fill the aquarium with the fish, saying the name of each picture as you place it in the aquarium. Use your good Z sound!

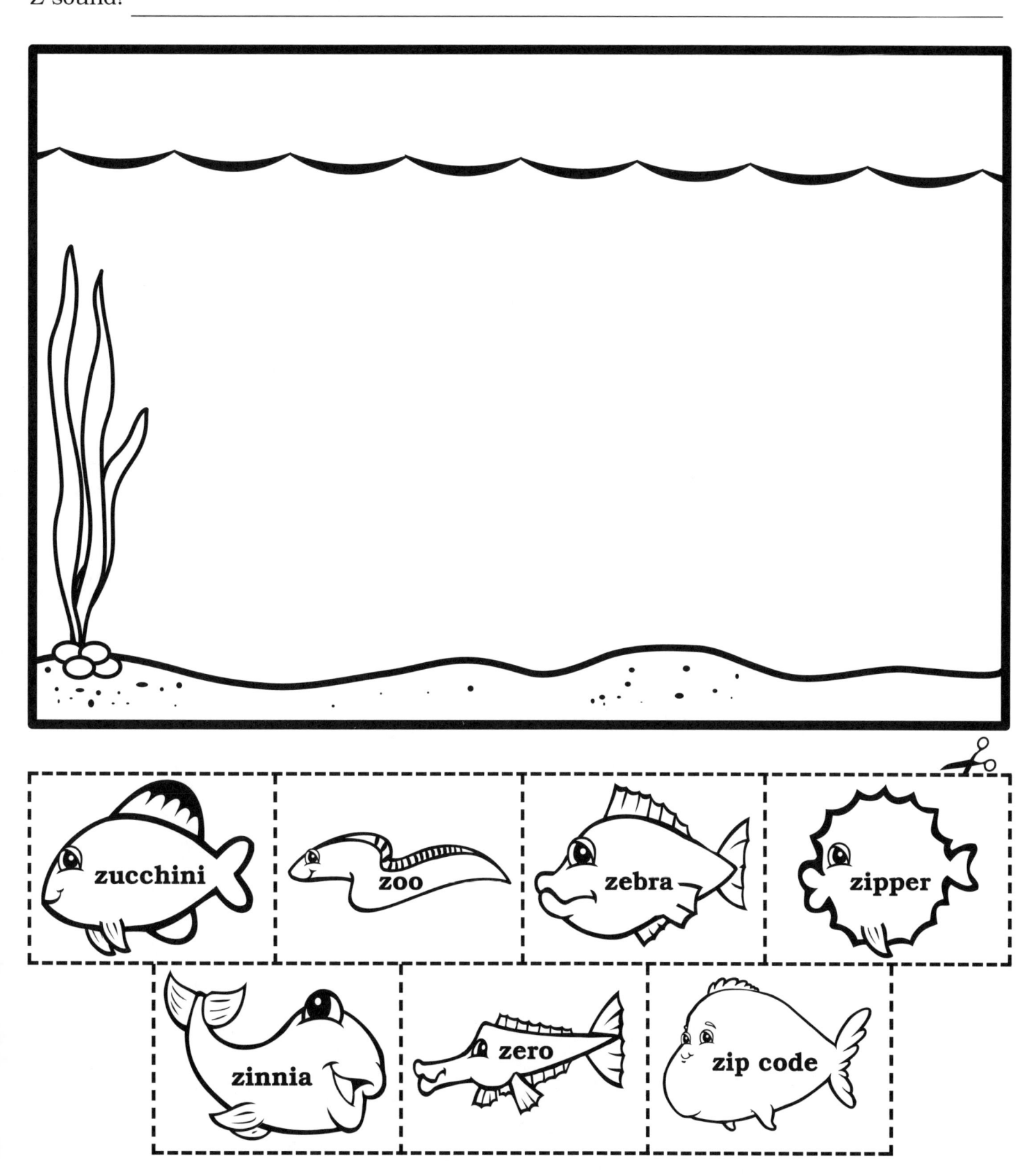

zucchini   zoo   zebra   zipper

zinnia   zero   zip code

Homework Partner   Date   Speech-Language Pathologist

Initial Z Words

Spinner Action

Directions: Read/say aloud the picture–words below. If you prefer, glue this page to construction paper for added durability. Cut out the arrow/dial. Use a brad to connect the dial to the circle. Spin the spinner. When you land on a picture, read/say the word aloud, using your best Z sound.

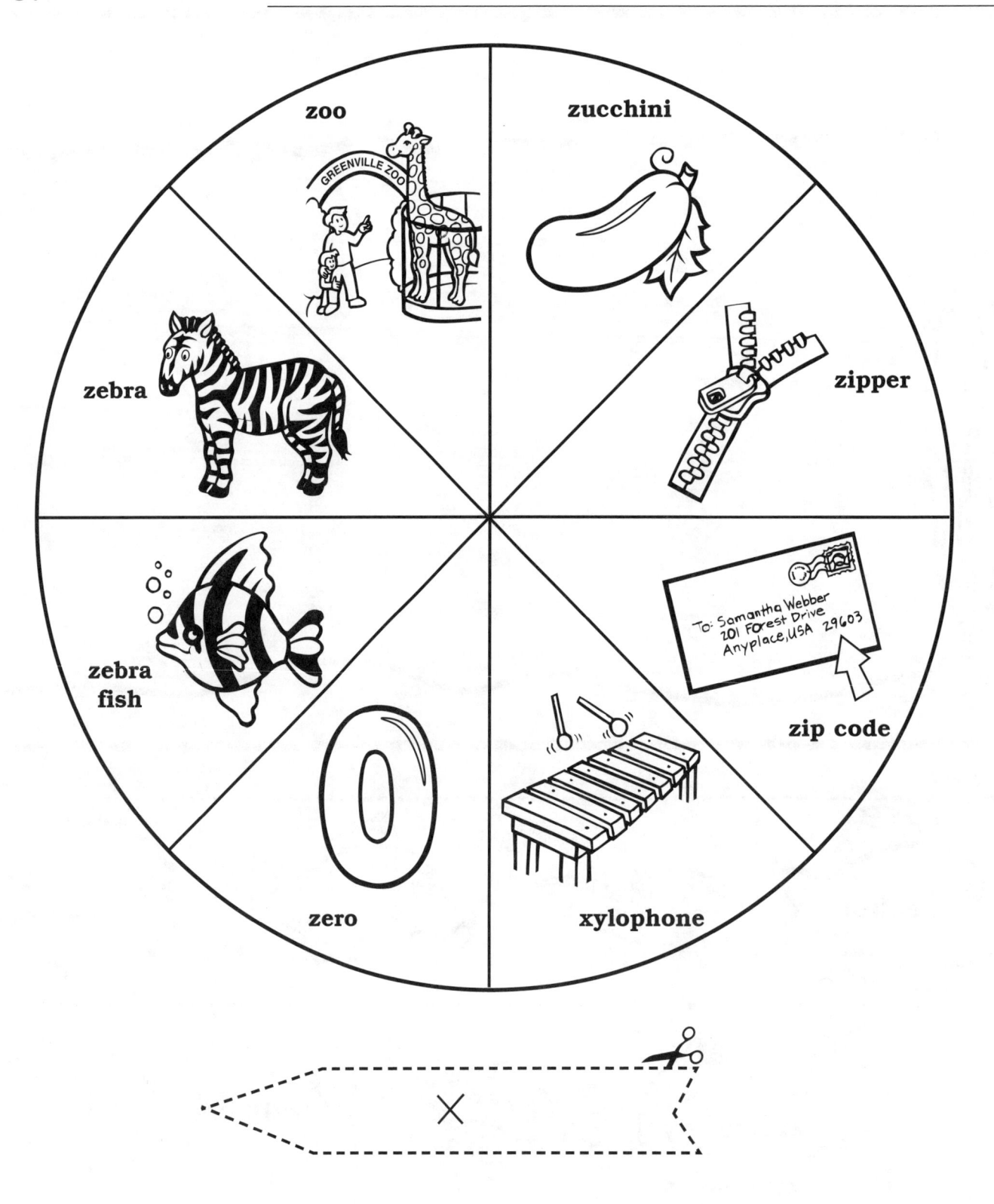

- zoo
- zucchini
- zipper
- zip code
- xylophone
- zero
- zebra fish
- zebra

Homework Partner   Date   Speech-Language Pathologist

Initial Z Words

Buzz Words

Directions: Let the bees help you read/say your Z words correctly. Circle the correct word containing the Z sound. Read/say the words aloud.

1. zoo / soo
2. zip code / sip code
3. sig zag / zig zag
4. sero / zero
5. zipper / sipper
6. sylophone / xylophone

Answers: 1. zoo, 2. zipcode, 3. zig zag, 4. zero, 5. zipper, 6. xylophone

Homework Partner   Date   Speech-Language Pathologist   Initial Z Words

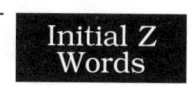

Ask and Answer

Directions: Cut along the dotted lines. Fold paper back along solid black line to cover up pictures. Read the questions and guess the answers. Say your answers aloud using your best Z sound.

1. What is the name of the numbers after the city and state on an envelope?

    zip code

2. What is the place where animals live?

    zoo

3. What is the name of the design that goes side to side?

    zig zag

4. What is the name of the animal with black and white stripes?

    zebra

5. What is a green vegetable that looks like a cucumber?

    zucchini

6. What is a number less than one?

    zero

7. What do you use to fasten pants and jackets?

    zipper

8. What is a type of flower?

    zinnia

Fold here

Homework Partner   Date   Speech-Language Pathologist

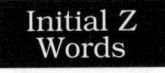

Initial Z Words

Riddle Detective

Directions: Read/say aloud the picture–words. Then, read the riddles below. Choose the correct answers from the Word Bank. Write the answers in the spaces. Read/say your answers aloud using your good Z sound.

Word Bank

- xylophone
- zero
- zebra
- zipper
- zinnia
- zebra fish

1. I have black and white stripes.
   You can catch me.
   I swim in a school.
   What am I?

   _____

2. I am round.
   I mean nothing.
   I can look like a doughnut.
   What am I?

   _____

3. I am colorful.
   I grow in dirt.
   People like to put me in a vase.
   What am I?

   _____

4. I can play a beautiful sound.
   People tap me with sticks.
   I can have different colors.
   What am I?

   _____

Answers: 1-zebra fish, 2-zero, 3-zinnia, 4-xylophone

Homework Partner   Date   Speech-Language Pathologist

Initial Z Words

X and O

Directions: Cut out each X and O below. Have each player/partner choose X or O. The first player reads/says a picture phrase aloud and places an X or O on the square. Play continues in turn. The first person to get three in a row wins.

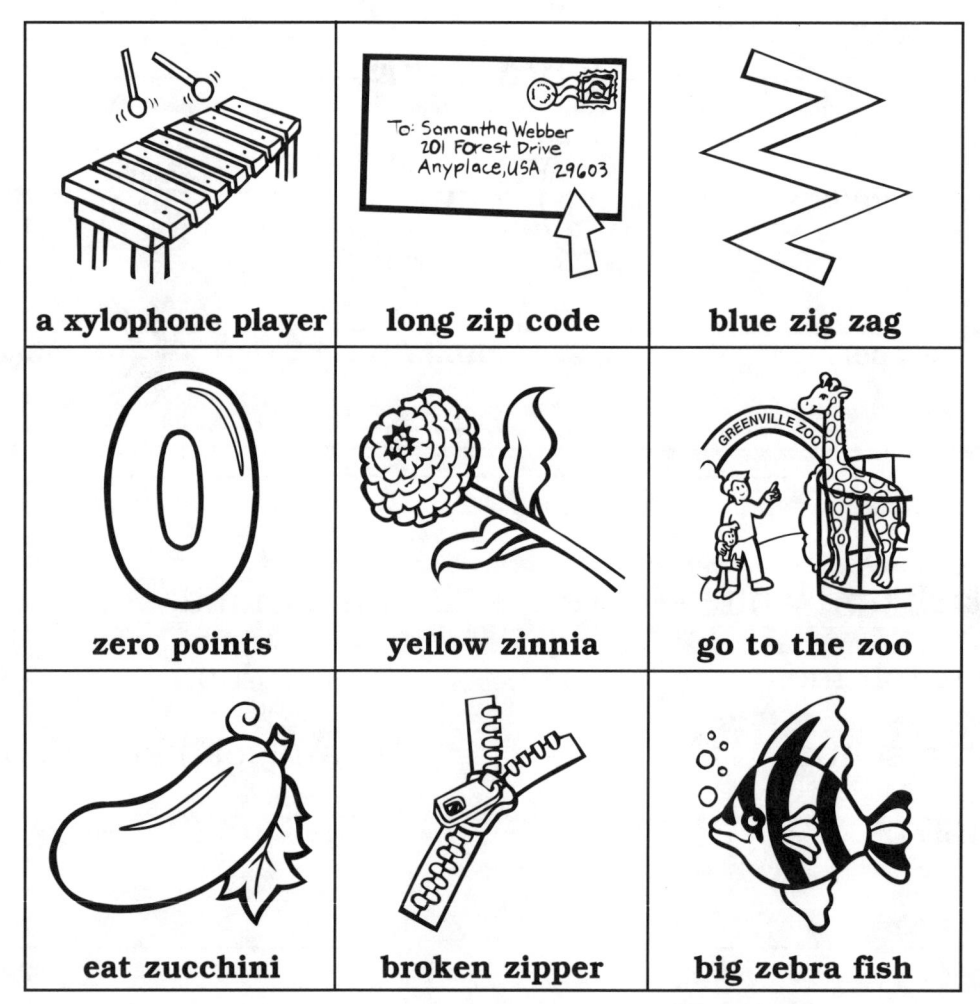

a xylophone player	long zip code	blue zig zag
zero points	yellow zinnia	go to the zoo
eat zucchini	broken zipper	big zebra fish

X X X X X

O O O O O

Homework Partner Date Speech-Language Pathologist

Initial Z Phrases

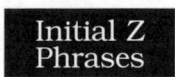

Q & A Match Up

Directions: Read the questions and find the answers at the bottom. Write the question number on the line of the matching answer. Then, read/say each answer aloud ("at the zoo"). Use your good Z sound!

1 Where do you go to see an animal in a cage?

2 What swims in the ocean?

3 What number is less than one?

4 What is found on pants?

5 What do you pick from a vine?

6 What looks like a horse?

7 What makes a beautiful sound?

8 What do you put on an envelope?

9 What do you pick to make a bouquet?

_____ at the zoo

_____ a silver zipper

_____ the xylophone

_____ a big, fat zero

_____ a green zucchini

_____ the long zip code

_____ a black & white zebra

_____ a zebra fish

_____ a pretty zinnia

Homework Partner   Date   Speech-Language Pathologist

Initial Z Phrases

Amaze Me

Directions: You are a zookeeper trying to find the zebra who got lost!! Try to solve the maze to find him. Say aloud the name of each Z picture you come across as you solve the maze. Find and save the zebra and you are the winner!

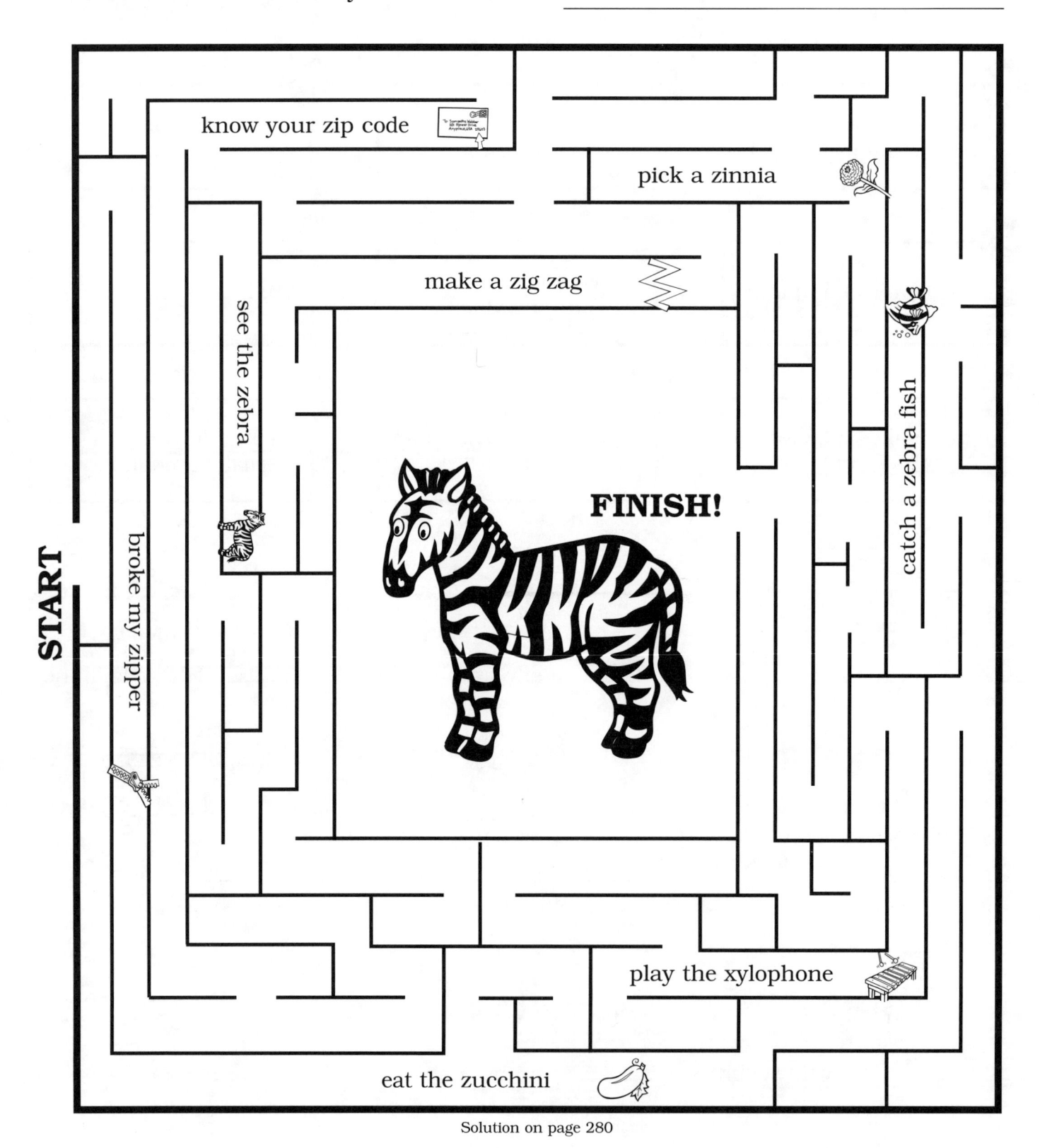

- know your zip code
- pick a zinnia
- make a zig zag
- see the zebra
- catch a zebra fish
- broke my zipper
- play the xylophone
- eat the zucchini

START

FINISH!

Solution on page 280

Homework Partner　　　Date　　　Speech-Language Pathologist

Initial Z Phrases

176　#BK-290 Webber® Artic Fun Sheets • ©2001 Super Duper® Publications • www.superduperinc.com • 1-800-277-8737

Our Zoo Trip

Directions: Draw a line from a puzzle piece on the left to the one that matches it on the right. Read/say both phrases aloud to make a complete sentence. Use your best Z sound.

1. On Saturday

2. John saw

3. Beautiful yellow zinnias

4. Sally was sad

5. The zebra fish

6. An iguana

7. We had fun

A. were growing everywhere.

B. ate a zucchini.

C. walking zig zag.

D. we went to the zoo.

E. there were zero monkeys.

F. a striped zebra.

G. were eating fish food.

Answers: 1.D, 2.F, 3.A, 4.E, 5.G, 6.B, 7.C

Homework Partner   Date   Speech-Language Pathologist

Initial Z Sentences

Hide 'n' Seek

Directions: Read/say aloud the picture–words. If you prefer, glue the pictures on a file folder/cardboard. Cut out the pictures and penny. Place the pictures face up. Have your partner hide the penny under a picture. Ask questions (using the name of the picture) to find the penny. ("Is it under zucchini?") Use your good Z sound!

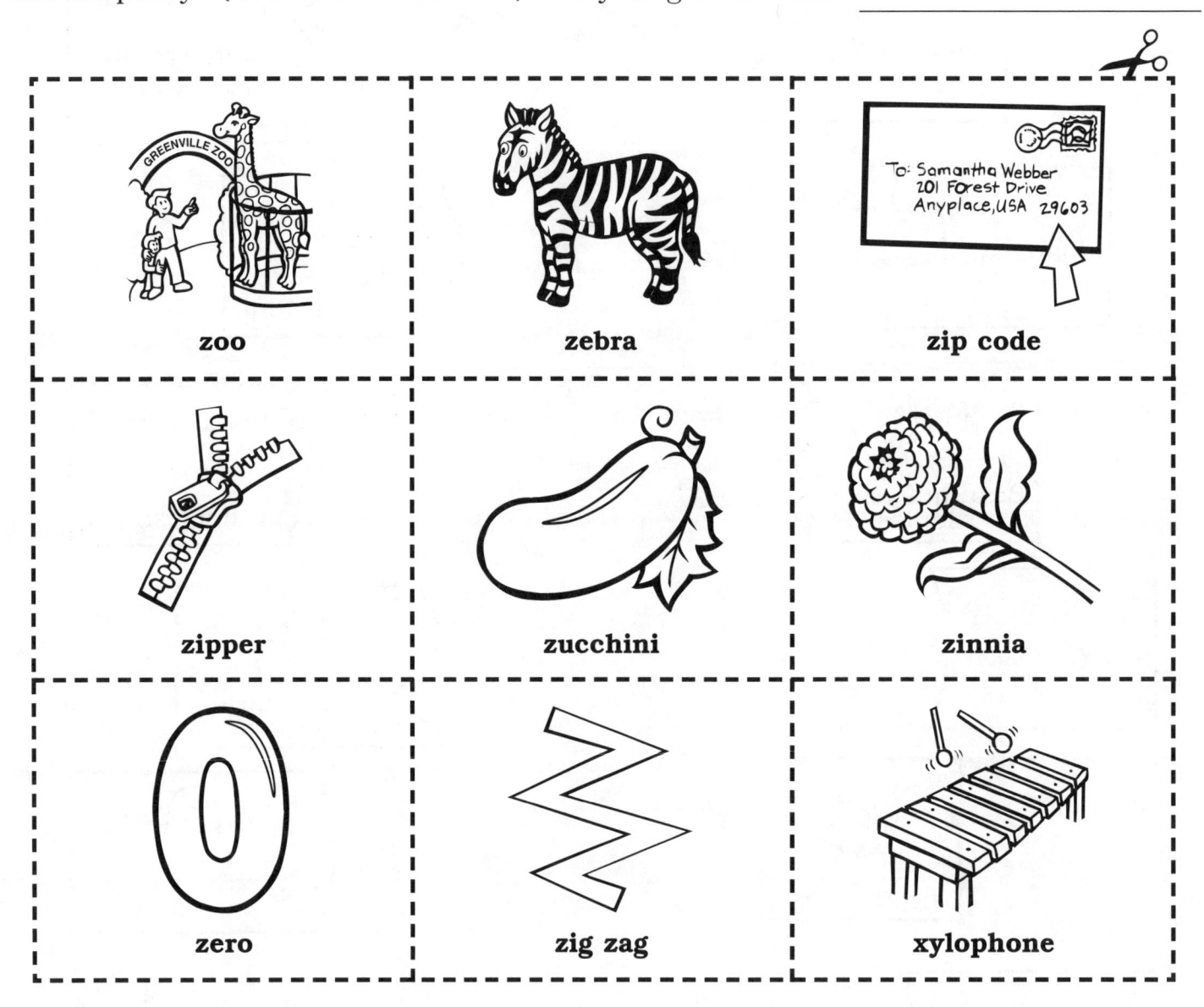

zoo	zebra	zip code
zipper	**zucchini**	**zinnia**
zero	**zig zag**	**xylophone**

Homework Partner   Date   Speech-Language Pathologist

Initial Z Sentences

178

Story Loop

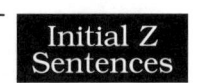

Directions: Read/say aloud each picture–word. Make up a story using all of the pictures in the circle. You can start anywhere in the circle and go in either direction, but you must always end where you started to complete the loop. Say your story aloud, using your good Z sound.

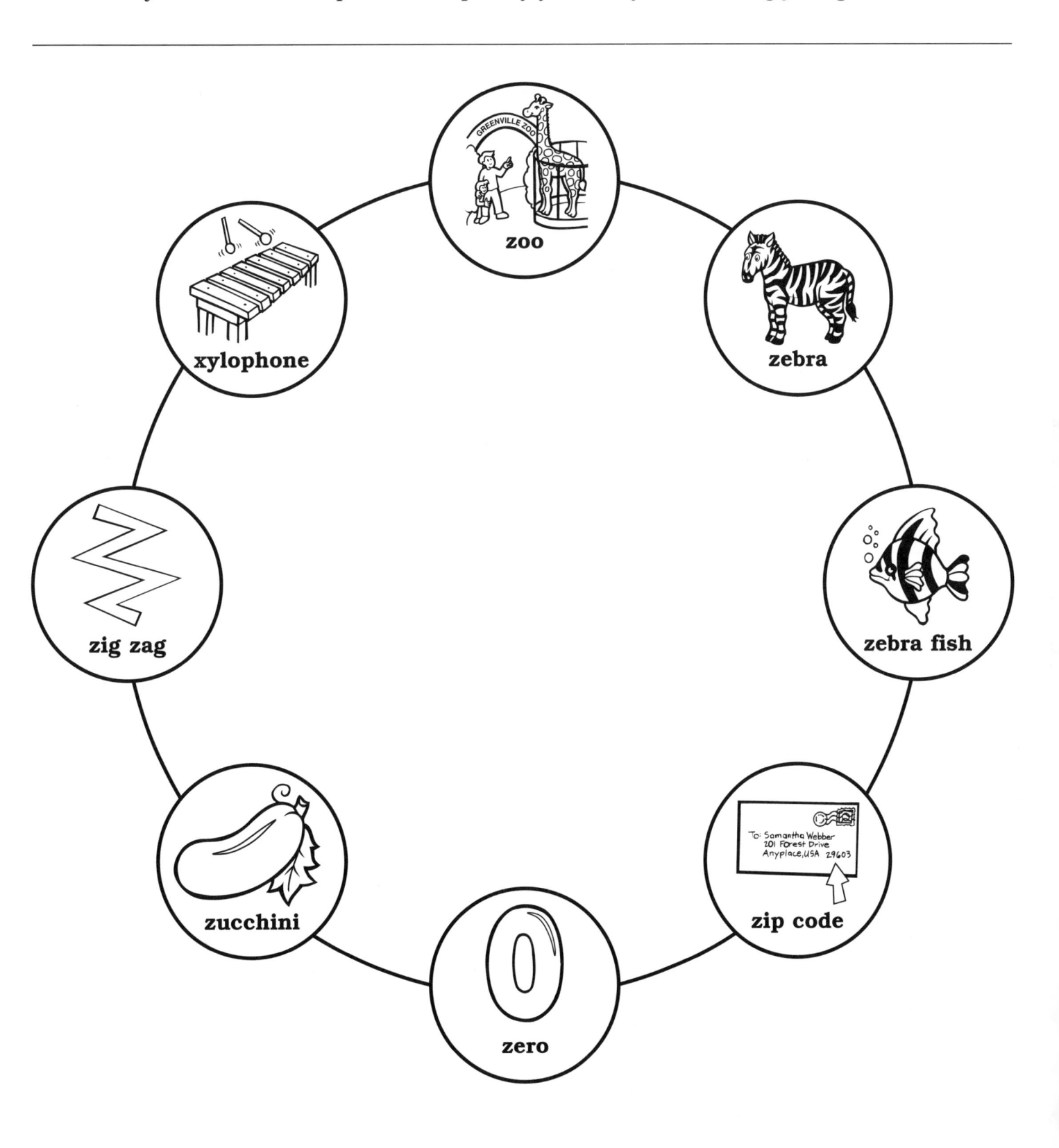

- zoo
- zebra
- zebra fish
- zip code
- zero
- zucchini
- zig zag
- xylophone

Homework Partner — Date — Speech-Language Pathologist

Initial Z Sentences

Memory Game

Directions: Read/say aloud each picture–word below. Cut out the pictures. Place all cards face down. Try to match the cards. Say each card as you pick it up, using your good Z sound. Keep all matches. Most matches wins!

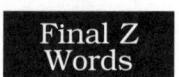

cheese	toes	bananas	girls
boys	apples	shoes	knees
eggs	pigs	eggs	pigs
cheese	toes	bananas	girls
boys	apples	shoes	knees

Homework Partner Date Speech-Language Pathologist

Final Z Words

Pick the Bananas

Directions: Copy this page and cut out the bananas. Pick a banana to place on the tree and read/say the word aloud using your best Z sound. Glue/place the bananas on the tree.

boys, toes, rose, girls, cheese, eggs, shoes, bananas, knees, apples, pigs, cows

Homework Partner   Date   Speech-Language Pathologist   Final Z Words

Apples to Apples

Directions: Read/say aloud the picture–words below. Then, cut out the apples. Cut "holes" as shown on the buckets. Read/say the name of the picture before placing it in the bucket. Remember to use your good Z sound!

cheese	girls	rose	pigs
eggs	shoes	boys	cows

Homework Partner   Date   Speech-Language Pathologist

Final Z Words

182   #BK-290 Webber® Artic Fun Sheets • ©2001 Super Duper® Publications • www.superduperinc.com • 1-800-277-8737

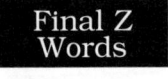

Z Cube Roll

Directions: Assemble the cube as follows: Glue onto construction paper for added durability. Cut along the dotted lines. Fold on solid lines and glue as indicated. To play: Roll the cube. Read/say aloud the word you see using your best Z sound.

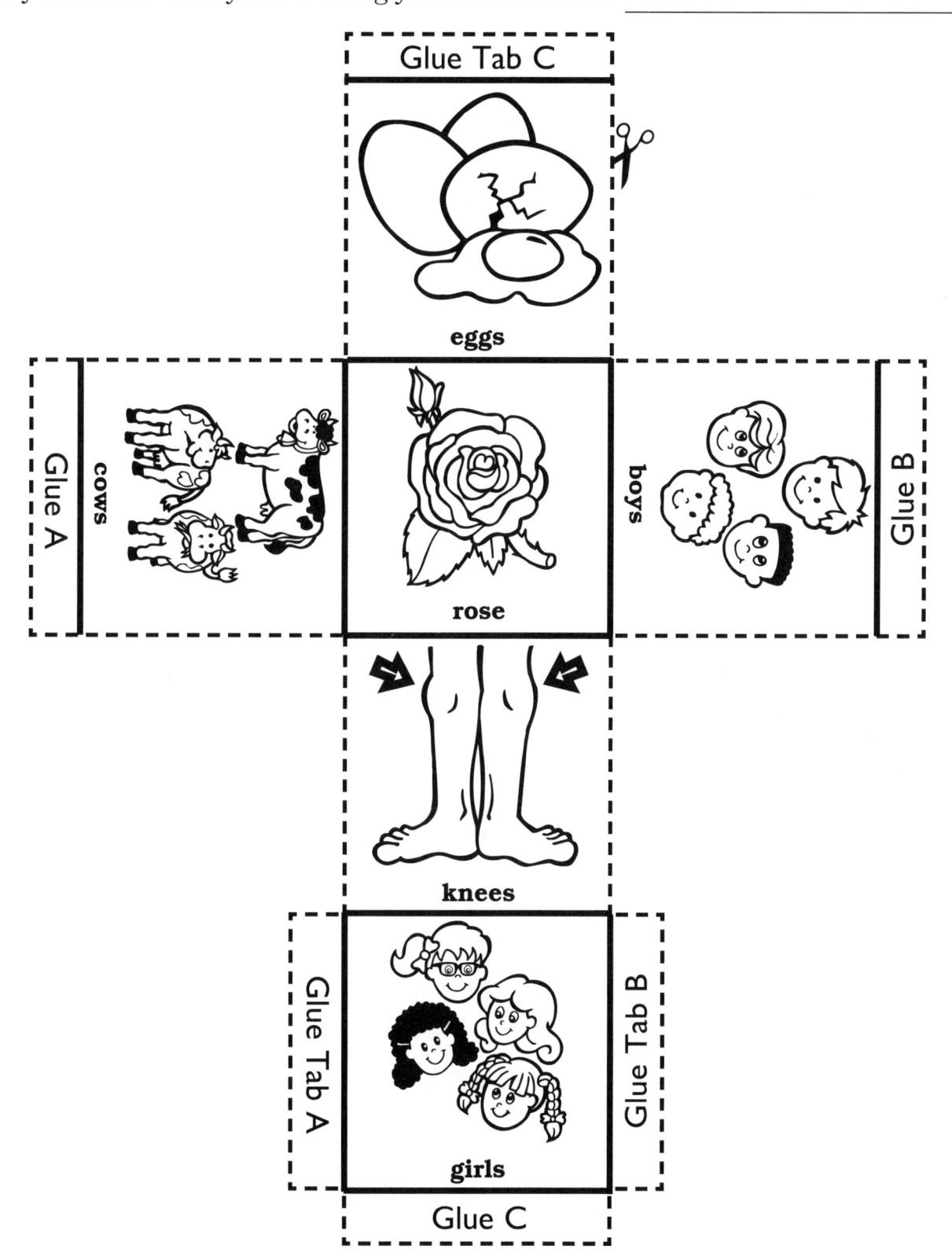

Glue Tab C

eggs

Glue A | cows | rose | boys | Glue B

knees

Glue Tab A | girls | Glue Tab B

Glue C

Homework Partner   Date   Speech-Language Pathologist

Final Z Words

#BK-290 Webber® Artic Fun Sheets • ©2001 Super Duper® Publications • www.superduperinc.com • 1-800-277-8737

183

Hide 'n' Seek

Directions: Read/say aloud the picture–words. If you prefer, glue the pictures on a file folder/cardboard. Cut out the pictures and present. Place the pictures face up. Have your partner hide the present under a picture. Ask questions (using the name of the picture) to find the penny. ("Is it under cheese?") Use your good Z sound!

knees	cheese	boys
girls	toes	cows
pigs	bananas	apples

Homework Partner   Date   Speech-Language Pathologist

Final Z Words

184   #BK-290 Webber® Artic Fun Sheets • ©2001 Super Duper® Publications • www.superduperinc.com • 1-800-277-8737

The Name Game

Directions: Read the words below, using your good Z sound. Then, answer each statement below with a word from the Word Bank. There may be more than one answer to a statement.

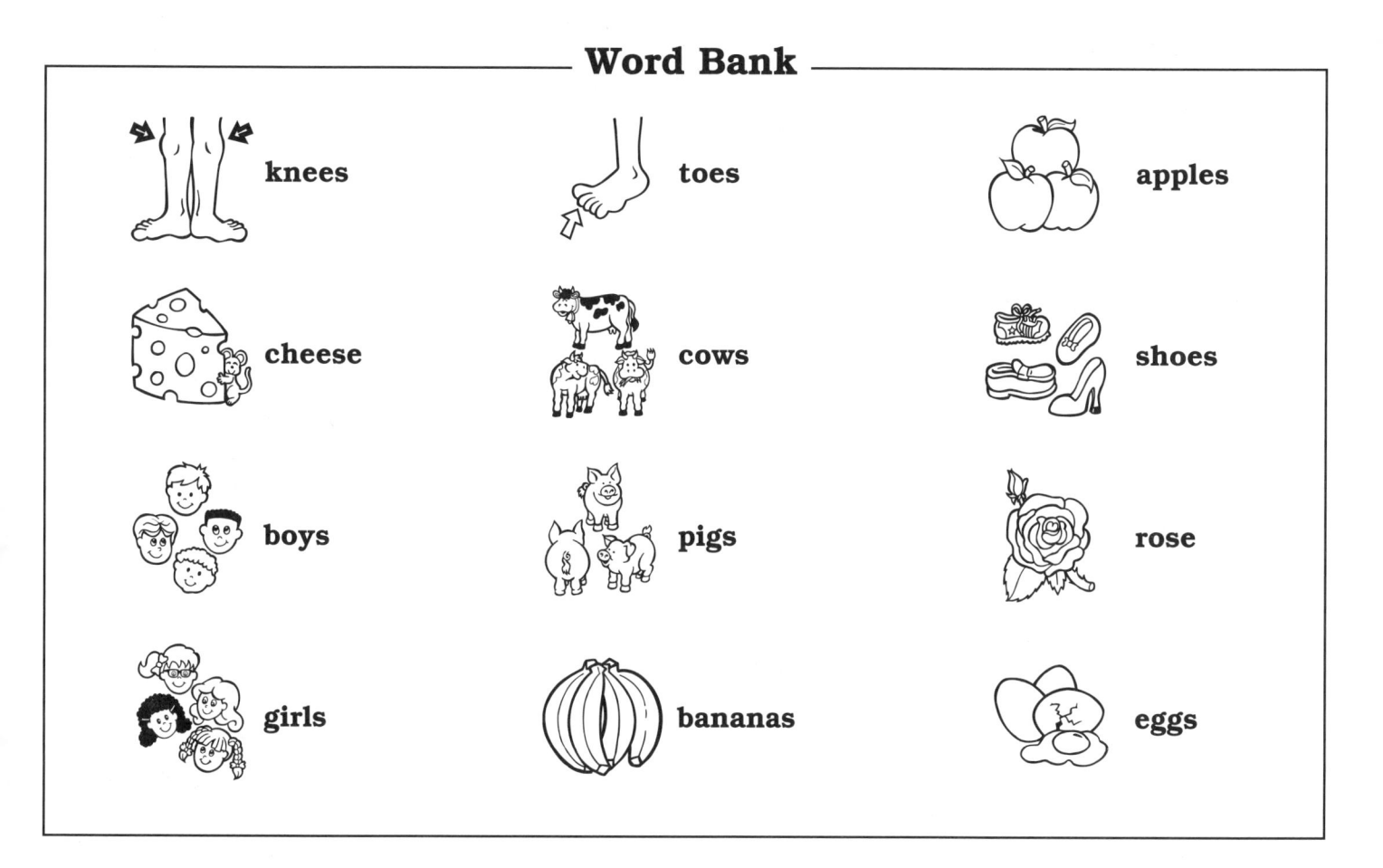

Word Bank

- knees
- toes
- apples
- cheese
- cows
- shoes
- boys
- pigs
- rose
- girls
- bananas
- eggs

1. Name something you eat.
2. Name something that walks.
3. Name something that grows on a tree.
4. Name something that lives on a farm.
5. Name something that is part of your body.
6. Name something that has petals.
7. Name something that you wear.
8. Name something that is a fruit.
9. Name something that comes in a carton.
10. Name something that talks.

Homework Partner   Date   Speech-Language Pathologist   Final Z Words

Paper Dolls

Directions: Cut out each doll, keeping the girls and the boys separate. Select one girl doll and one boy doll to make a phrase ("silly apples"). Read/say each phrase aloud, using your best Z phrase.

Boys

- silly
- two
- my
- yummy
- happy

Girls

- bananas
- apples
- pigs
- cows
- knees

Final Z Phrases

Cheese Hunt

Directions: Read/say aloud the picture–words below. Then, cut out the markers. Flip a coin (heads=1, tails=2) to determine how many spaces to move. As you move, read/say each phrase aloud, using your good Z sound. First player to reach the finish wins.

START

- sleepy boys
- little toes
- big brown cows
- the yellow bananas
- crunchy apples
- yummy cheese
- happy little girls
- on my knees
- tie your shoes
- a red rose
- the pink pigs
- lay the eggs
- clean clothes
- beautiful balloons
- shiny braces

FINISH

Homework Partner   Date   Speech-Language Pathologist

Final Z Phrases

How Many?

Directions: Look at the pictures and count the number of items in each box. Write the number on the line. Then, read/say the phrase aloud using your best Z sound ("four apples").

1. _____

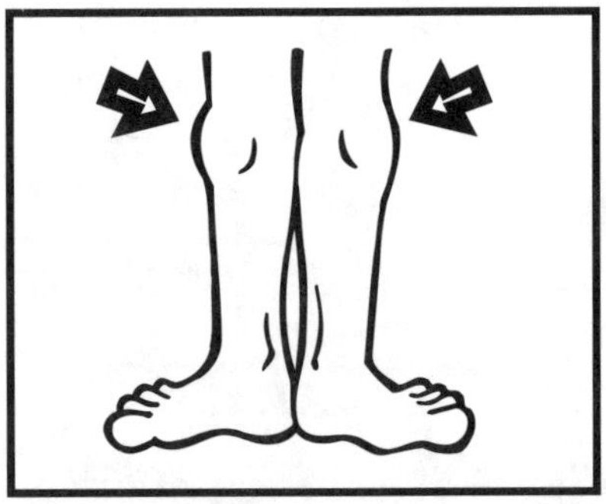

2. _____

3. _____

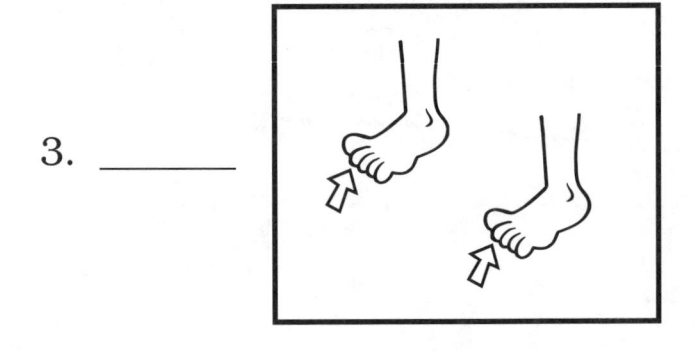

4. _____

5. _____

6. _____

7. _____

8. _____

Homework Partner   Date   Speech-Language Pathologist

Final Z Phrases

Scrambled Sentences

Directions: Try to unscramble each sentence. Write it on the line below the egg. Then read/say the sentence aloud using your best Z sound.

1. _He read the Three Little Pigs._

2. _The monkey ate the bananas._

3. _We cut the apples to make pie._

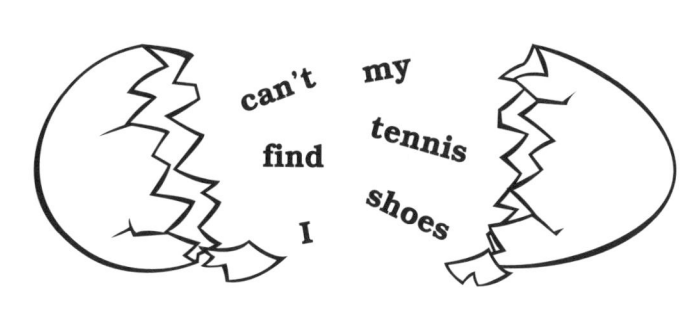

4. _I can't find my tennis shoes._

5. _Mom and Dad gave a rose._

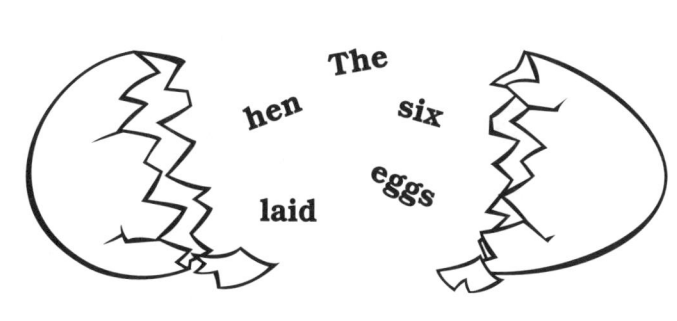

6. _The hen laid six eggs._

Answer Key on Page 279

Homework Partner — Date — Speech-Language Pathologist

Final Z Sentences

189

Scrambled Sentences

Directions: Try to unscramble each sentence. Write it on the line below the egg. Then read/say the sentence aloud using your best Z sound.

1. The boy fell on his knees.

2. Please make me a cheese sandwich.

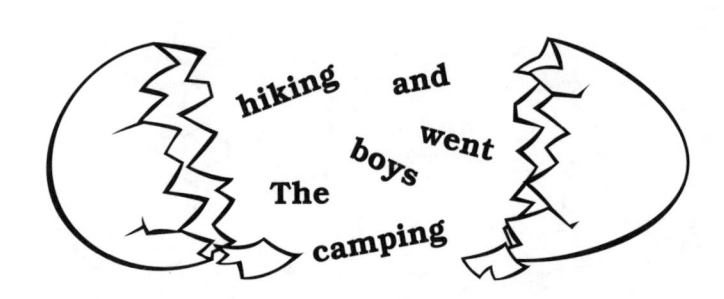

3. The boys went hiking and camping.

4. The three girls love to play dress-up.

5. We have five toes on each foot.

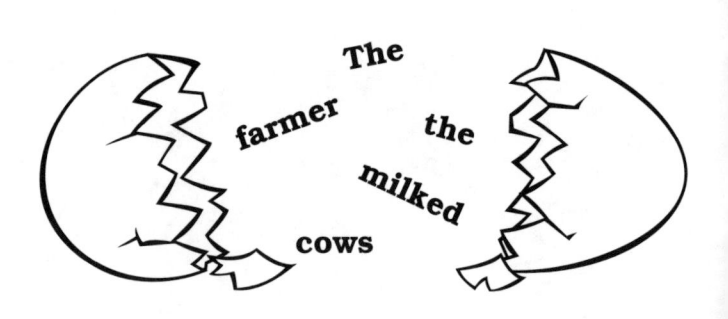

6. The farmer milked the cows.

Answer Key on Page 279

Homework Partner   Date   Speech-Language Pathologist

Final Z Sentences

Analogies

Directions: Read/say aloud the picture-words below. Then, read each analogy and choose an answer from the Word Bank. Read/say your answer aloud using your best Z sound.

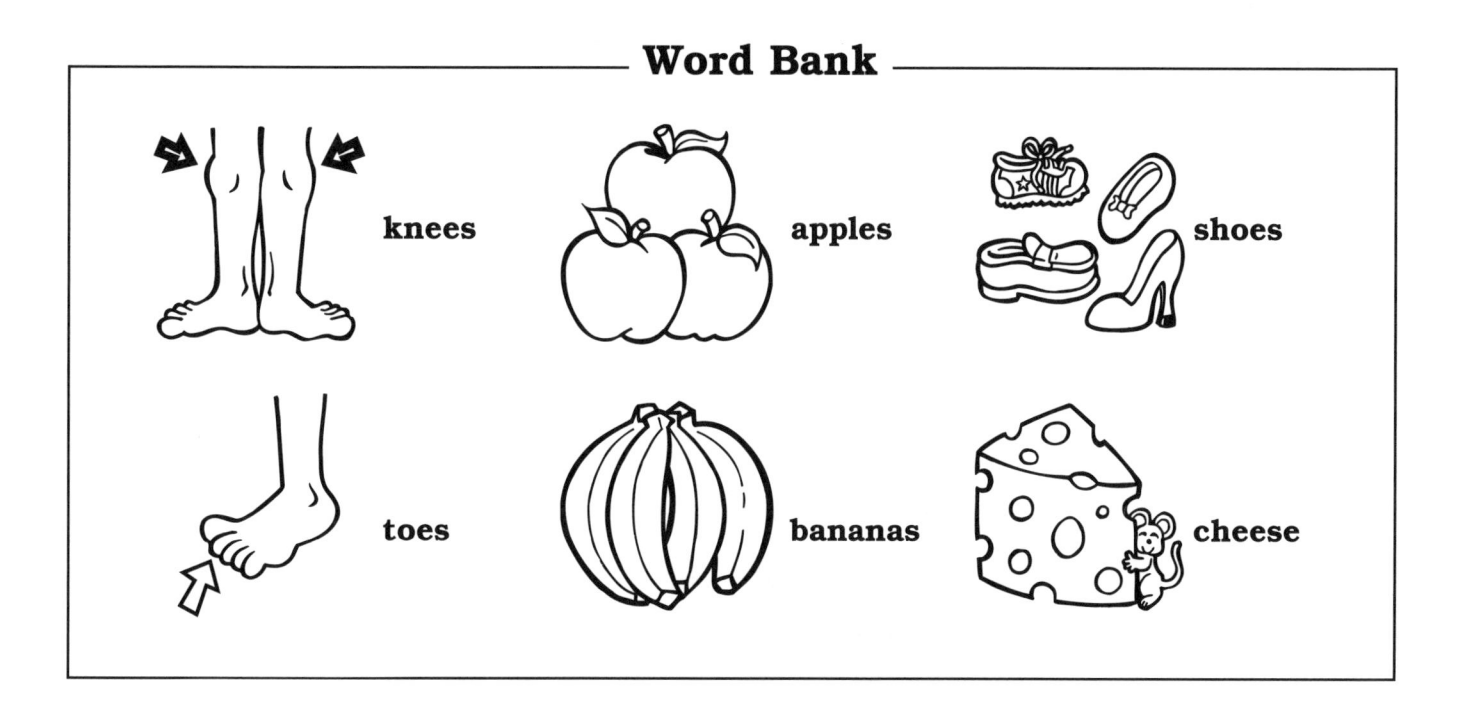

Word Bank

knees   apples   shoes

toes   bananas   cheese

---

1. Arms are to elbows as legs are to _____.

2. Hands are to fingers as feet are to _____.

3. Yellow is to lemons as red is to _____.

4. Vine is to watermelon as trees are to _____.

5. Hands are to gloves as feet are to _____.

6. Elephant is to peanuts as mouse is to _____.

Answer Key: 1-knees, 2-toes, 3-apples, 4-bananas, 5-shoes, 6-cheese

Homework Partner   Date   Speech-Language Pathologist

Final Z Sentences

Petal Pusher

Directions: Read/say aloud each picture–word below. Then, cut out the flower petals. As you glue/tape or place each petal to make a flower, say each picture–word again using your best Z sound.

present   bulldozer   clothesline

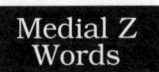

music   measles   grizzly bear

buzzard   puzzle   lizard

Homework Partner   Date   Speech-Language Pathologist

Medial Z Words

Clothesline

Directions: Cut out clothes below. Read/say aloud each picture–word. Then, glue/tape or place the clothes on the clothesline.

- music
- lizard
- newspaper
- grizzly bear
- puzzle
- present
- buzzard
- bulldozer

Homework Partner　　Date　　Speech-Language Pathologist

Medial Z Words

Puzzle Mania

Directions: Draw a line from the puzzle piece on the left to the puzzle piece on the right to complete the word. Read/say the word aloud after you have "put" the pieces together.

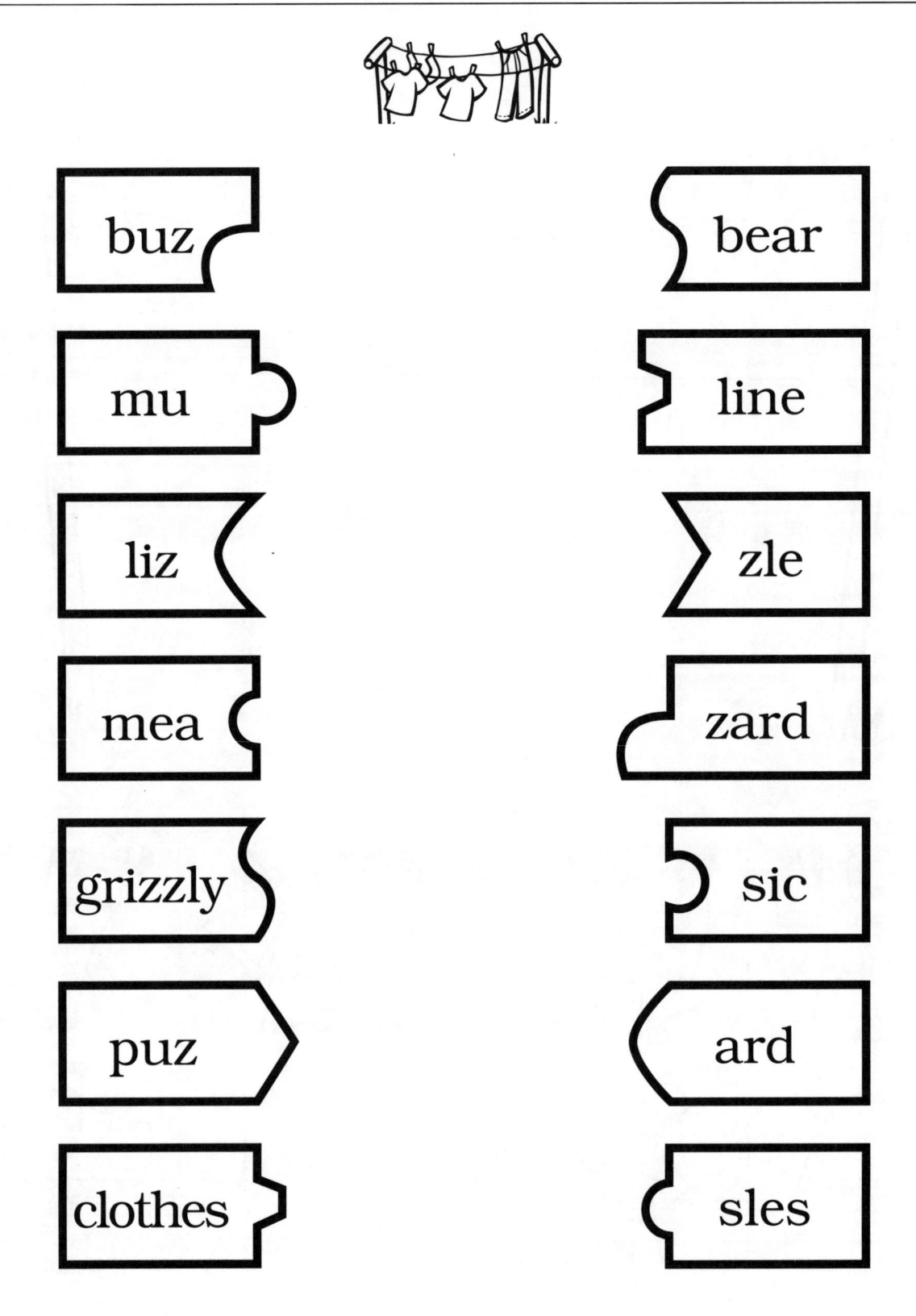

buz	bear
mu	line
liz	zle
mea	zard
grizzly	sic
puz	ard
clothes	sles

Homework Partner   Date   Speech-Language Pathologist   Medial Z Words

Newspaper Search

Directions: Read/say aloud each picture–word below. Then, search for and circle the same pictures and/or words in the newspaper. Read/say aloud each one you find.

Word Bank

- clothesline
- measles 
- buzzard 
- lizard 
- bulldozer 
- grizzly bear 
- music 
- puzzle 

Bulldozer Times

Thief steals neighbor's clothesline!

Grizzly Bear and Buzzard Escape from Zoo!

Mike has the Measles!

Largest Lizard Caught!

Music Concert Tonight

Lost Puzzle Piece Found!

Homework Partner   Date   Speech-Language Pathologist

Medial Z Words

Which One?

Directions: Read the questions. Then, circle the correct answer to the questions. Read/say each answer aloud using your best Z sound.

1. Which one has a small body and a long tail?

   bulldozer   lizard

2. Which one do you read?

   buzzard   newspaper

3. Which one do you give at a birthday?

   clothesline   present

4. Which one do you listen to?

   music   puzzle

5. Which one lives in the forest?

   grizzly bear   measles

6. Which one makes you sick?

   lizard   measles

7. Which one do you hang clothes on?

   present   clothesline

8. Which one does a construction worker drive?

   bulldozer   music

Homework Partner   Date   Speech-Language Pathologist

Medial Z Words

Crazy Crossword

Directions: Read/say the picture–words below. Then, complete the crossword puzzle by reading and answering the clues. Use the pictures to help you. Then, use your good Z sound and read/say the Z words aloud, as you fill in your answers.

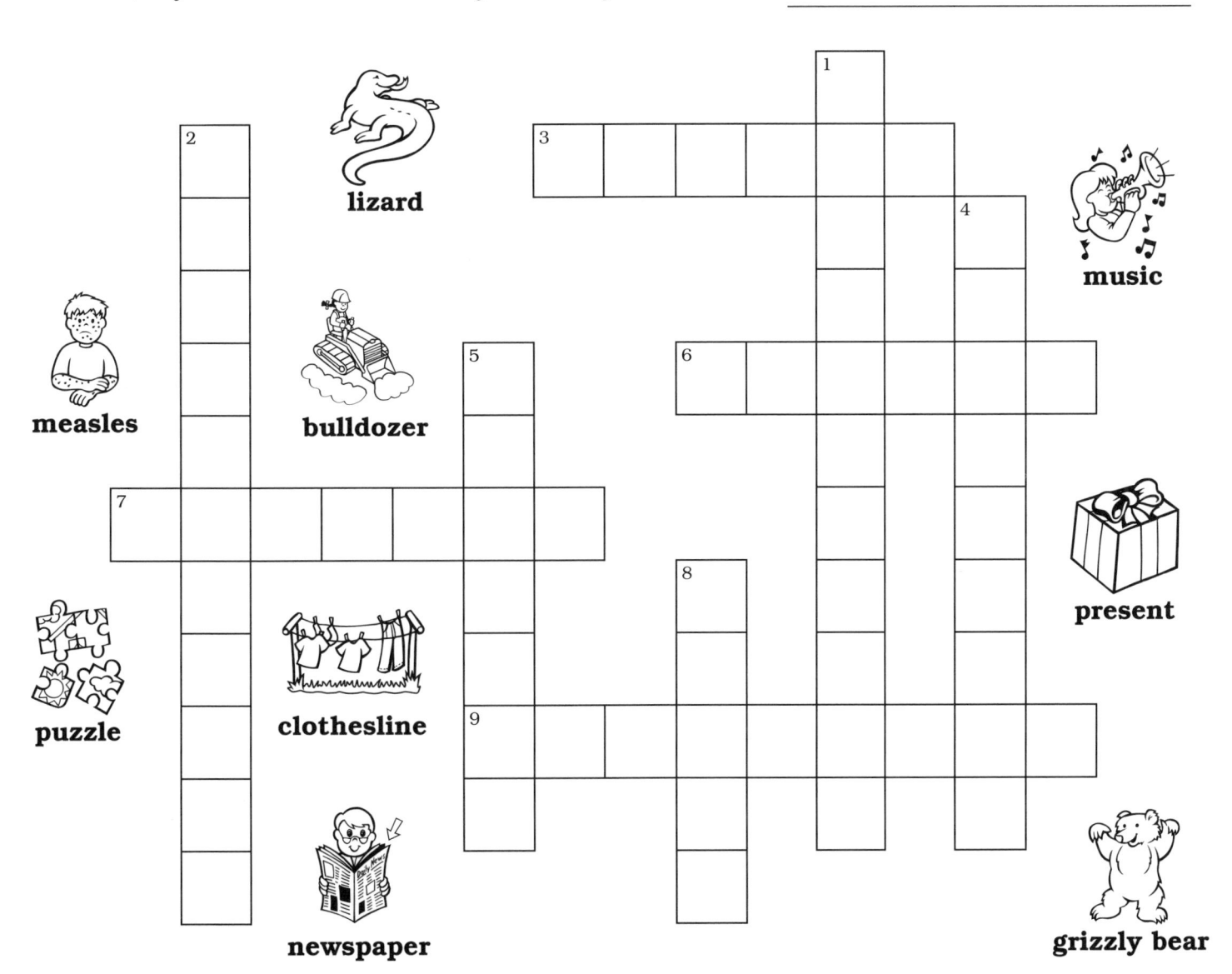

lizard

music

measles

bulldozer

present

puzzle

clothesline

grizzly bear

newspaper

Across

3. A small, green reptile
6. A picture in many pieces
7. An illness
9. You read it in the morning.

Down

1. An animal found in the forest
2. Hang wet laundry on it
4. A heavy machine
5. Another word for gift
8. A beautiful sound

Answer on page 279

Homework Partner   Date   Speech-Language Pathologist   Medial Z Words

Z Phrase It

Directions: Assemble the cube as follows: Glue onto construction paper for added durability. Cut along the dotted lines. Fold on solid lines and glue as indicated. To play: Roll both cubes. Read/say the word and picture together aloud to make up a phrase ("small lizard"). Use your good Z sound.

Cube 1 (pictures):
- Glue B
- clothesline
- buzzard | present | puzzle | bulldozer
- Glue Tab C / Glue Tab B / Glue C / Glue Tab A
- lizard
- Glue A

Cube 2 (words):
- Glue B
- big
- long | broken | green | small
- Glue Tab C / Glue Tab B / Glue C / Glue Tab A
- heavy
- Glue A

Medial Z Phrases

198 #BK-290 Webber® Artic Fun Sheets • ©2001 Super Duper® Publications • www.superduperinc.com • 1-800-277-8737

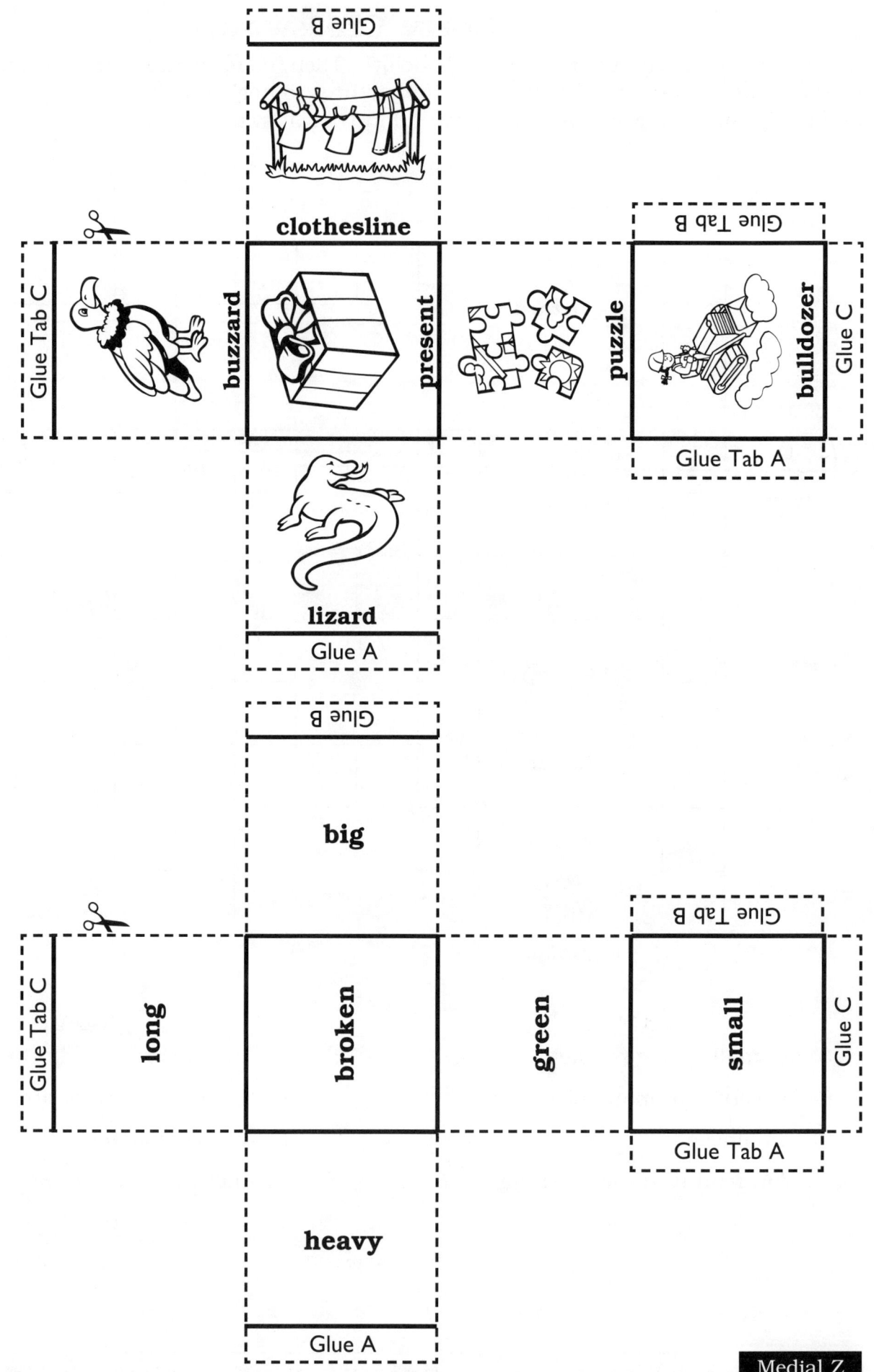

Say What?

Directions: Read/say aloud each B picture–word. Then, cut out the cards. Keep the A and B cards in separate piles. Place them face down. Flip over one A and one B card and make up a phrase. Read/say each phrase aloud.

A	A	A
growling	loud	big

A	A	A
old	itchy	long

B	B	B
bulldozer	lizard	grizzly bear

B	B	B
music	puzzle	measles

B	B	B
newspaper	buzzard	clothesline

Homework Partner   Date   Speech-Language Pathologist

Medial Z Phrases

#BK-290 Webber® Artic Fun Sheets • ©2001 Super Duper® Publications • www.superduperinc.com • 1-800-277-8737

199

All the Same

Directions: Read/say aloud the picture–words. Then, cut out the pictures. Shuffle and place the cards face down. Pick a card, and create a phrase with words starting with the same letter/sound as the one on the card ("baby - bouncing baby boy"). _____

buzzard	lizard	present
music	newspaper	clothesline
grizzly bear	puzzle	bulldozer

Homework Partner   Date   Speech-Language Pathologist

Medial Z Phrases

200   #BK-290 Webber® Artic Fun Sheets • ©2001 Super Duper® Publications • www.superduperinc.com • 1-800-277-8737

Category Action

Directions: Read/say aloud the words in bold. Then, fill in the blank with words that complete the sentence. Say/read the sentence aloud. Use your best Z sound.

A. reptile

1. A buzzard is a _____?

2. A puzzle is a _____?

B. illness

3. A lizard is a _____?

4. A present is for _____?

C. giving

5. A bulldozer is a _____?

6. Music is for _____?

7. A clothesline is for _____?

D. listening

8. Measles are an _____?

9. A grizzly bear is a _____?

I. machine

10. A newspaper is a _____?

E. bird

F. laundry

G. mammal

H. reading

J. game

Answer: 1. E, 2. J, 3. A, 4. C, 5. I, 6. D, 7. F, 8. B, 9. G, 10. H

Homework Partner | Date | Speech-Language Pathologist

Medial Z Sentences

Story Loop

Directions: Read/say aloud each picture–word. Make up a story using all of the pictures in the circle. You can start anywhere in the circle and go in either direction, but you must always end where you started to complete the loop. Say your story aloud, using your good Z sound.

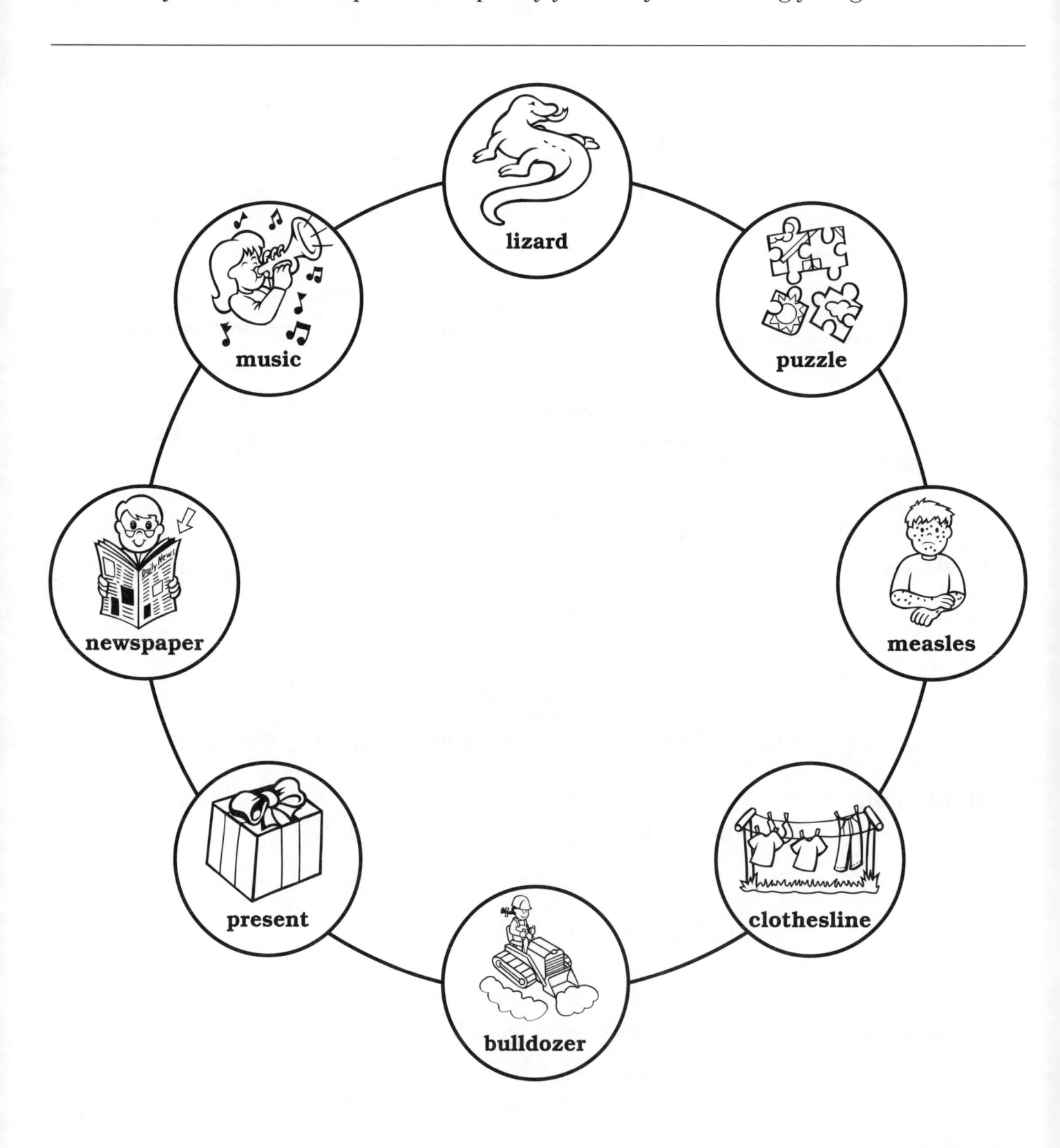

- lizard
- puzzle
- measles
- clothesline
- bulldozer
- present
- newspaper
- music

Homework Partner   Date   Speech-Language Pathologist

Medial Z Sentences

202   #BK-290 Webber® Artic Fun Sheets • ©2001 Super Duper® Publications • www.superduperinc.com • 1-800-277-8737

Make It Up

Directions: Make up sentences using the Z words below. Write each sentence on the lines below the picture. Say/read your sentences aloud using your good Z sound.

music

measles

grizzly bear

present

newspaper

puzzle

bulldozer

clothesline

Homework Partner | Date | Speech-Language Pathologist

Medial Z Sentences

Which One Fits?

Directions: Choose the picture that best completes each sentence. Then, read each sentence aloud. Remember to use your good Z sound.

1. Katie was sick with the _____ .

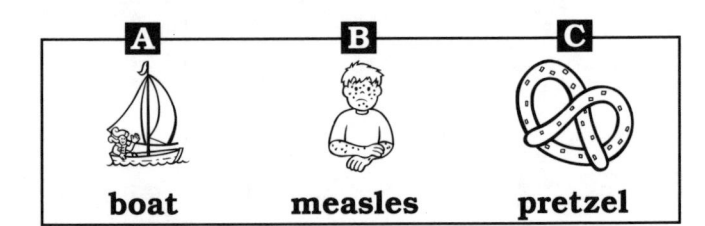

   A. boat   B. measles   C. pretzel

2. I saw a big green _____ .

   A. lizard   B. cereal   C. dog

3. Put the wash on the _____ .

   A. apple   B. bike   C. clothesline

4. I lost a piece of my _____ .

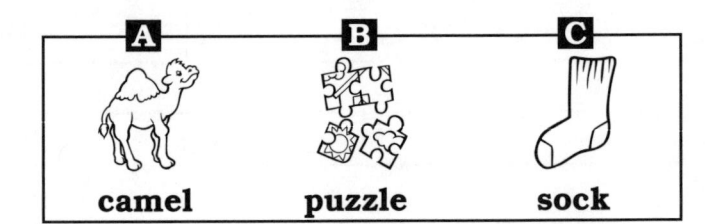

   A. camel   B. puzzle   C. sock

5. I brought her a birthday _____ .

   A. present   B. bunny   C. bats

6. Dad likes to read the _____ .

   A. octopus   B. beard   C. newspaper

Homework Partner   Date   Speech-Language Pathologist

Medial Z Sentences

Z Cube Roll

Directions: Assemble the cube as follows: Glue onto construction paper for added durability. Cut along the dotted lines. Fold on solid lines and glue as indicated. To play: Roll the cube. Read/say aloud the word you see using your best Z sound.

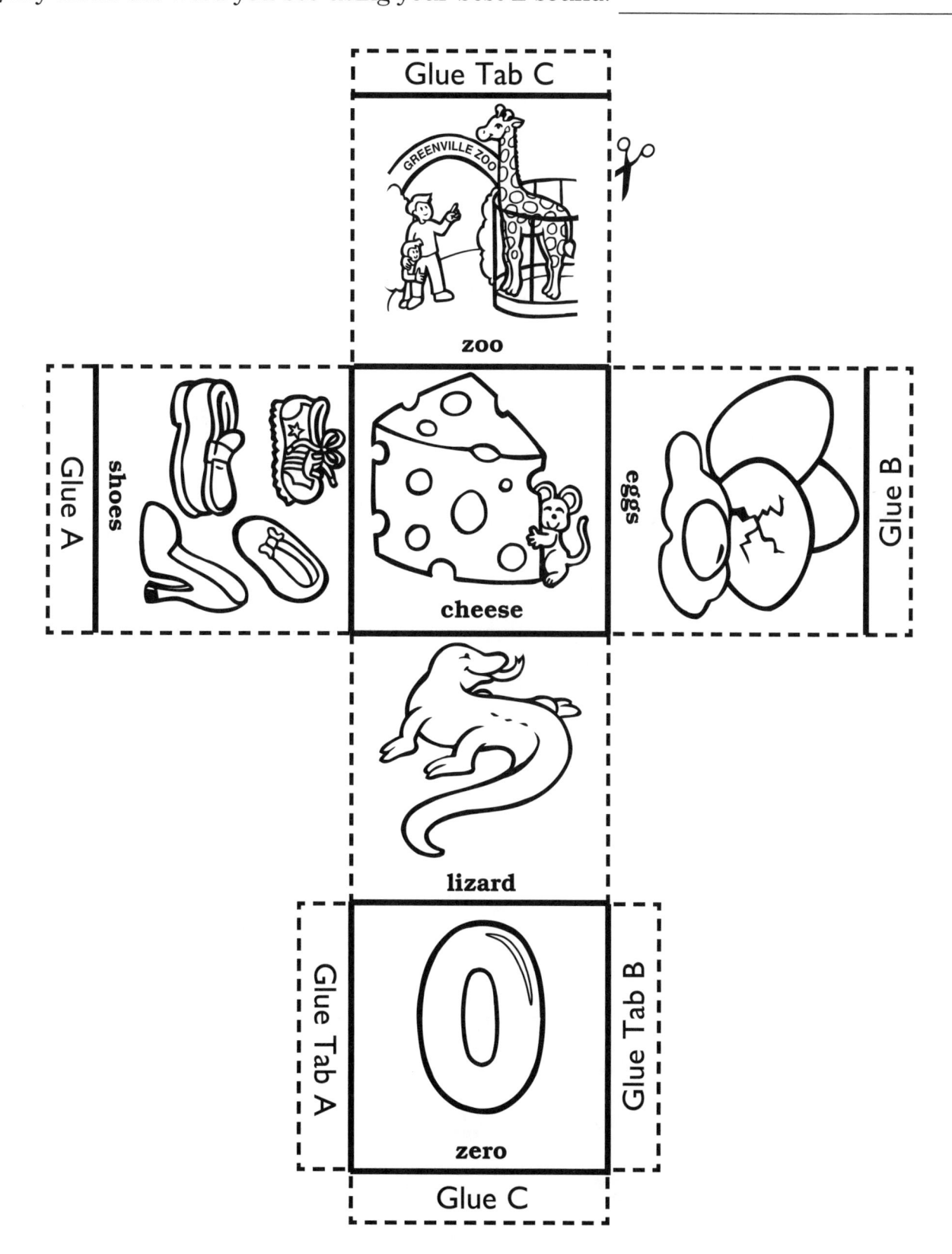

Glue Tab C

zoo

Glue A | shoes | cheese | eggs | Glue B

lizard

Glue Tab A | zero | Glue Tab B

Glue C

Homework Partner Date Speech-Language Pathologist

Combo Z Words

205

#BK-290 Webber® Artic Fun Sheets • ©2001 Super Duper® Publications • www.superduperinc.com • 1-800-277-8737

What Am I?

Directions: Read/say aloud each picture–word below. Then, read each clue. Fill in the blank with the appropriate word. Read/say each answer aloud, using your good Z sound.

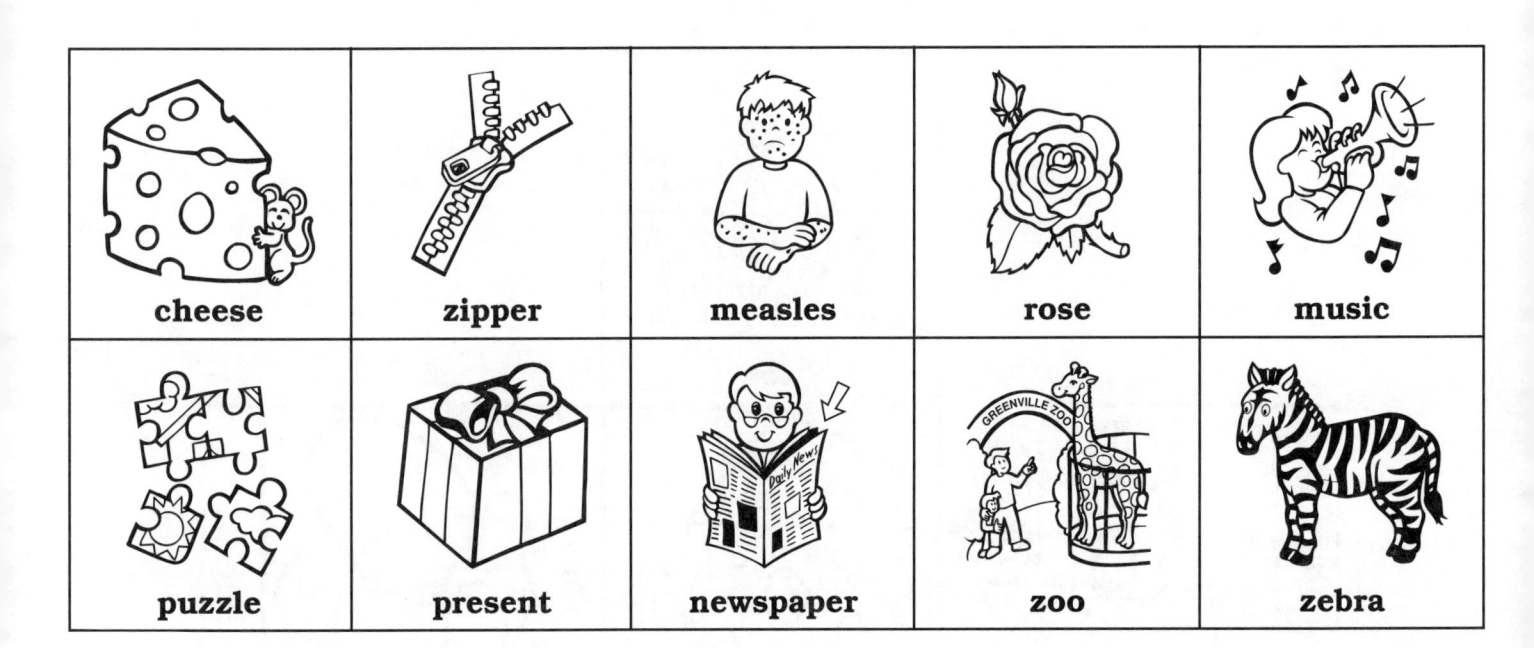

cheese	zipper	measles	rose	music
puzzle	present	newspaper	zoo	zebra

1. I am a place where animals live. I am a _____.
2. I am something on your pants or coat that you pull. I am a _____.
3. I am a food mice like to eat. I am _____.
4. I am a pretty flower with thorns. I am a _____.
5. I am something you give at a birthday. I am a _____.
6. I am a toy that has pieces you put together. I am a _____.
7. I am an illness that causes a red rash. I am the _____.
8. I am something you read. I am a _____.
9. I am something you listen to. I am _____.
10. I am an animal with black and white stripes. I am a _____.

Answers: 1-zoo, 2-zipper, 3-cheese, 4-rose, 5-present, 6-puzzle, 7-measles, 8-newspaper, 9-music, 10-zebra

Homework Partner   Date   Speech-Language Pathologist

Combo Z Words

X and O

Directions: Cut out each X and O below. Have each player/partner choose X or O. The first player reads/says a picture–word aloud and places an X or O on the square. Play continues in turn. The first person to get three in a row wins.

apples	grizzly bear	bulldozer
music	zoo	bananas
zucchini	toes	zip code

X X X X X

O O O O O

Homework Partner   Date   Speech-Language Pathologist

Combo Z Words

Category Match

Directions: Read/say each word aloud. Then, choose the correct category from the choices below. Write the letter of the answer in the space provided. Use your good Z sound. ___

1. zebra

2. cows

3. bananas

4. grizzly bear

5. zucchini

6. cheese

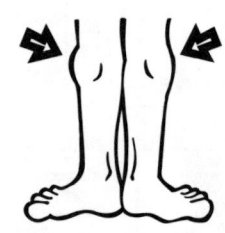

7. knees

8. pigs

9. toes

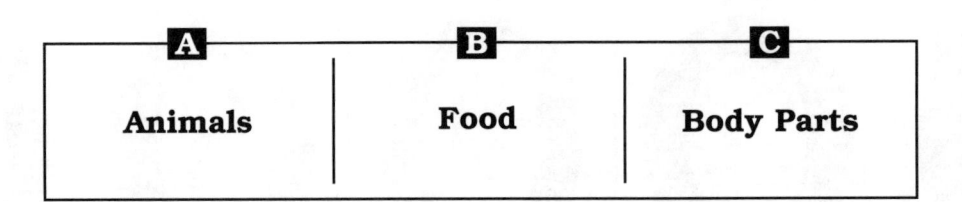

A	**B**	**C**
Animals	Food	Body Parts

Answers: 1-A, 2-A, 3-B, 4-A, 5-B, 6-B, 7-C, 8-A, 9-C

Homework Partner   Date   Speech-Language Pathologist

Combo Z Words

Spinner Action

Directions: Read/say aloud the picture–words below. If you prefer, glue this page to construction paper for added durability. Cut out the arrow/dial. Use a brad to connect the dial to the circle. Spin the spinner. When you land on a picture, read/say the word aloud, using your best Z sound.

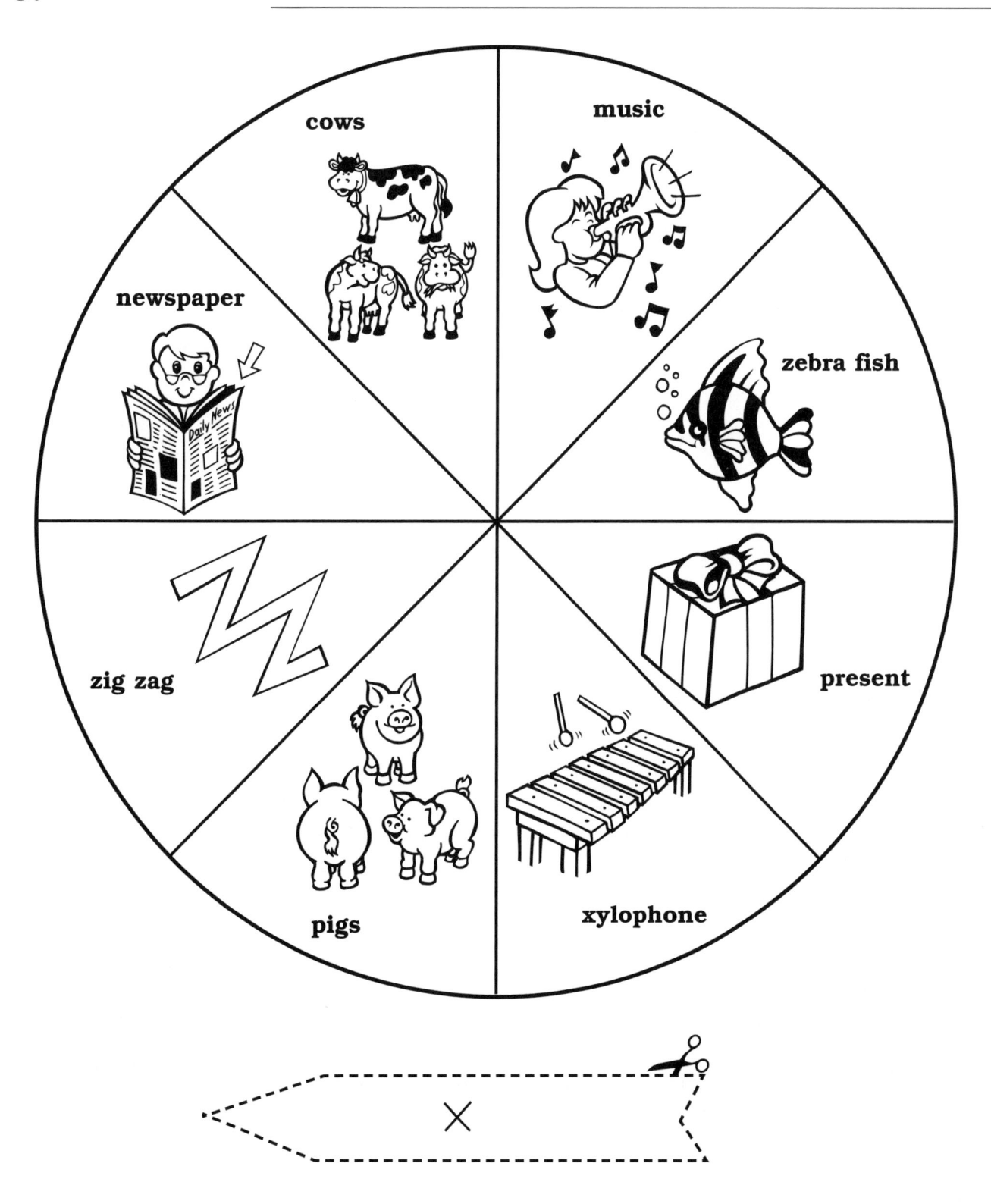

- cows
- music
- zebra fish
- present
- xylophone
- pigs
- zig zag
- newspaper

Homework Partner   Date   Speech-Language Pathologist

Combo Z Words

#BK-290 Webber® Artic Fun Sheets • ©2001 Super Duper® Publications • www.superduperinc.com • 1-800-277-8737

209

Who Said That?

Directions: Read/say each Z picture–word aloud. Read the statements in the middle. Then, ask, **"Who said that?"** Answer with the correct word. Then, draw a line from the sentence to the correct picture.

present

zip code

knees

zebra

I help your letters get there.

I am a yummy green vegetable.

I am yellow and monkeys like me.

Hang your clothes on me so they will dry.

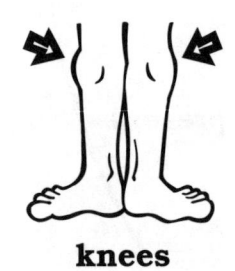

Wrap me up and take me to a birthday party.

I am white with black stripes.

Read me to find out what's happening.

Bend me to walk, run, and exercise.

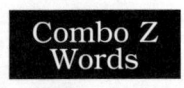

clothesline

newspaper

zucchini

bananas

Homework Partner   Date   Speech-Language Pathologist

Combo Z Words

210   #BK-290 Webber® Artic Fun Sheets • ©2001 Super Duper® Publications • www.superduperinc.com • 1-800-277-8737

Crazy Phrase

Directions: Read/say aloud the picture–words on the right. Then, draw a line from the describing word in column "A" to a picture–word in column "B." Read/say each phrase aloud ("leaping lizard"). Make the phrases as silly as you want.

A		B
leaping		cheese
broken		zipper
big		bulldozer
loud		present
squealing		eggs
pretty		zinnia
cracked		lizard
birthday		pigs

Homework Partner   Date   Speech-Language Pathologist

Combo Z Phrases

Phrase Race

Directions: Read/say aloud the picture–words below. Then, cut out the markers. Flip a coin (heads=1, tails=2) to determine how many spaces to move. As you move, read/say each word aloud, using your good Z sound. First player to reach the finish wins.

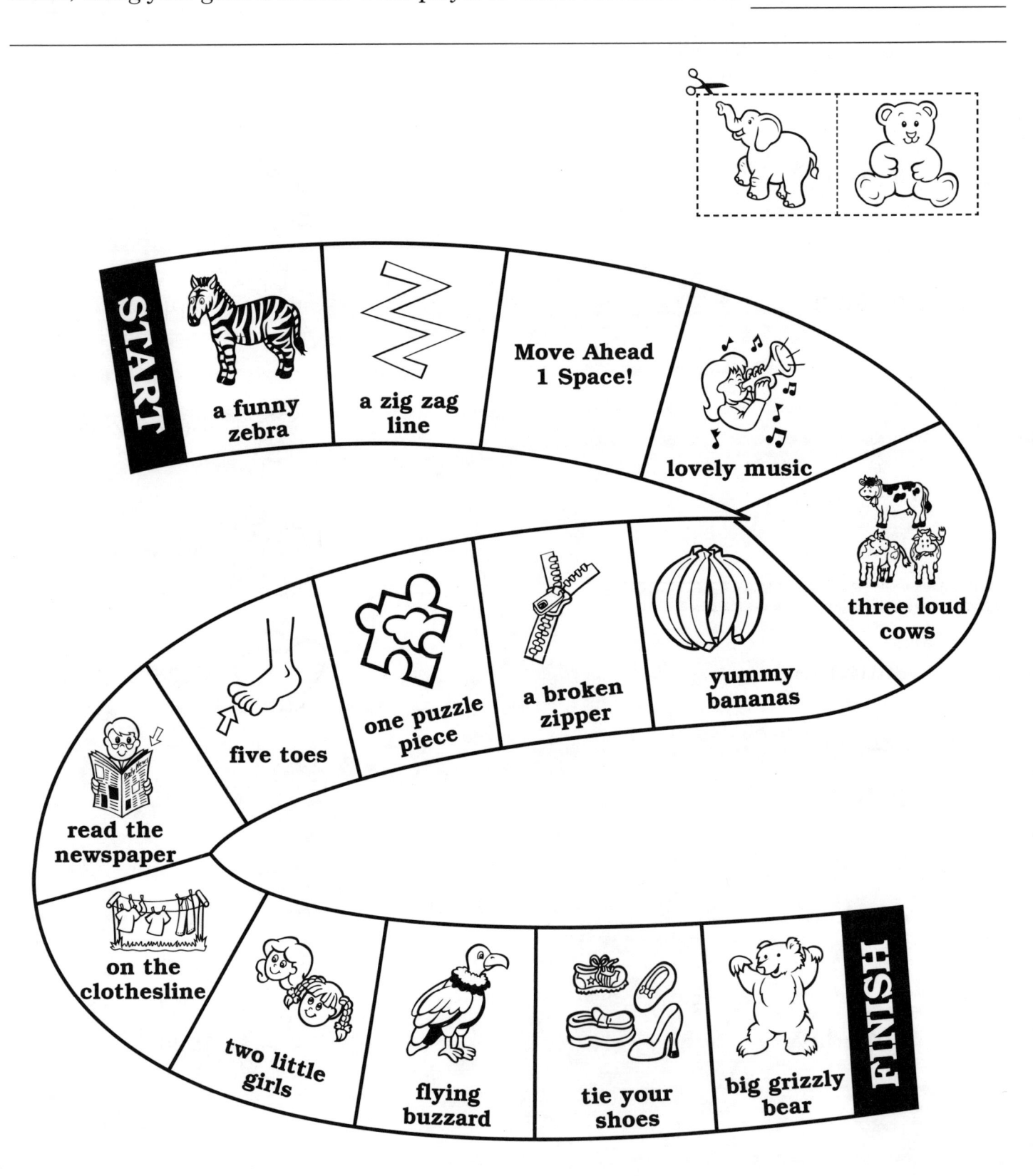

START — a funny zebra — a zig zag line — Move Ahead 1 Space! — lovely music — three loud cows — yummy bananas — a broken zipper — one puzzle piece — five toes — read the newspaper — on the clothesline — two little girls — flying buzzard — tie your shoes — big grizzly bear — **FINISH**

Homework Partner — Date — Speech-Language Pathologist

Combo Z Phrases

Act It Out!

Directions: Practice each Z phrase aloud. Then, cut the squares out and place them face down on a table. The students/helpers take turns picking a card, acting it out, and guessing what the actor is doing. Variations:

1. Pick two cards to act out to have the students use longer phrases ("reading a newspaper and tapping your toes").
2. Homework partner/teacher acts out all cards and student(s) guess the activities.

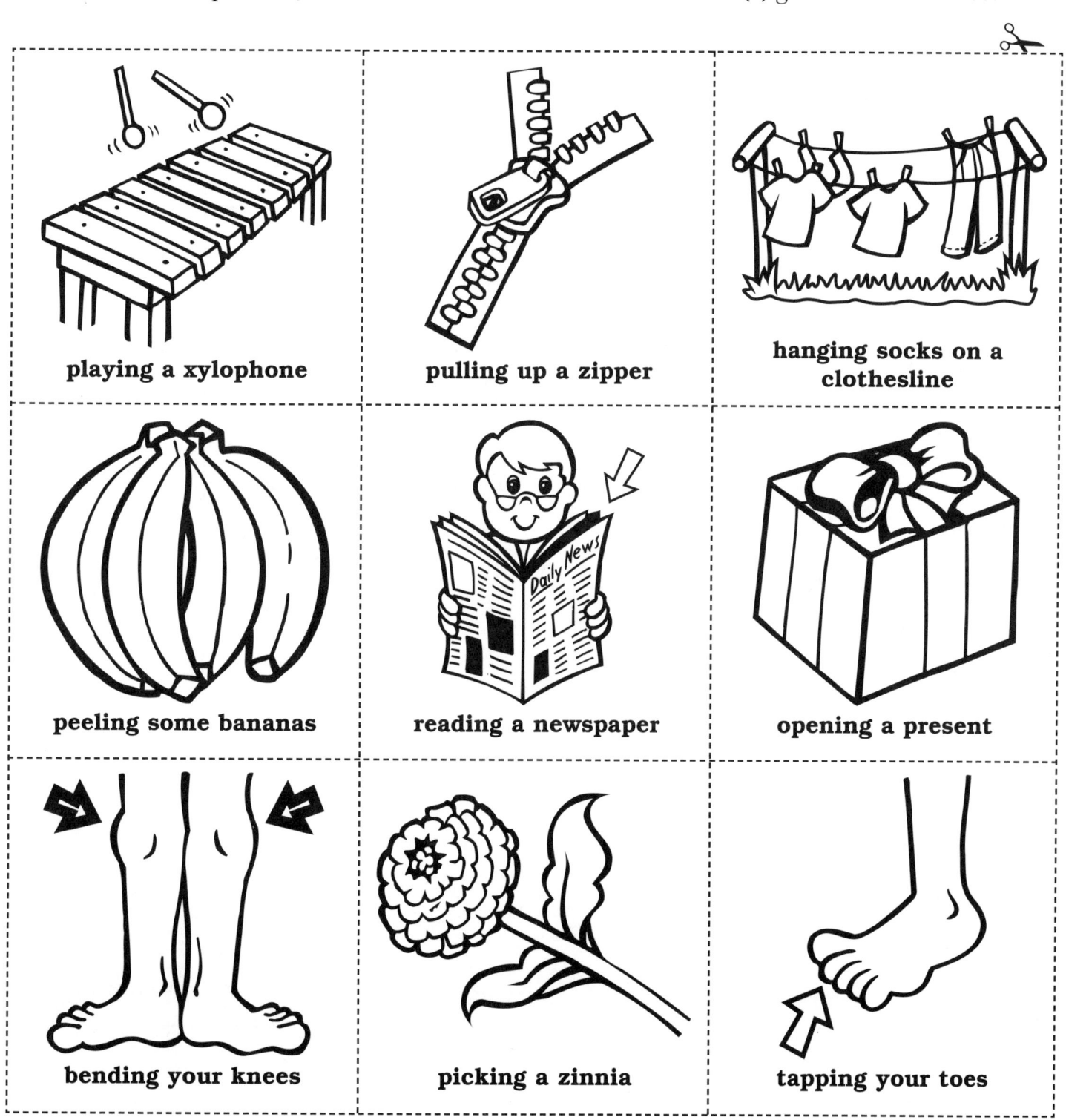

playing a xylophone	pulling up a zipper	hanging socks on a clothesline
peeling some bananas	reading a newspaper	opening a present
bending your knees	picking a zinnia	tapping your toes

Homework Partner | Date | Speech-Language Pathologist

Combo Z Phrases

Search-A-Word

Directions: Read/say the picture–words aloud. Then, complete the phrases below. Use the picture-words for hints. Find and circle each word answer in the word search box. Then, read/say the complete phrases aloud. Use your good Z sound. _____

cheese

newspaper

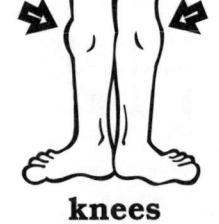

zero

knees

```
H S K H B T P L U W W T Q N O
C O A L G R S W A K U G O H Y
O L H I E M R X S U R N Z I U
F H E S B C Z V H U S D U E C
J T E L I Q A T F N L N C K A
E N A S Z N V Y W P O T C S P
T F U E R Z E E D Q X A H B O
I M N T F L U W Z B P T I G F
E S E E H C S P S O T O N H K
Z E R O A Q E B O P Q X I W J
T G B M R R E H H S A M P O W
O B I D Y I N I X T B P E L B
Q H Y K F R K O K B H W E I W
I N K U B Z E G T X U I T R I
F E F L A V K J T H C J S R L
```

Answer Key on Page 280

present

zucchini

music

puzzle

1. One minus _____

2. Birthday _____

3. Bending _____

4. Eats _____

5. A green _____

6. _____ piece

7. _____ delivery

8. Listening to _____

_____ _____ _____ | Combo Z Phrases |
Homework Partner   Date   Speech-Language Pathologist

214 #BK-290 Webber® Artic Fun Sheets • ©2001 Super Duper® Publications • www.superduperinc.com • 1-800-277-8737

Finish the Sentence

Directions: Complete each sentence by telling what you would do. Say the complete sentence aloud, using your best Z sound.

1. If I had a zebra... _____
_____.

2. If I drove a bulldozer... _____
_____.

3. If I broke my zipper... _____
_____.

4. If I had some bananas... _____
_____.

5. If I had more than ten toes... _____
_____.

6. If I was a lizard... _____
_____.

7. If I had the measles... _____
_____.

8. If I opened a present... _____
_____.

_____ _____ _____ Combo Z
Homework Partner   Date   Speech-Language Pathologist   Sentences

What Do You Think?

Directions: Read the sentences and circle the correct answers. Then, read/say the correct sentence aloud. Remember to use your good Z sound.

1. You **do/don't** see animals at the zoo.

2. A lizard **is/isn't** a reptile.

3. You **do/don't** hang hats on a clothesline.

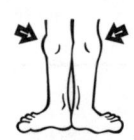

4. Your knees **are/aren't** on your head.

5. A buzzard **is/isn't** a bird.

6. The measles **are/aren't** an illness.

7. Boys **do/don't** wear dresses.

8. Cheese **is/isn't** a food.

9. You **do/don't** play with a grizzly bear.

10. You **do/don't** drive a bulldozer.

Homework Partner   Date   Speech-Language Pathologist

Combo Z Sentences

Number It Up!

Directions: Read/say aloud the picture-words. Number the words in the Word Bank below 1-8 in any order you desire. Then, put the words on the line below that match the corresponding numbers ("I stubbed my toes"). Read/say the sentences aloud using your good Z sound.

Word Bank

zoo ___   measles ___   boys ___   bulldozer ___

newspaper ___   zip code ___   toes ___   zinnia ___

1. I stubbed my _____.

2. Dad reads the _____.

3. The _____ has/have lots of animals.

4. I was home sick with the _____.

5. She gave the ball to the _____.

6. The _____ is/are in the vase.

7. The _____ make/makes a loud noise.

8. Put the _____ on the envelope.

Homework Partner   Date   Speech-Language Pathologist

Combo Z Sentences

Sentence Cards

Directions: Read/say the picture-words below. Cut out the cards, keeping the A and the B cards separate. Place the cards face down in two piles. Flip over one A and one B card and make up a silly sentence. Read/say aloud each sentence using your good Z sound.

A	A	A
loud	striped	wrinkled
hungry	itchy	yummy

B	B	B
measles	zebra	newspaper
pigs	music	bananas

Homework Partner Date Speech-Language Pathologist

Combo Z Sentences

S, R, L Blends

S Blend Cube Roll

Directions: Assemble the cube as follows: Glue onto construction paper for added durability. Cut along the dotted lines. Fold on solid lines and glue as indicated. To play: Roll the cube. Read/say aloud the word you see using your best S blend sound. _____

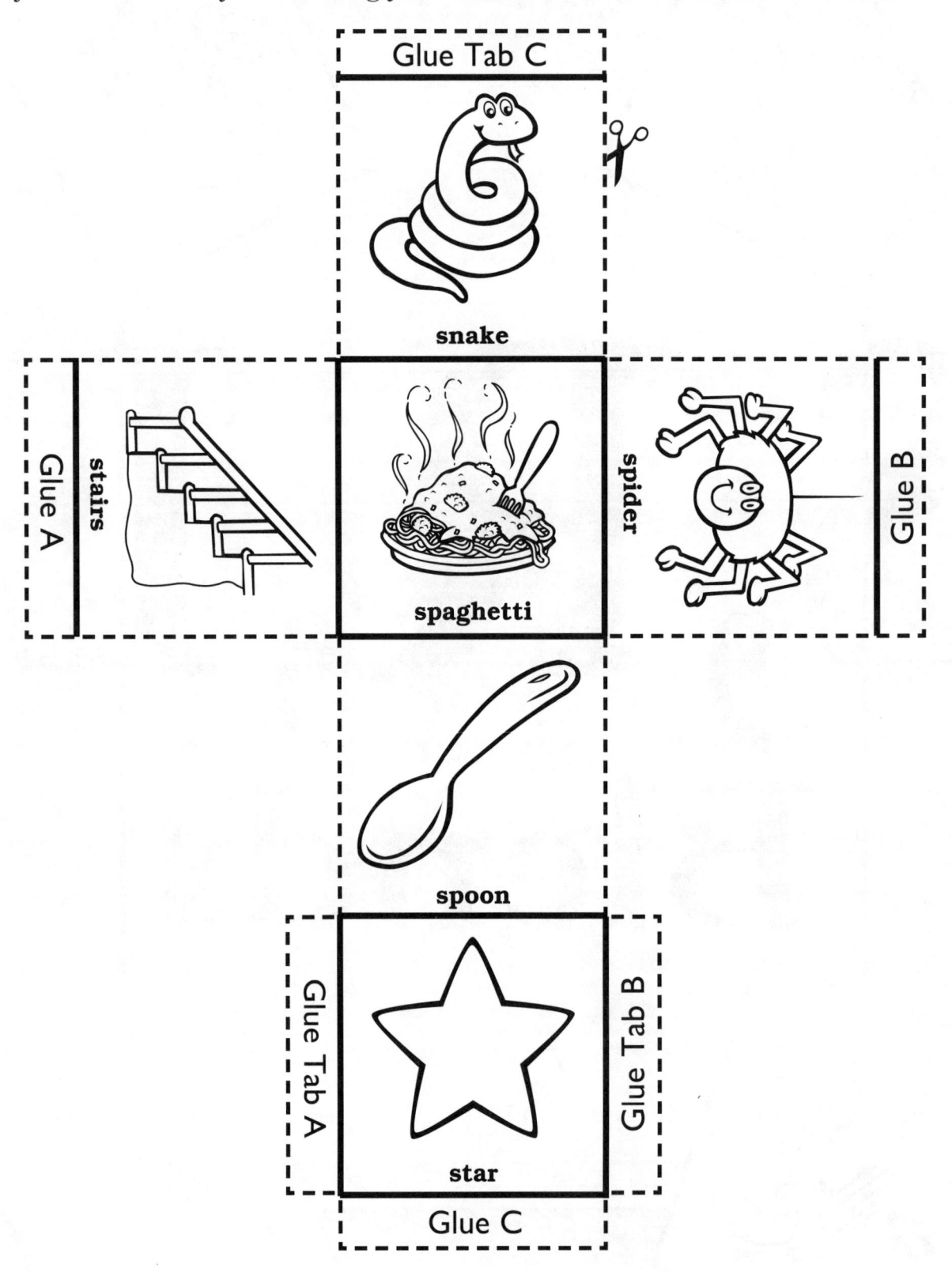

Glue Tab C

snake

Glue A | stairs | spaghetti | spider | Glue B

spoon

Glue Tab A | star | Glue Tab B

Glue C

Homework Partner　　　　Date　　　　Speech-Language Pathologist

S Blend Words

220　　#BK-290 Webber® Artic Fun Sheets • ©2001 Super Duper® Publications • www.superduperinc.com • 1-800-277-8737

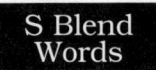

S Blend Rhymes

Directions: Read/say aloud the words in column A. Then, draw a line to find a matching rhyme in column B. There may be more than one match. Say/read both words aloud using your best S blend voice.

A

snake

snail

spoon

skirt

string

stick

square

swing

skunk

star

B

moon

kick

shirt

car

rake

ring

hair

pail

bunk

sing

Snail Trail

Directions: Read/say aloud the picture–words below. Then, cut out the markers. Flip a coin (heads=1, tails=2) to determine how many spaces to move. As you move, read/say each word aloud, using your good S blend sound. First player to reach the finish wins. _____

START: screwdriver, station wagon, skeleton, spaceship, strawberries, swimsuit, scarecrow, slippers, squirrel, stop sign, scarf, string, snail, snake, sled **FINISH**

Homework Partner — Date — Speech-Language Pathologist

S Blend Words

Finger Hopscotch

Directions: Read/say aloud the picture–words below. Then, slide a penny across the hopscotch board. Hop your finger to the square it lands on. Read/say the name of the picture–word again, practicing your good S blend sound. Play again until you have landed on all the words.

spoon

square | slide

string

skunk | sweater

skirt

swing | school

stairs

START

Homework Partner　　　　Date　　　　Speech-Language Pathologist

S Blend Words

Answer This!

Directions: Read/say aloud the picture-words below. Then, answer the questions using words from the Word Bank. Write the answers in the correct spaces. Some questions may have more than one answer. Read/say your answers aloud, using your good S blend sound.

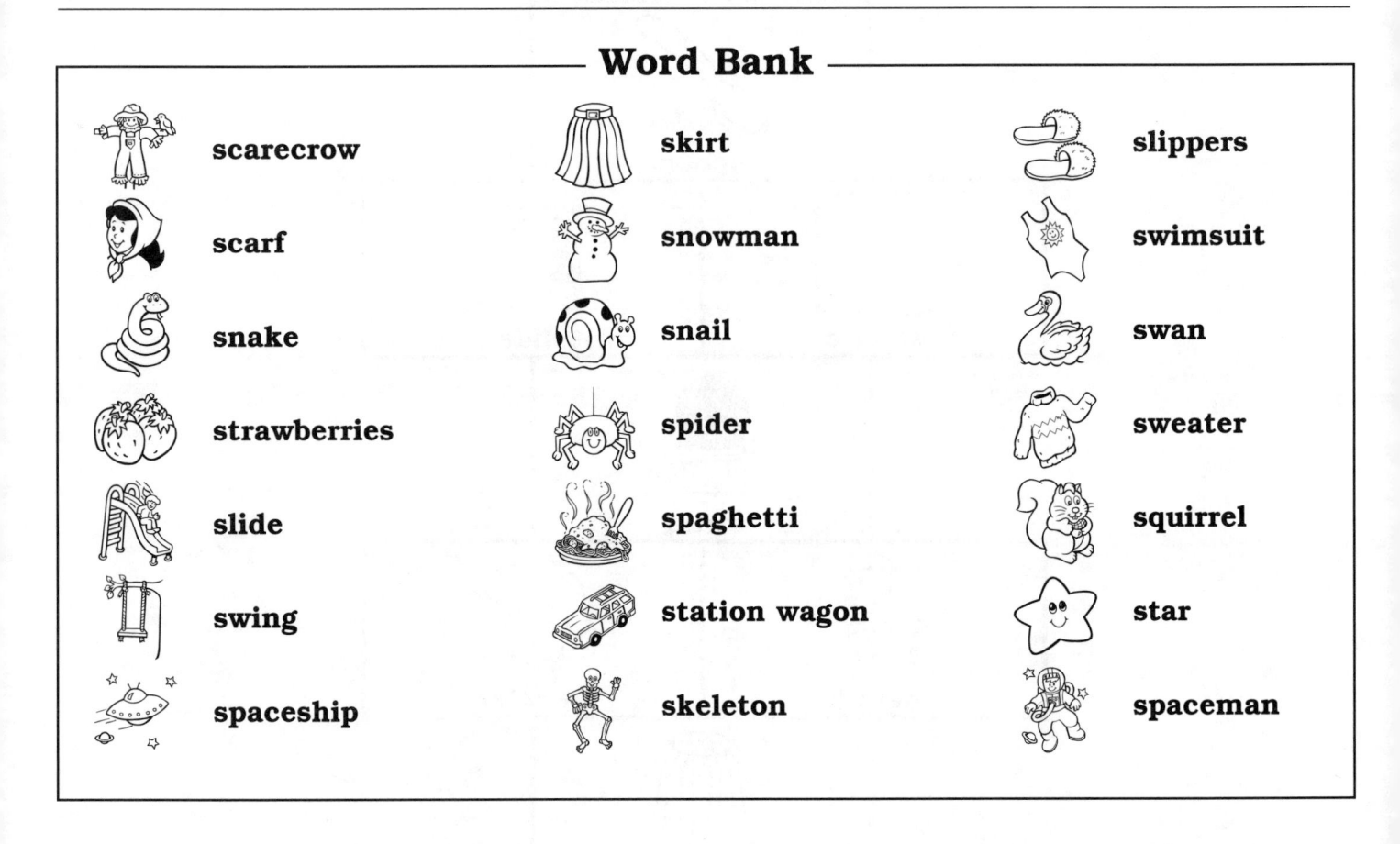

Word Bank

scarecrow	skirt	slippers
scarf	snowman	swimsuit
snake	snail	swan
strawberries	spider	sweater
slide	spaghetti	squirrel
swing	station wagon	star
spaceship	skeleton	spaceman

1. Name some clothes.

2. Name some animals.

3. What can you eat?

4. Name some things you find in space.

5. Name some things that remind you of Halloween.

6. What are some things you find on a playground?

7. What are some winter things?

8. What are some vehicles?

Homework Partner   Date   Speech-Language Pathologist   **S Blend Words**

Slide and Say

Directions: Read/say aloud the picture–words below. Then, cut out all the cards. "Slide" the cards down the slide, reading/saying each word aloud as you slide. Remember to use your good S blend sound.

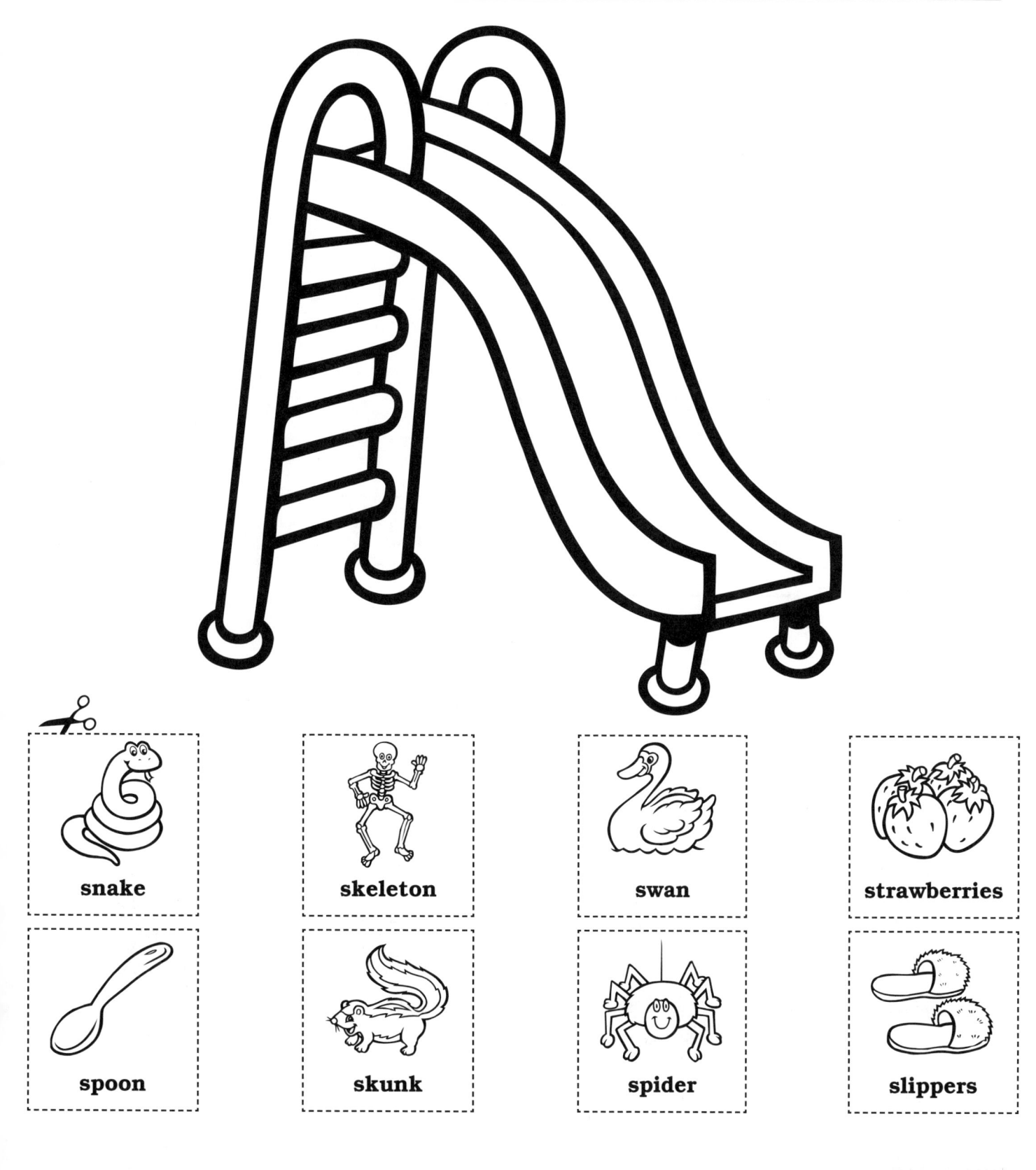

snake	skeleton	swan	strawberries
spoon	skunk	spider	slippers

Homework Partner Date Speech-Language Pathologist S Blend Words

Unscramble The Words

Directions: Read/say the picture–words on the page. Then, unscramble the words on the left and write the answers in the blanks. Read/say your answers aloud. Say the words again using your good S blend sound.

1. **nsoop** __ __ __ __ __

2. **kkuns** __ __ __ __ __

3. **loohcs** __ __ __ __ __ __

4. **awsn** __ __ __ __

5. **psderi** __ __ __ __ __ __

6. **tsra** __ __ __ __

7. **strik** __ __ __ __ __

8. **dseli** __ __ __ __ __

spoon

skirt

swan

skunk

star

school

spider

slide

Answers: 1-spoon, 2-skunk, 3-school, 4-swan, 5-spider, 6-star, 7-skirt, 8-slide

Homework Partner   Date   Speech-Language Pathologist   S Blend Words

226   #BK-290 Webber® Artic Fun Sheets • ©2001 Super Duper® Publications • www.superduperinc.com • 1-800-277-8737

Float in Space

Directions: Choose S blends from the stars to fill in the blanks. Write the S blend to make a word on each line below. Then, say the words aloud using your good S blend sound.

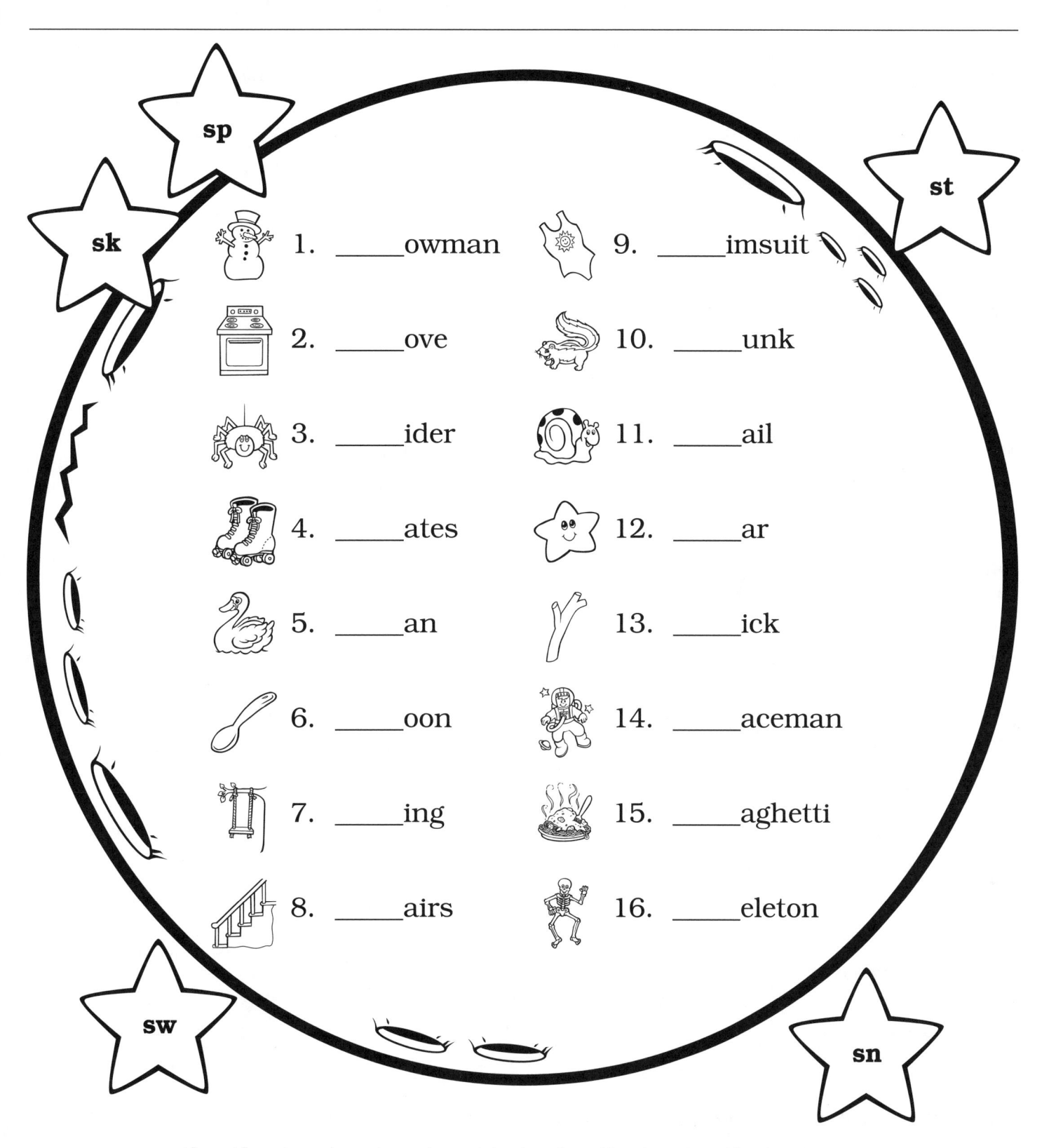

sp
sk
st

1. ____owman
2. ____ove
3. ____ider
4. ____ates
5. ____an
6. ____oon
7. ____ing
8. ____airs
9. ____imsuit
10. ____unk
11. ____ail
12. ____ar
13. ____ick
14. ____aceman
15. ____aghetti
16. ____eleton

sw
sn

Answers: 1-sn, 2-st, 3-sp, 4-sk, 5-sw, 6-sp, 7-sw, 8-st, 9-st, 10-sk, 11-sn, 12-st, 13-st, 14-sp, 15-sp, 16-sk

Homework Partner   Date   Speech-Language Pathologist

S Blend Words

#BK-290 Webber® Artic Fun Sheets • ©2001 Super Duper® Publications • www.superduperinc.com • 1-800-277-8737

227

Matching

Directions: Read/say aloud the B card phrases. Then, cut out the cards. Keep the A and B cards in separate piles and place face down. Flip over one A and one B card. Read both cards aloud. If you make a correct match, you score a point. Play continues in turn. Most points wins!

A	A	A	A
What do you wear around the house?	Where do you climb?	What has sauce and meatballs on it?	Who flies to the moon?
A What do you eat cereal or soup with?	**A** What do you drive?	**A** What does a dog fetch?	**A** What do you wear to the beach?
A What bird likes the water?	**A** What has four equal sides?	**A** What has eight legs and crawls?	**A** What animal eats nuts?
A What animal has a bad odor?	**A** What do you cook food on?	**A** What keeps birds out of the garden?	**A** What do you wear in the winter?

B	B	B	B
a red swimsuit	a beautiful swan	some fuzzy slippers	a wooden stick
B up the stairs	**B** a hungry squirrel	**B** a shiny spoon	**B** a big skunk
B a warm sweater	**B** a silly spider	**B** the family station wagon	**B** the intelligent spaceman
B a funny scarecrow	**B** yummy spaghetti	**B** a perfect square	**B** a hot stove

Homework Partner   Date   Speech-Language Pathologist   **S Blend Phrases**

Find the Falling Star

Directions: Read/say aloud the B cards below. Then, cut out the cards. Keep the A and B cards in separate piles and place face down. Flip over one A and one B card and make up a phrase. If your phrase is "a falling star," you win! Read/say each phrase aloud using your good S blend sound.

A	A	A
a falling	a melting	a chubby
a bouncing	a singing	a heavy

B	B	B	B	B
sweater	spider	spaceship	snowman	squirrel
skeleton	station wagon	star	snake	stick

Homework Partner   Date   Speech-Language Pathologist

S Blend Phrases

Phrase Race

Directions: Read/say aloud the picture–phrases below. Then, cut out the markers. Flip a coin (heads=1, tails=2) to determine how many spaces to move. As you move, read/say each phrase aloud, using your good S blend sound. First player to reach the finish wins.

START
- a pretty skirt
- my roller skates
- eat more spaghetti
- ball of string
- wish on a star
- a hairy spider
- lick the spoon
- up the stairs
- a baby swan
- ride the swing
- on the stove
- wear your swimsuit
- the squirrel's nut
- a winter scarf
- at the stop sign

FINISH

Homework Partner   Date   Speech-Language Pathologist

S Blend Phrases

Story Loop

Directions: Read/say aloud each picture-word. Make up a story using all of the pictures in the circle. You can start anywhere in the circle and go in either direction, but you must always end where you started to complete the loop. Say your story aloud, using your good S blend sound. _____

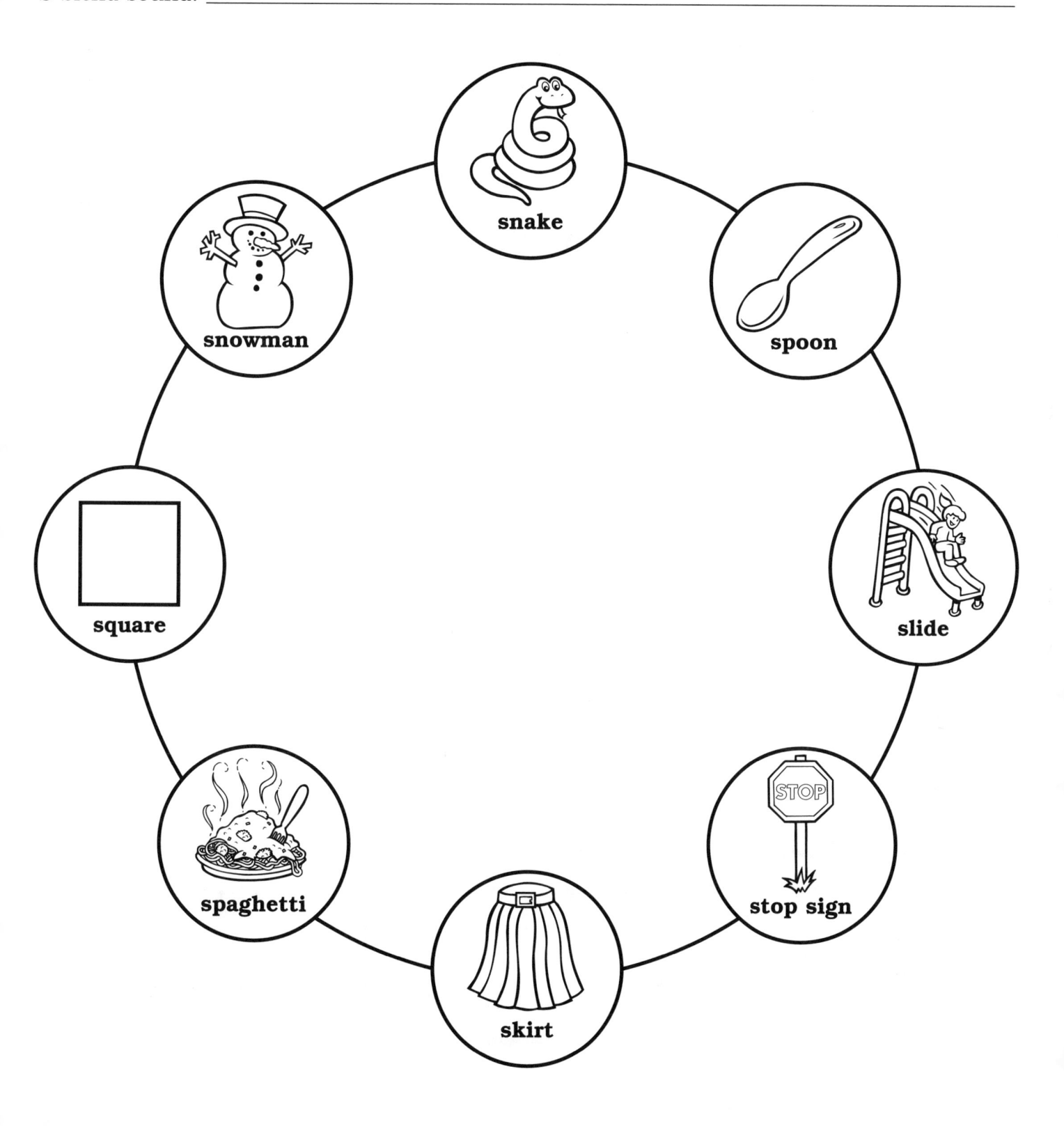

- snake
- spoon
- slide
- stop sign
- skirt
- spaghetti
- square
- snowman

Homework Partner   Date   Speech-Language Pathologist

S Blend Sentences

Pick a Toy

Directions: Finish the phrase, "I will catch a(n) ____," with a toy from the machine below. Read/say the completed sentence aloud using your best S blend sound.

"I will catch a(n) _____."

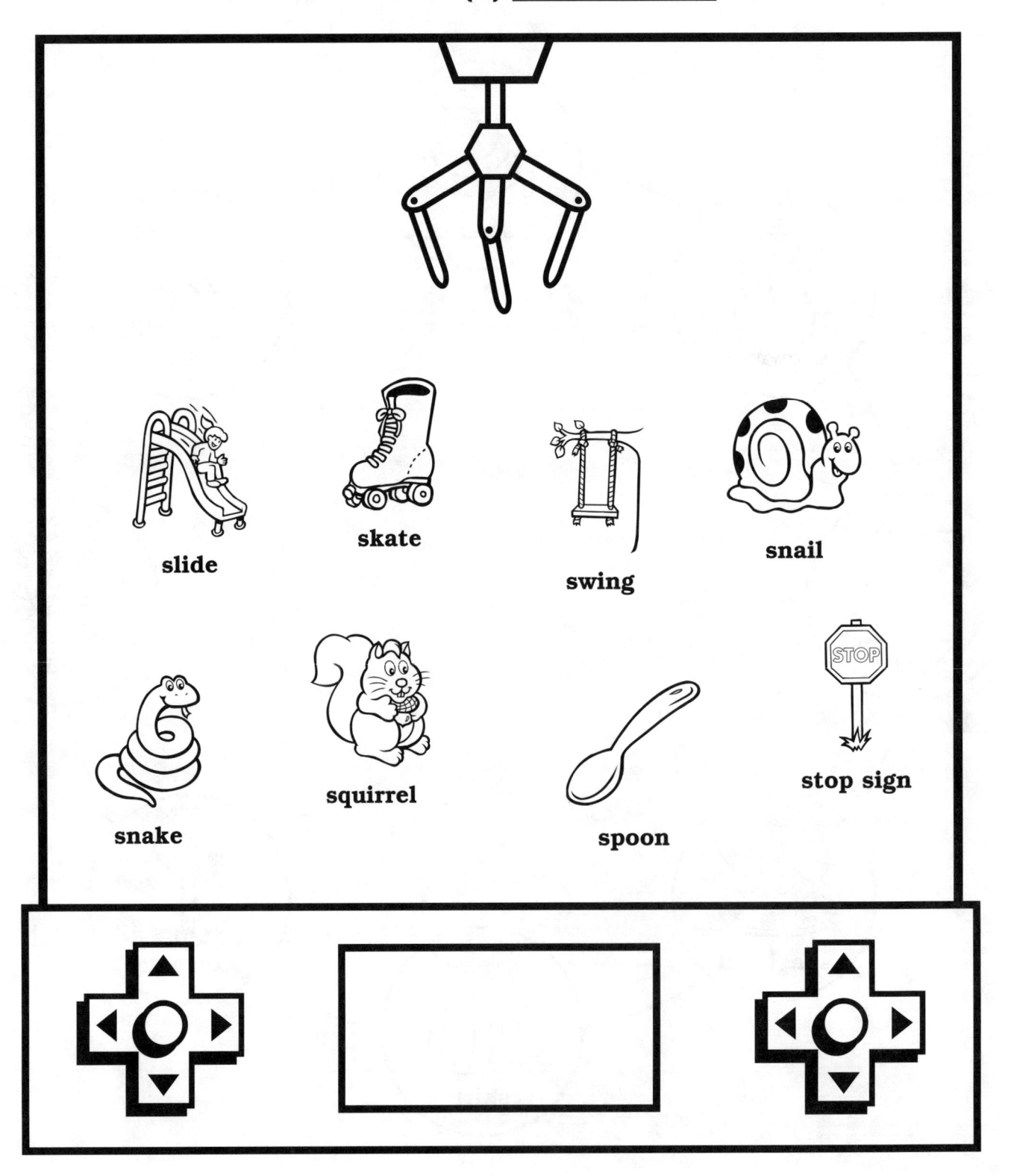

- slide
- skate
- swing
- snail
- snake
- squirrel
- spoon
- stop sign

Homework Partner   Date   Speech-Language Pathologist

S Blend Sentences

Make a Sentence

Directions: Read/say aloud each picture–word. Then, write a sentence on the line below each picture using the word. Read/say each sentence aloud using your best S blend sound.

_____
_____

snowman

spaceship

spider

school

skeleton

swan

Homework Partner　　　Date　　　Speech-Language Pathologist

S Blend Sentences

Which Is?

Directions: Read/say the following questions aloud. Then, answer each question using your best R blend sound.

1. Which is smaller - a **frog** or a **dragon**?

2. Which is louder - a **drum** or **grass**?

3. Which is faster - a **frog** or a **dragon**?

4. Which is older - your **friends** or your **grandmother**?

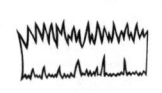

5. Which is harder - a **crane** or **grass**?

6. Which is prettier - a **dress** or a **drum**?

7. Which is longer - a **crane** or a **dragon's** neck?

8. Which is softer - a **frog** or **grass**?

Answers: 1.frog 2.drum 3.dragon 4.grandmother 5.crane 6.dress 7.crane 8.grass

Homework Partner   Date   Speech-Language Pathologist   R Blend Words

Riddle Detective

Directions: Read/say aloud the picture–words. Then, read the riddles below. Choose the correct answers from the Word Bank. Write the answers in the spaces. Read/say your answers aloud using your best R blend sound.

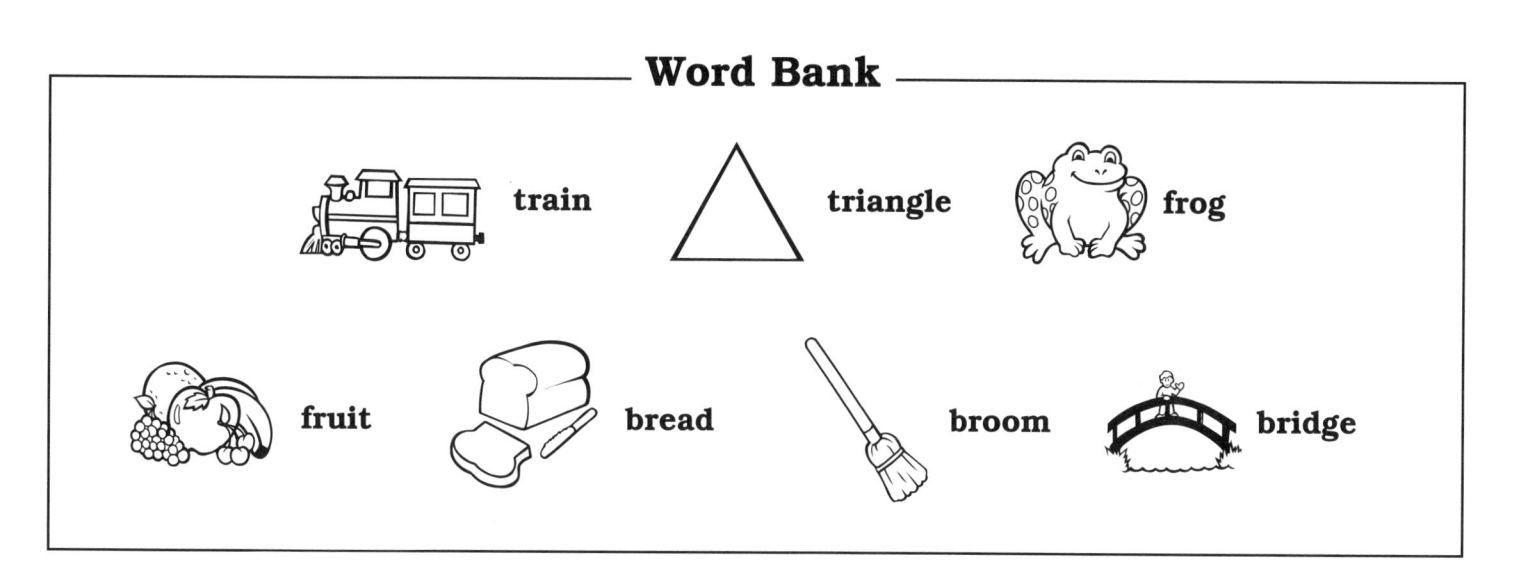

Word Bank

train   triangle   frog

fruit   bread   broom   bridge

1. I am green and hop.
   I like to eat flies and
   swim in water.
   What am I?

2. I move fast when I go.
   I carry a lot of people and
   I am very large.
   What am I?

3. Use me to make a sandwich.
   I can be white or wheat.
   Kids love to eat me.
   What am I?

4. I am built over water.
   Boats travel under me
   and cars travel on me.
   I can be long or covered.
   What am I?

Answers: 1. frog 2. train 3. bread 4. bridge

Homework Partner   Date   Speech-Language Pathologist

R Blend Words

What Am I?

Directions: Read/say aloud each picture–word below. Then, read each question. Fill in the blank with the appropriate word. Read/say each answer aloud, using your best R blend sound.

frog	dragon	grapes	bread	braces
broom	bride	crab	french fries	dress

1. I am hanging from a vine. I am _____.

2. I am hopping on a lily pad. I am a _____.

3. I am getting married. I am a _____.

4. I help sweep the floor. I am a _____.

5. I am worn by girls and women. I am a _____.

6. I live in the water. I am a _____.

7. I can be toasted or eaten in a sandwich. I am _____.

8. I go on people's teeth. I am _____.

9. I am eaten with hamburgers and hot dogs. I am _____.

10. I am a big animal with a long tail. I am a _____.

Answers: 1-grapes, 2-frog, 3-bride, 4-broom, 5-dress, 6-crab, 7-bread, 8-braces, 9-french fries, 10-dragon

Homework Partner Date Speech-Language Pathologist

R Blend Words

Gumball Fun

Directions: Read/say aloud each picture-word. Cut out the gumballs and glue/tape or place them in the gumball machine. As you do this, read/say the words aloud again using your best R blend sound.

- tree
- crane
- pretzel
- bridge
- braid

- dress
- frog
- crab
- traffic
- tricycle

Gum

Homework Partner Date Speech-Language Pathologist

R Blend Words

Football Mania!

Directions: Read/say aloud the picture–words. Cut out the footballs and place them at the 10 yard line on opposite sides of the field. First player flips a coin and moves 10 yards (heads) or 20 yards (tails). Say the word you land on aloud. Play continues in turn. First player to score a touchdown wins. Next time you play, switch sides. _____

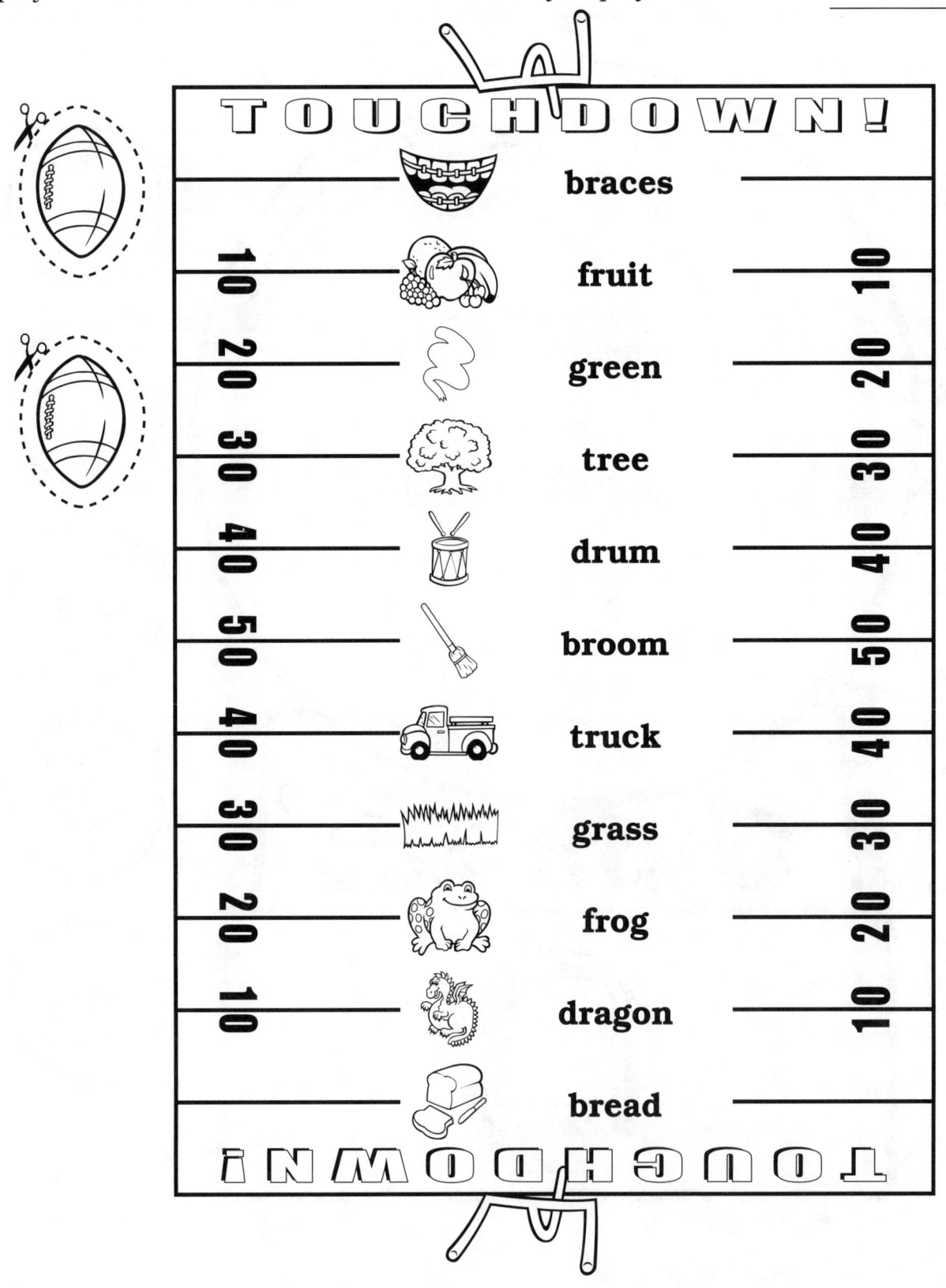

TOUCHDOWN!

- braces
- fruit
- green
- tree
- drum
- broom
- truck
- grass
- frog
- dragon
- bread

TOUCHDOWN!

_____ Homework Partner   _____ Date   _____ Speech-Language Pathologist

R Blend Words

238

Win the Trophy!

Directions: Read/say aloud the words on the trophies. Then, cut out the trophies and place them face down. Roll a die (heads=1, tails=2) and pick up a trophy/trophies. Say the name of the picture on each trophy aloud using your best R blend sound.

crab	pretzel	traffic
friends	bread	trash can
drum	dress	bracelet
crane	green	grass

Homework Partner Date Speech-Language Pathologist

R Blend Words

Spinner Action

Directions: Read/say aloud the picture–words below. If you prefer, glue this page to construction paper for added durability. Cut out the arrow/dial. Use a brad to connect the dial to the circle. Spin the spinner. When you land on a picture, read/say the word aloud, using your best R blend sound.

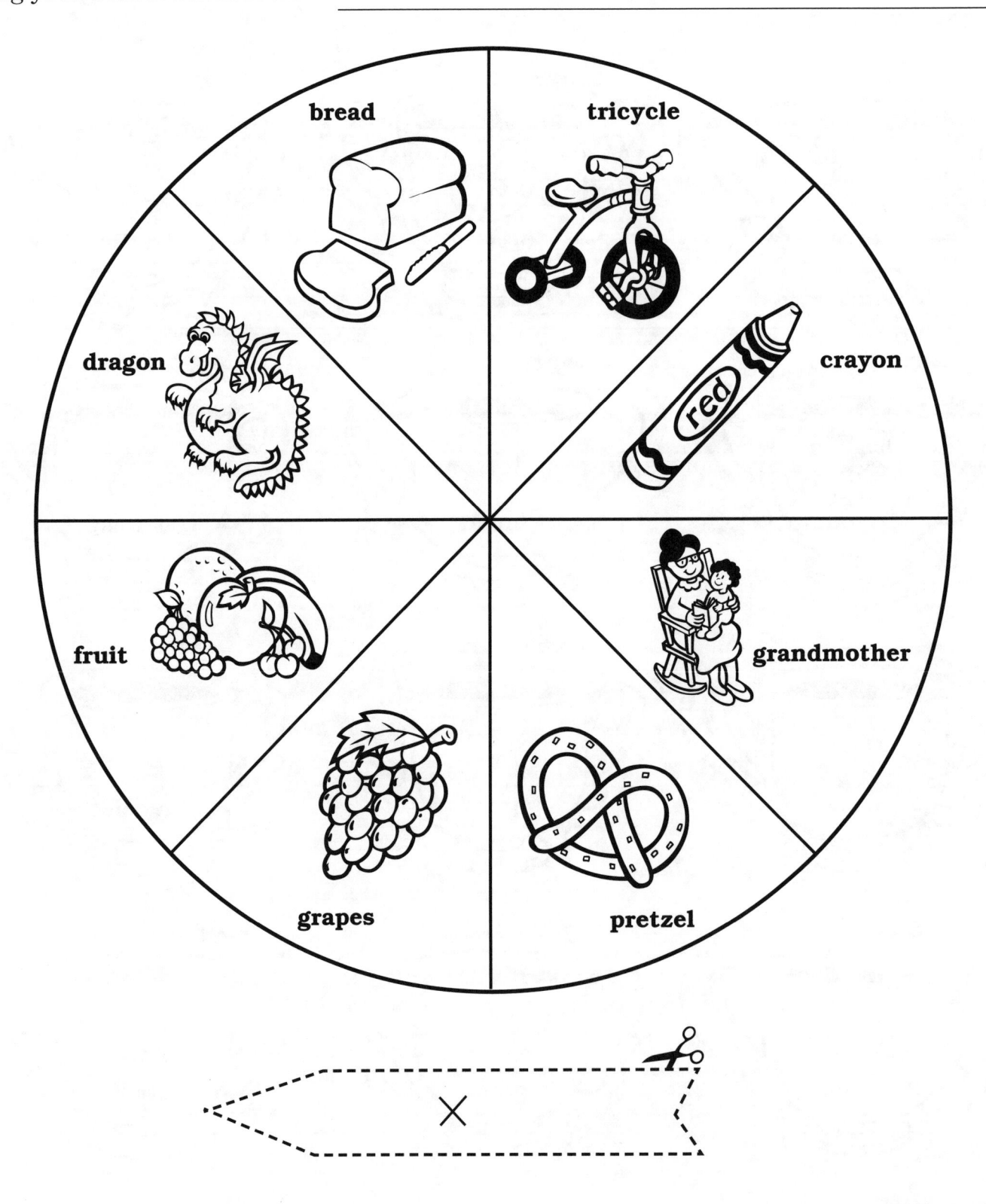

- bread
- tricycle
- crayon
- grandmother
- pretzel
- grapes
- fruit
- dragon

Homework Partner   Date   Speech-Language Pathologist

R Blend Words

240

R Cube Roll

Directions: Assemble the cube as follows: Glue onto construction paper for added durability. Cut along the dotted lines. Fold on solid lines and glue as indicated. To play: Roll the cube. Read/say aloud the word you see using your best R blend sound.

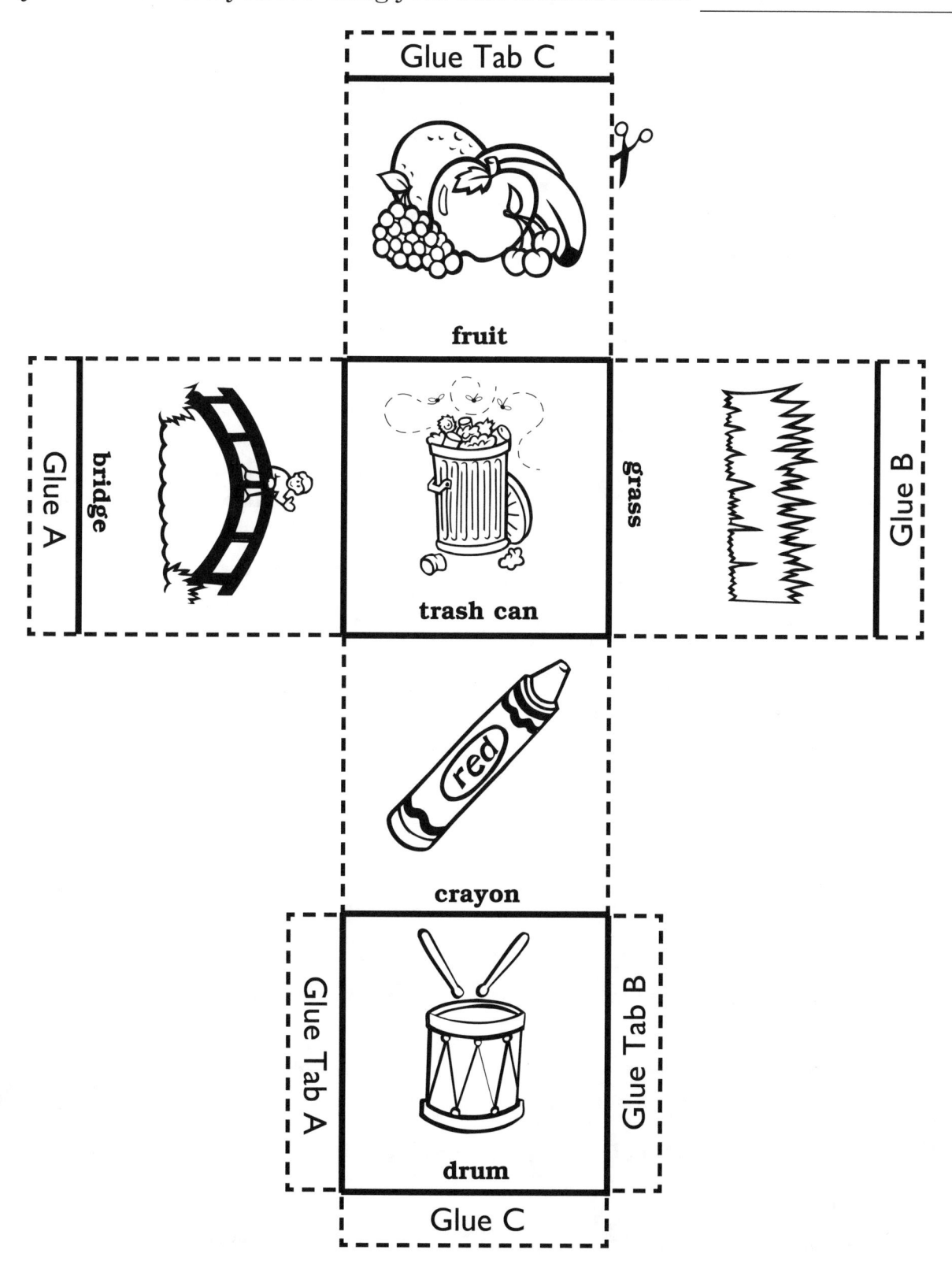

Glue Tab C

fruit

Glue A | bridge | trash can | grass | Glue B

crayon

Glue Tab A | drum | Glue Tab B

Glue C

Homework Partner | Date | Speech-Language Pathologist | R Blend Words

Color It

Directions: Read/say the picture-words below. Then, color each crayon. Use a different color for each one. Then say a phrase aloud about each crayon, using the color on that crayon ("a blue triangle").

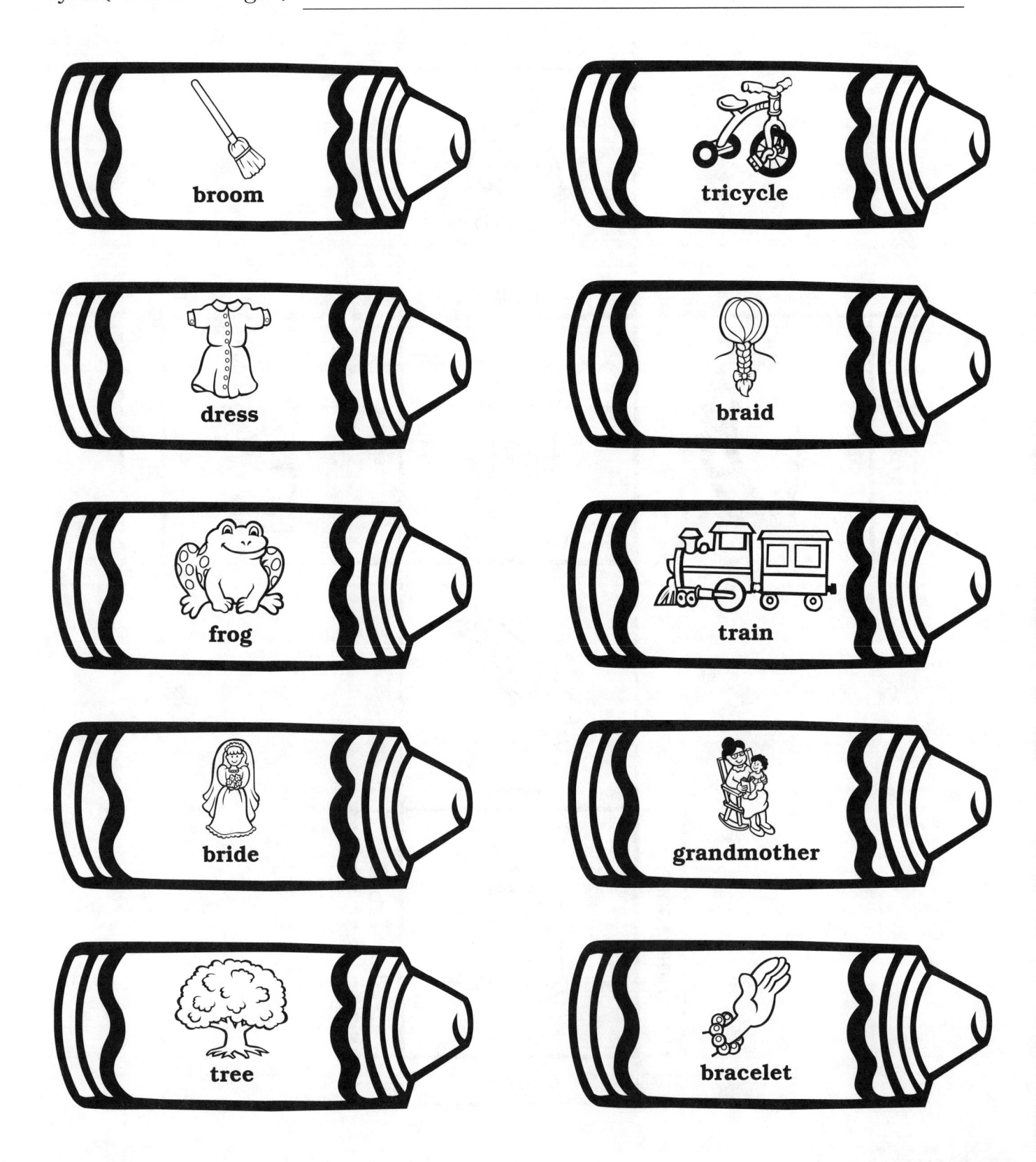

- broom
- tricycle
- dress
- braid
- frog
- train
- bride
- grandmother
- tree
- bracelet

Homework Partner   Date   Speech-Language Pathologist

R Blend Phrases

Bridge Over Troubled Water

Directions: Read/say aloud the picture–words below. Then, choose a ship and use the picture–word in the phrase, "Save the_____." Read/say each phrase aloud using your best R blend sound.

"Save the..."

- train
- dinosaur
- broom
- crayon
- trash can
- friends
- brush
- drum

Homework Partner   Date   Speech-Language Pathologist

R Blend Phrases

#BK-290 Webber® Artic Fun Sheets • ©2001 Super Duper® Publications • www.superduperinc.com • 1-800-277-8737

243

X and O

Directions: Cut out each X and O below. Have each player/partner choose X or O. The first player reads/says a picture–phrase aloud and places an X or O on the square. Play continues in turn. The first person to get three in a row wins.

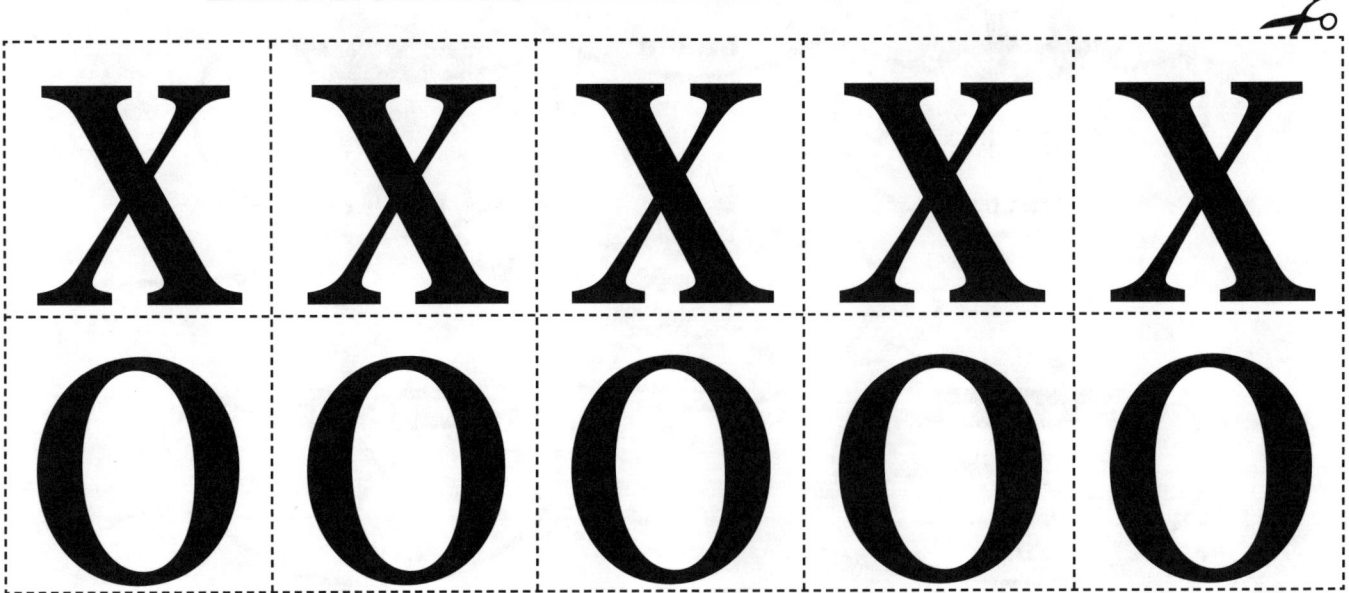

eat the fruit	a new dress	beat the drum
a new crayon	a yummy pretzel	use the brush
get the broom	move the trash can	cut the bread

X X X X X

O O O O O

Homework Partner   Date   Speech-Language Pathologist

R Blend Phrases

244   #BK-290 Webber® Artic Fun Sheets • ©2001 Super Duper® Publications • www.superduperinc.com • 1-800-277-8737

To Grandmother's House We Go

Directions: Read/say aloud the picture–words below. Then, cut out the markers. Flip a coin (heads=1, tails=2) to determine how many spaces to move. As you move, read/say each sentence aloud, using your good R blend sound. First player to reach the finish wins.

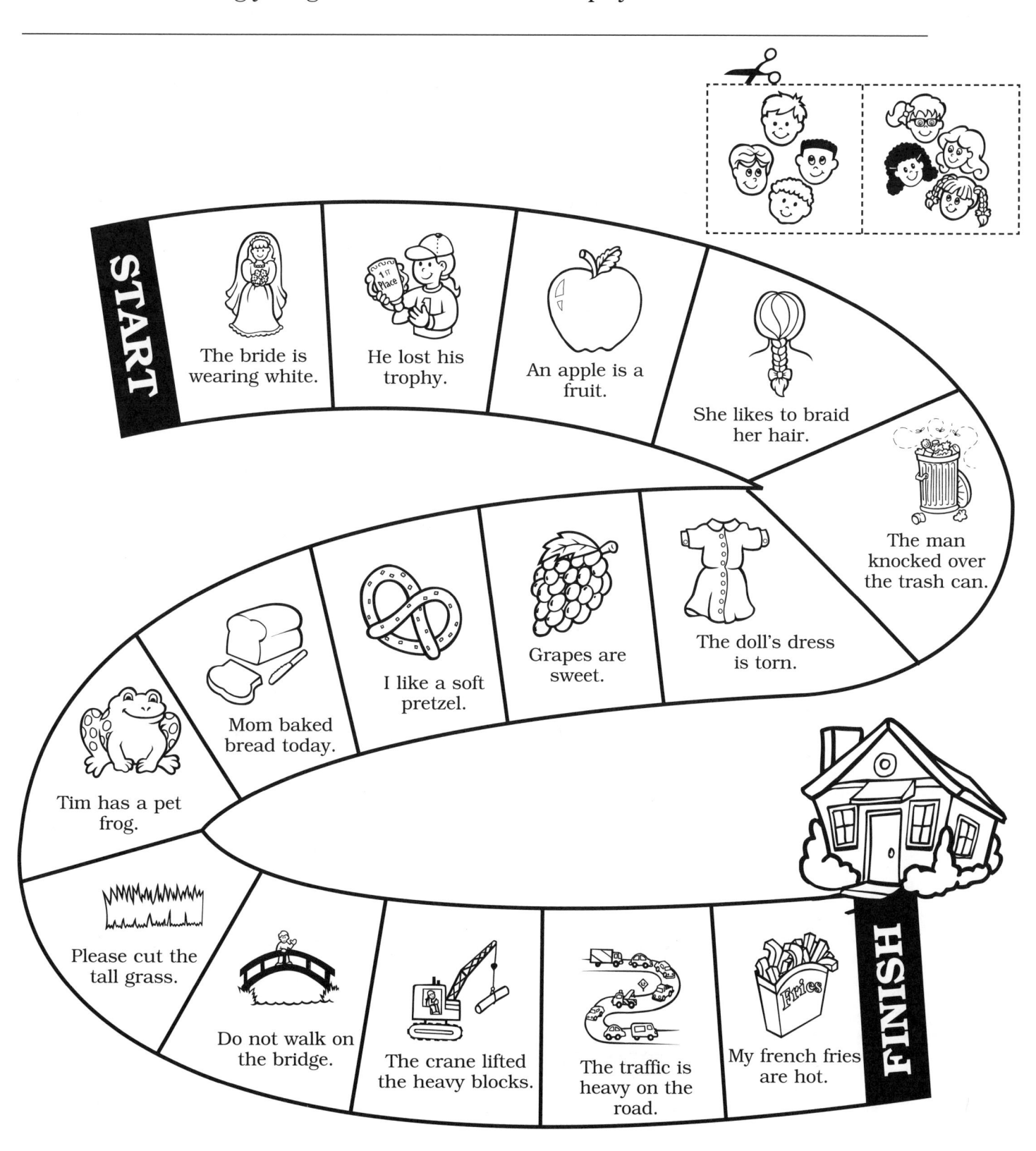

START

- The bride is wearing white.
- He lost his trophy.
- An apple is a fruit.
- She likes to braid her hair.
- The man knocked over the trash can.
- The doll's dress is torn.
- Grapes are sweet.
- I like a soft pretzel.
- Mom baked bread today.
- Tim has a pet frog.
- Please cut the tall grass.
- Do not walk on the bridge.
- The crane lifted the heavy blocks.
- The traffic is heavy on the road.
- My french fries are hot.

FINISH

Homework Partner   Date   Speech-Language Pathologist

R Blend Sentences

What Do You Think?

Directions: Read the sentences and circle the correct answers. Then, read/say the correct sentence aloud. Remember to use your good R blend sound.

1. You **do/don't** use a broom to sweep.
2. Frogs **do/don't** wear dresses. 
3. A triangle **is/isn't** a shape. 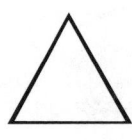
4. A pretzel **is/isn't** a food. 
5. A tricycle **does/doesn't** have four wheels. 
6. Braces **do/don't** go on your ears. 
7. You **do/don't** use a brush to fix your hair. 
8. A train **does/doesn't** have a whistle. 
9. French fries **are/aren't** made of potatoes. 
10. Grapes **are/aren't** green. 

Homework Partner   Date   Speech-Language Pathologist

R Blend Sentences

Make it Fit

Directions: Circle the words that best finish the sentences below. Then, read/say the sentences aloud using your best R blend sound.

1. I got stuck in _____ .

A	B	C
butterfly	traffic	jelly

2. I went to a wedding and saw a _____ .

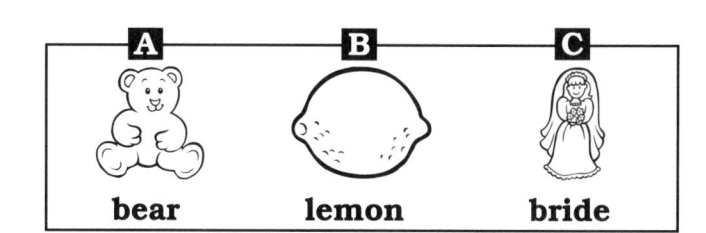

A	B	C
bear	lemon	bride

3. She has _____ on her teeth.

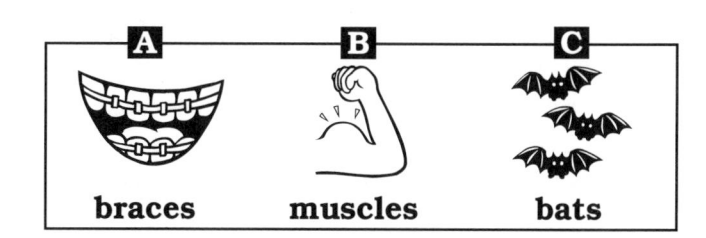

A	B	C
braces	muscles	bats

4. A _____ is a shape.

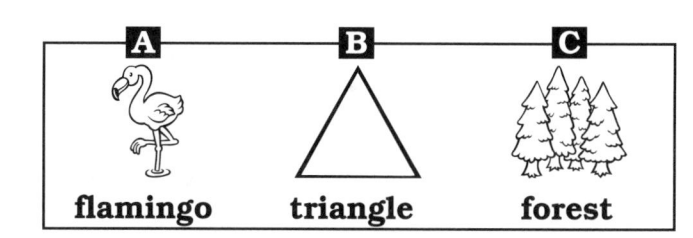

A	B	C
flamingo	triangle	forest

5. The cat climbed up the _____ .

A	B	C
lobster	cereal	tree

6. She wants to put on a new _____ .

A	B	C
dress	book	mouse

Homework Partner   Date   Speech-Language Pathologist

R Blend Sentences

Slide and Climb

Directions: Read/say aloud the picture–words below. Then, cut out the markers. Flip a coin (heads=1, tails=2) to determine how many spaces to move. As you move, read/say each word aloud, using your good L blend sound. First player to reach the finish wins.

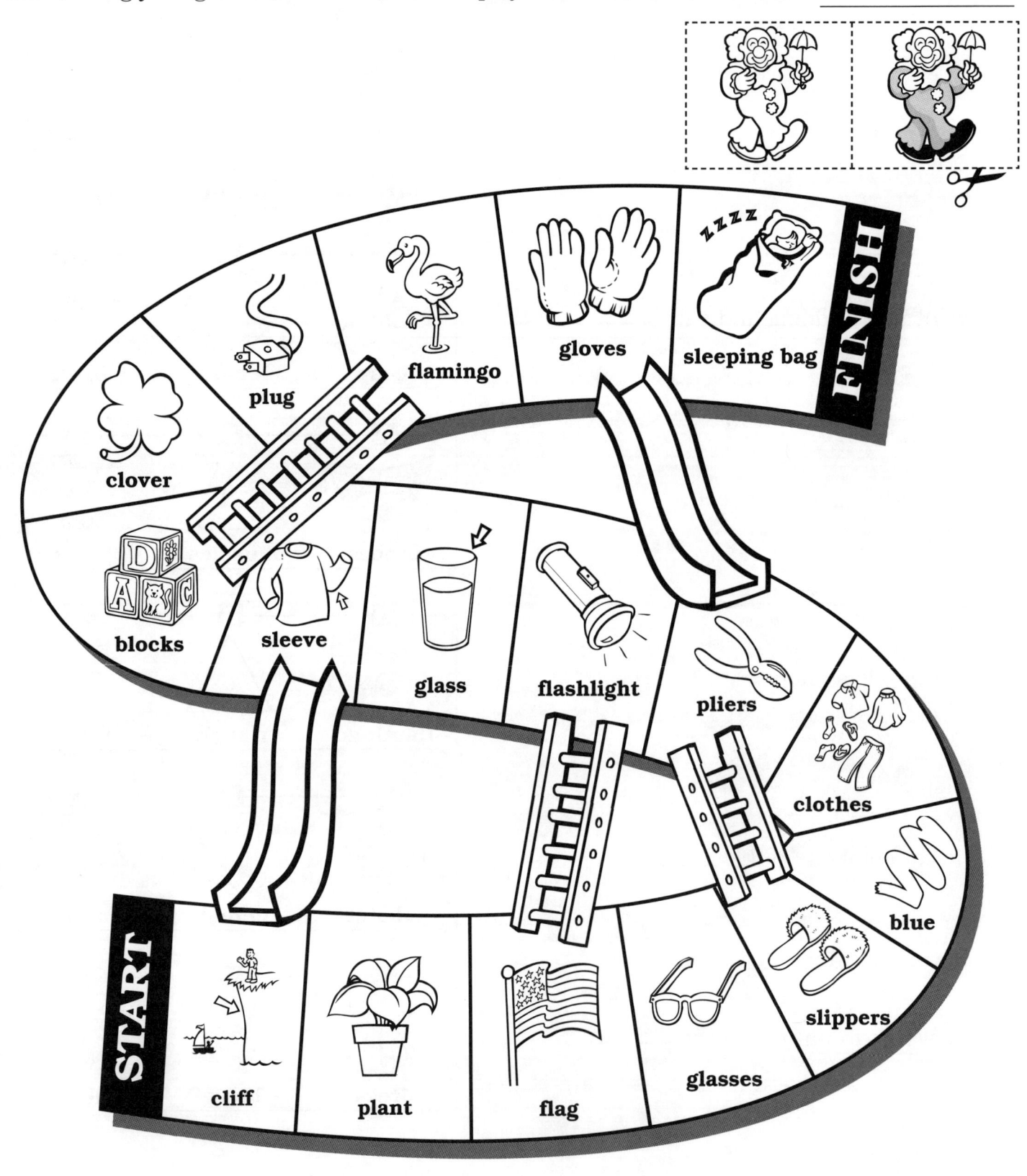

Board spaces from START to FINISH:
cliff, plant, flag, glasses, slippers, blue, clothes, pliers, flashlight, glass, sleeve, blocks, clover, plug, flamingo, gloves, sleeping bag, FINISH

Homework Partner Date Speech-Language Pathologist

L Blend Words

248

Flamingo Walk

Directions: Read/say aloud the picture–words below. Then, cut out the markers. Flip a coin (heads=1, tails=2) to determine how many spaces to move. As you move, read/say each word aloud, using your good L blend sound. First player to reach the finish wins.

START

| clam | gloves | flashlight | blanket | pliers | sleeve | cliff | glass | flag | blue | plum | slippers | clown | blocks | fly |

FINISH

Homework Partner | Date | Speech-Language Pathologist

L Blend Words

Who Said That?

Directions: Read/say each L blend picture–word aloud. Read the statements in the middle. Then, ask, **"Who said that?"** Answer with the correct word. Then, draw a line from the sentence to the correct picture.

"I keep your hands warm."

"I am found in the ocean."

flower

blocks

"You walk on top of me."

"Kids build towers with me."

blue

clam

"I am the color of the sky."

"I bloom in the spring."

floor

gloves

Homework Partner   Date   Speech-Language Pathologist

L Blend Words

See, Say, Do!

Directions: Read/say aloud the picture–words below. Then, put a △ around the pictures that are found at school. Put a ☐ around the pictures of things that grow and put a ○ around the pictures of things that people wear. As you follow these directions, read/say each word aloud. Use your good L blend sound.

| gloves | blocks | plant | clothes |

| glue | glasses | slippers | slide |

| flower | flag | clock | clover |

| sleeve | plum | cloak |

Homework Partner   Date   Speech-Language Pathologist

L Blend Words

Cookie Jar

Directions: Read/say aloud each word below. Then, cut out the cookies. Glue/tape or place them on the jar. Read/say each word aloud using your best L blend sound. _____

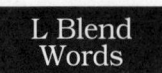

slippers · glasses · black · pliers · plant

clothesline · flamingo · cloak · blanket · clown

Homework Partner   Date   Speech-Language Pathologist

L Blend Words

Memory Game

Directions: Read/say aloud each picture–word below. Cut out the pictures. Place all cards face down. Try to match the cards. Say each card as you pick it up, using your good L blend sound. Keep all matches. Most matches wins!

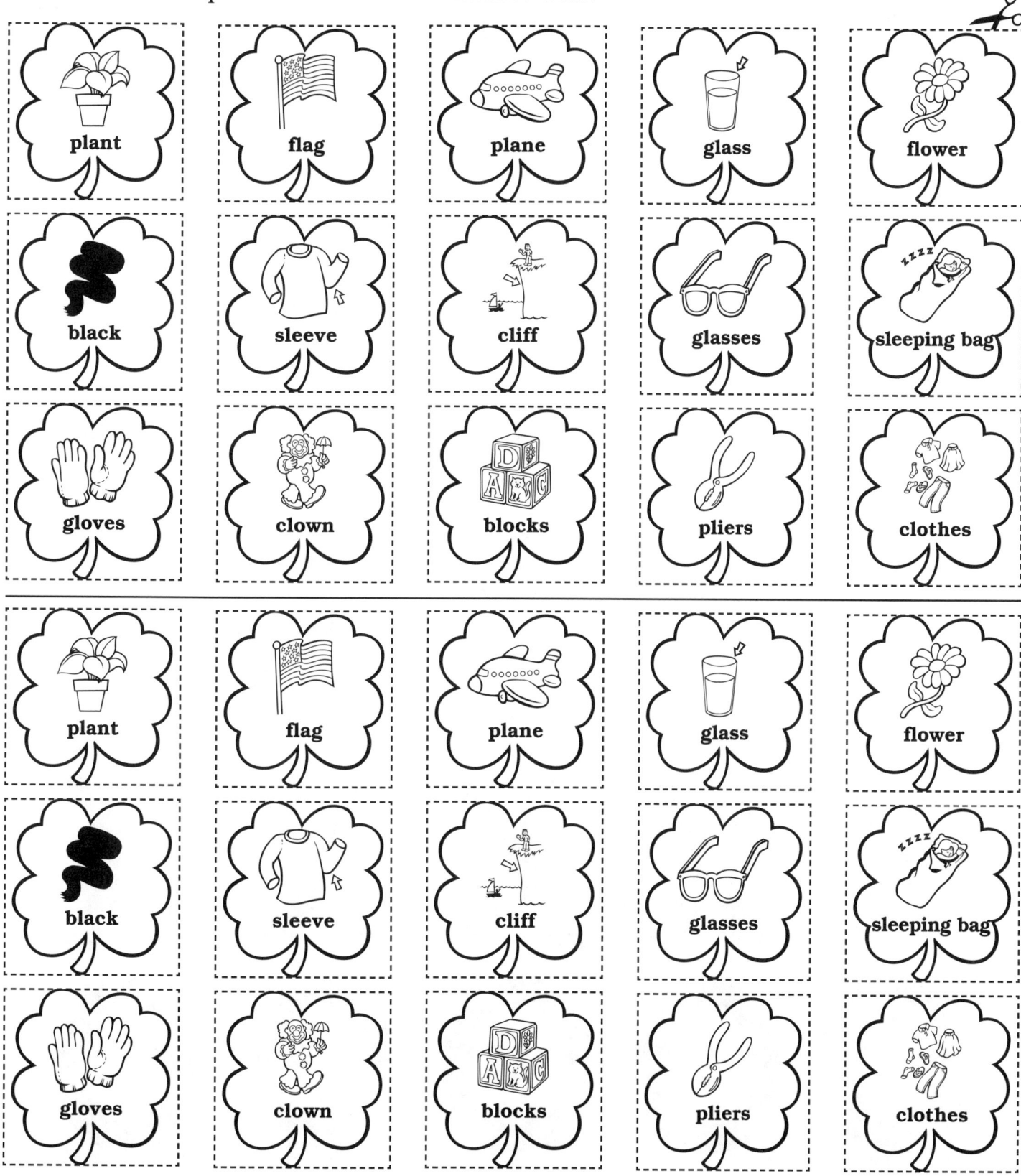

plant	flag	plane	glass	flower
black	sleeve	cliff	glasses	sleeping bag
gloves	clown	blocks	pliers	clothes
plant	flag	plane	glass	flower
black	sleeve	cliff	glasses	sleeping bag
gloves	clown	blocks	pliers	clothes

Homework Partner   Date   Speech-Language Pathologist

L Blend Words

X and O

Directions: Cut out each X and O below. Have each player/partner choose X or O. The first player reads/says a picture–word aloud and places an X or O on the square. Play continues in turn. The first person to get three in a row wins.

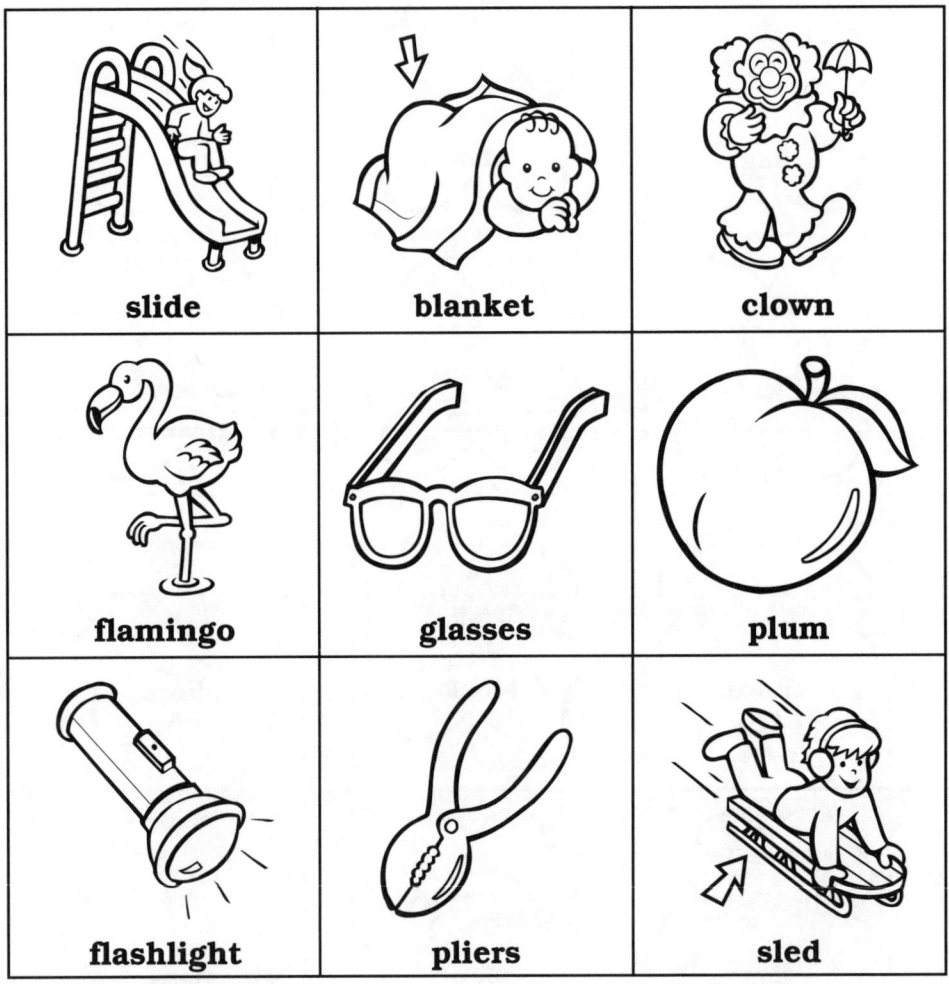

slide	blanket	clown
flamingo	glasses	plum
flashlight	pliers	sled

X X X X X

O O O O O

Homework Partner Date Speech-Language Pathologist

L Blend Words

Search-A-Word

Directions: Read/say the picture–words aloud. Using the picture–words for hints, find and circle each word answer in the word search box. Then, read/say the words again. Use your good L blend sound.

blocks **sled** **sleeve**

clothes

L G C R H F B K E V J B V B T
D I O L L O Z L G X C L R N E
N U M O O S Z H U L M O J D T
O T W K Y T M E A E B C N O P
T E M Z X H M V M M K F L S
R L H Q P S T E P E P S N W S
U N J T E L F I S Z E B W V A
M X M N O E U T Y T U L I T L
Q H A K Z D Z S D E S R S Y G
W L D X Y C C N A E J O Q T S
P K Q I Q B M O V D P I N L Y
P L U M R I R E V O L C O B E
J W B O I U B M D E X N Q Y X
S R G F L A S H L I G H T D Z
H L S Z H R M F Z P Z J F G I

plane

flower

flashlight

plum

clam

blue **clover** **glass**

Answer Key on Page 280

Homework Partner — Date — Speech-Language Pathologist

L Blend Words

Feed the Elephant

Directions: Cut out the peanuts. Read/say the L blend phrases aloud while you feed the elephant. Remember to use your good L blend sounds.

on a cliff	on the clothesline	wash the slippers
the American flag	sweep the floor	a funny clown
yummy steamed clams	the loud plane	all the dirty clothes
a bright flashlight	sticky glue	a pink flamingo

Homework Partner Date Speech-Language Pathologist

L Blend Phrases

Flag Together

Directions: Draw a line from the flagpoles to the matching flags. Match the flags to make complete phrases. Read/say each phrase aloud, using your good L blend sound.

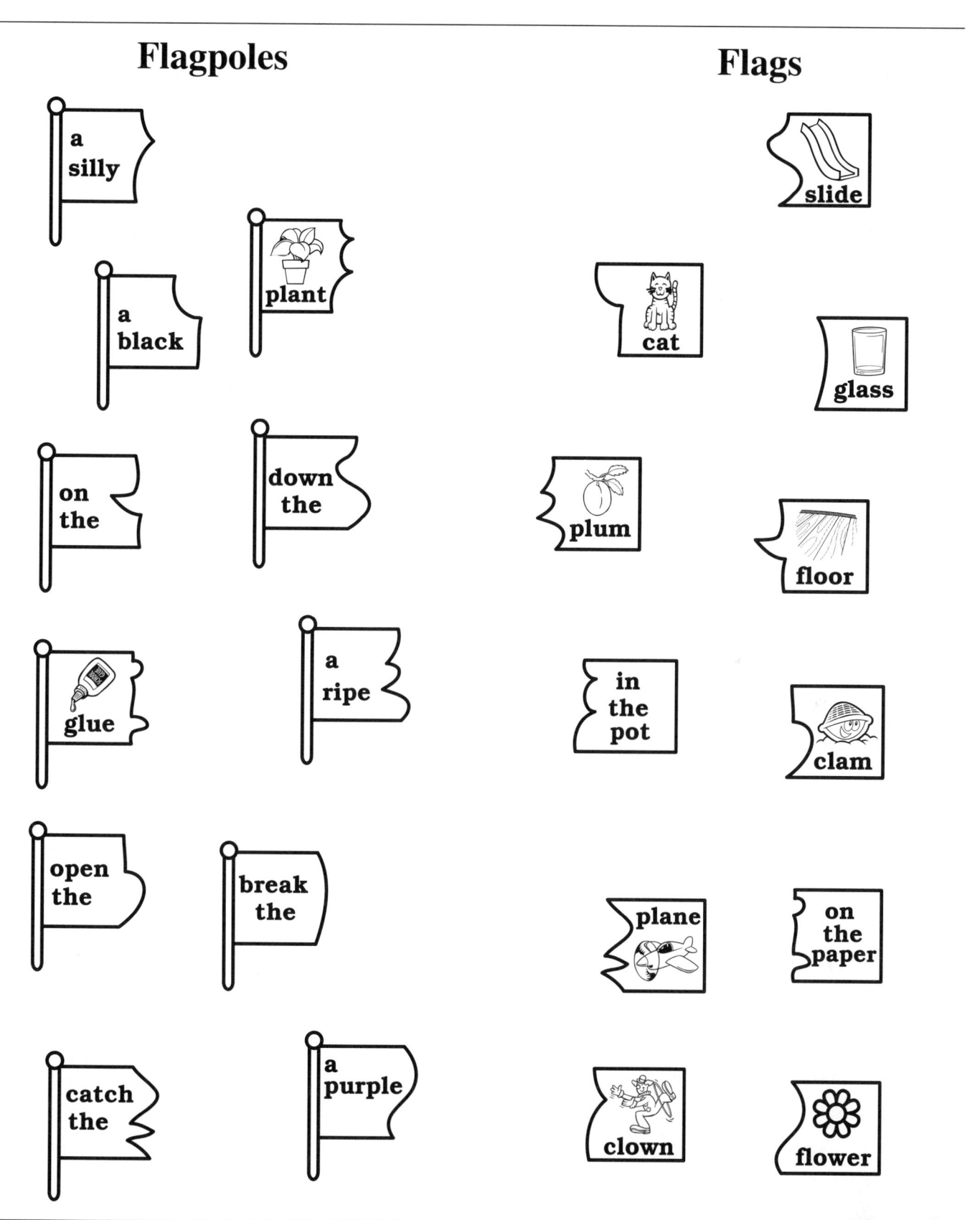

Flagpoles

- a silly
- a black
- plant
- on the
- down the
- glue
- a ripe
- open the
- break the
- catch the
- a purple

Flags

- slide
- cat
- glass
- plum
- floor
- in the pot
- clam
- plane
- on the paper
- clown
- flower

Homework Partner Date Speech-Language Pathologist

L Blend Phrases

Phrase Matches

Directions: Read/say aloud each noun below. Then, draw a line from an adjective to a noun. Read/say each phrase aloud using your best L blend sound. _____

Adjective	Noun
happy	 plane
tall	 floor
fast	 clown
big	 flashlight
loud	 sled
small	 fly
soft	 flamingo
heavy	 blanket
dirty	 cliff

_____ _____ _____ Medial L
Homework Partner   Date   Speech-Language Pathologist   Phrase

Make a Wish

Directions: Read/say each picture–word aloud. Then, make up a sentence with each word by saying, "I wish I had a _____." Use your best L blend sound.

- sled
- blanket
- flashlight
- plane
- flamingo
- plant
- clam
- plum
- flag
- clown
- clock
- sleeping bag

Homework Partner　　　Date　　　Speech-Language Pathologist

L Blend Sentences

L Spinner Action

Directions: Read/say aloud the picture–words below. If you prefer, glue this page to construction paper for added durability. Cut out the arrow/dial. Use a brad to connect the dial to the circle. Spin the spinner. When you land on a picture, say a sentence aloud using the target word in the picture. Use your best L sound.

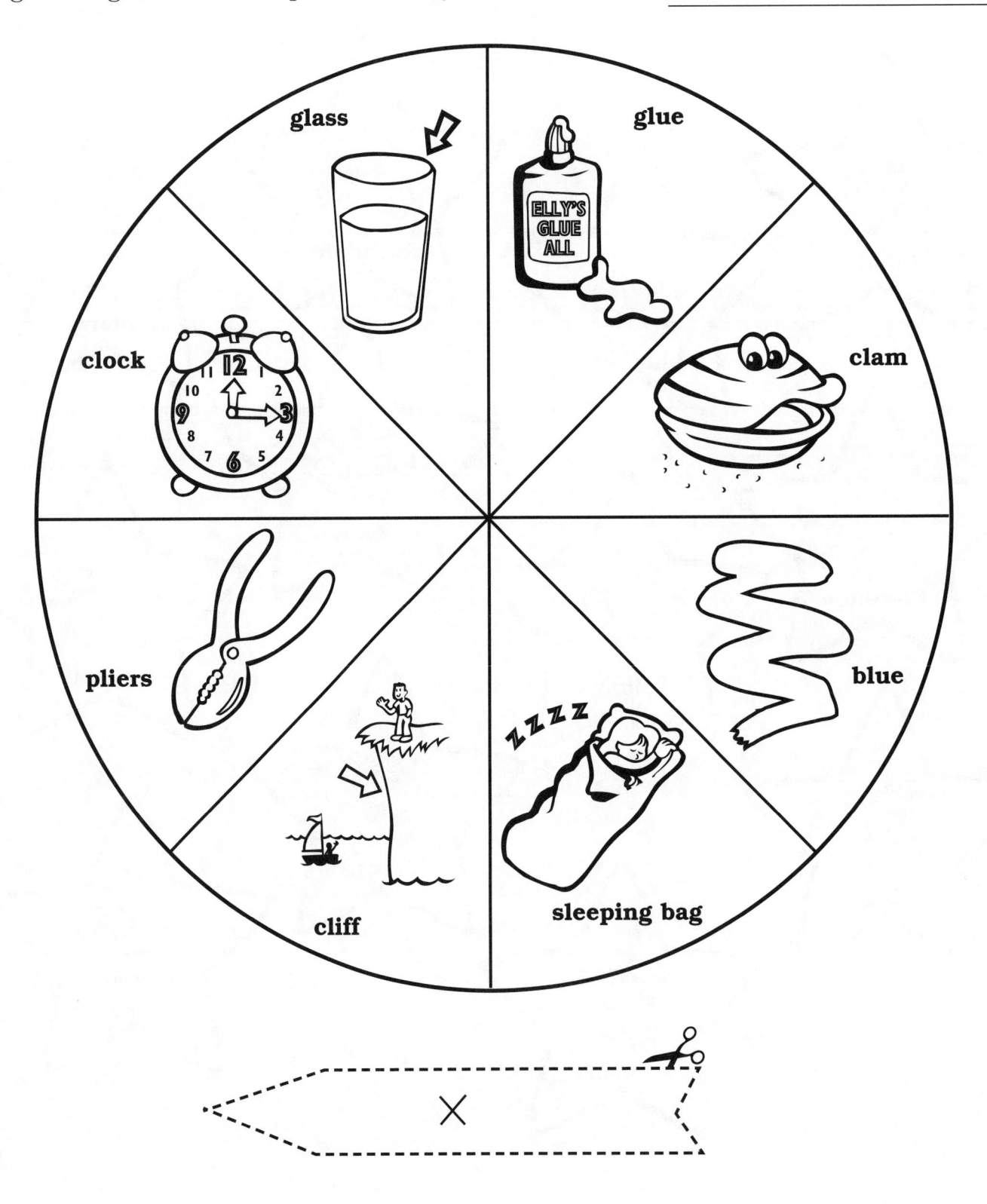

- glass
- glue
- clam
- blue
- sleeping bag
- cliff
- pliers
- clock

Homework Partner   Date   Speech-Language Pathologist

L Blend Words

Plant Town

Directions: Read/say aloud each phrase below. Cut out the plants and pots. Match the plants to the correct pot to make a sentence. Say/read each sentence aloud. Use your good L blend sound.

Plants:
- In the winter
- Pour chocolate milk
- We can build
- Rob gave Ali
- At the circus
- Shirt, pants and socks
- In the tool box
- Michelle is sitting
- A zebra is
- Put some batteries

Pots:
- is a pair of pliers.
- we like to sled.
- in the glass.
- on the floor.
- are all clothes.
- a purple flower.
- we saw a clown.
- with blocks.
- black and white.
- in the flashlight.

Homework Partner   Date   Speech-Language Pathologist

L Blend Sentences

What Am I?

Directions: Read/say aloud each picture–word. Then, read each clue. Fill in the blanks with the appropriate word. Read/say your answers aloud using your good blend sounds. _____

clothes	braid	skunk	star	pliers
tricycle	swimsuit	cloak	blanket	pretzel

1. I am something you wear. I am _____.
2. I am something that covers you to keep you warm. I am a _____.
3. I am something that shines in the sky at night. I am a _____.
4. I am something you wear in the pool. I am a _____.
5. I am a three–wheeled bike. I am a _____.
6. I am a way to fix a girl's hair. I am a _____.
7. I am a yummy snack that's twisted. I am a _____.
8. I am a black and white animal with an odor. I am a _____.
9. I am an old-fashioned coat. I am a _____.
10. I am a tool to fix things. I am _____.

Answers: 1-clothes, 2-blanket, 3-star, 4-swimsuit, 5-tricycle, 6-braid, 7-pretzel, 8-skunk, 9-cloak, 10-pliers

Homework Partner   Date   Speech-Language Pathologist

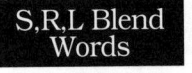

S,R,L Blend Words

Category Match

Directions: Read/say each picture–word aloud. Then, choose the correct category from the choices below. Write the letter of the answer in the space provided.

1. plum

2. skirt

3. french fries

4. grapes

5. flamingo

6. dress

7. sweater

8. skunk

9. spaghetti

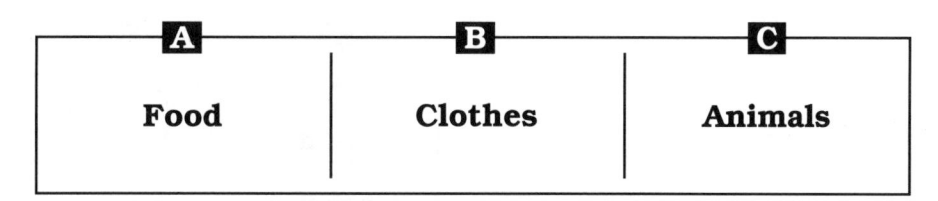

A	B	C
Food	Clothes	Animals

Answers: 1-A, 2-B, 3-A, 4-A, 5-C, 6-B, 7-B, 8-C, 9-A

Homework Partner Date Speech-Language Pathologist

S,R,L Blend Words

Which Is?

Directions: Read/say the following questions aloud. Say the answers aloud, using your best blend sounds.

1. Which is fastest? _____

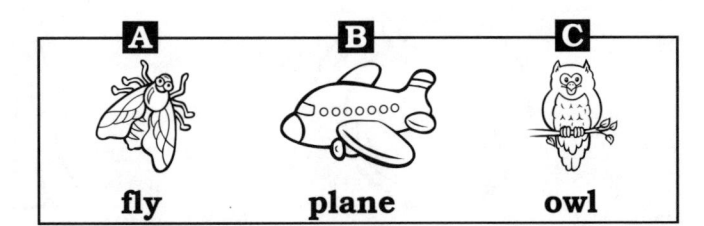

A	B	C
fly	plane	owl

2. Which is smallest? _____

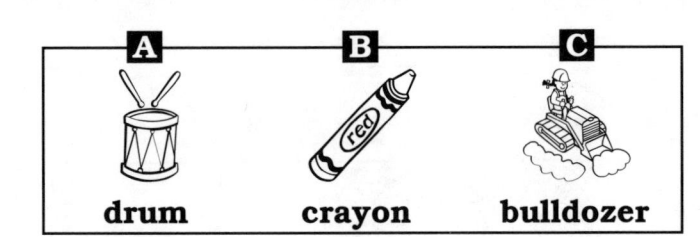

A	B	C
drum	crayon	bulldozer

3. Which is loudest? _____

A	B	C
spaceship	spider	owl

4. Which is longest? _____

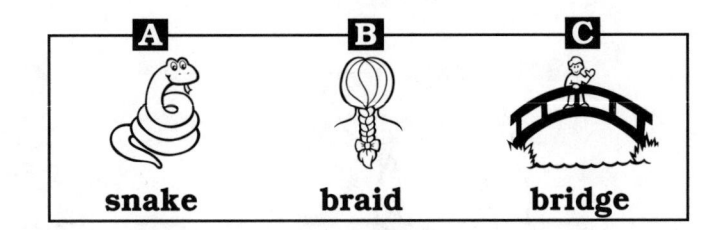

A	B	C
snake	braid	bridge

5. Which is stickiest? _____

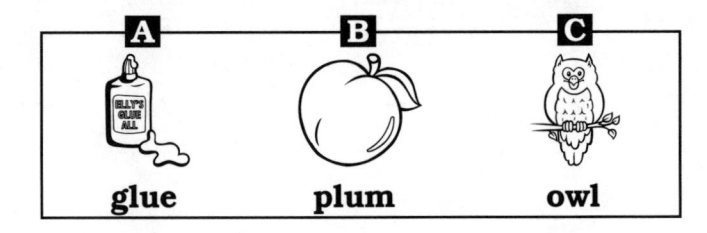

A	B	C
glue	plum	owl

6. Which is warmest? _____

A	B	C
scarf	apple	sweater

Answers: 1-B, 2-B, 3-A, 4-C, 5-A, 6-C

Homework Partner   Date   Speech-Language Pathologist

S,R,L Blend Words

Riddle Detective

Directions: Read/say aloud the picture–words. Then, read the riddles. Choose the correct answers from the Word Bank. Write the answers in the spaces. Read/say your answers aloud using your good blend sounds.

Word Bank

- clock
- floor
- sleeping bag
- apple
- crane
- french fries
- swan
- bats
- balloon

1. I am used for camping.
   I keep you warm.
   I am a bed that rolls up.
   What am I? _____

2. I like water.
   I am a beautiful bird.
   I am usually white.
   What am I? _____

3. I can be straight or curly.
   I go with hamburgers.
   I am made from potatoes.
   What am I? _____

4. I can be mopped.
   You walk on me.
   I rhyme with door.
   What am I? _____

5. I am very tall.
   I lift heavy items.
   I am a machine.
   What am I? _____

6. I have two hands.
   I have numbers on my face.
   I tell you the time.
   What am I? _____

Answers: 1. sleeping bag, 2. swan, 3. french fries, 4. floor, 5. crane, 6. clock

Homework Partner   Date   Speech-Language Pathologist   **S,R,L Blend Words**

How Many?

Directions: Look at the pictures and count the number of items in each box. Write the number on the line. Then, read/say the phrase aloud, using your good blend sounds ("four apples"). _____

1. _____ 
2. _____ 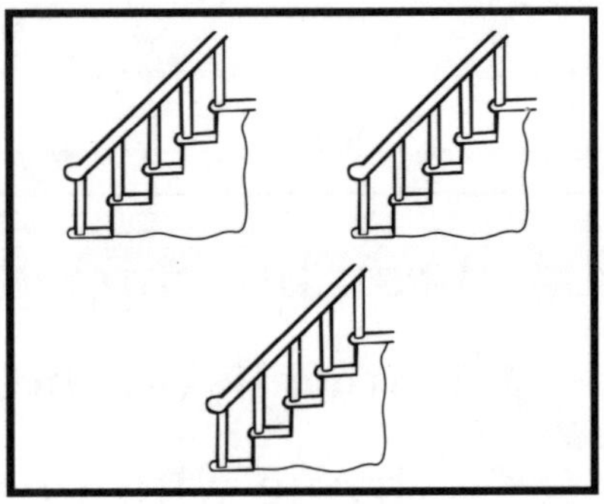
3. _____ 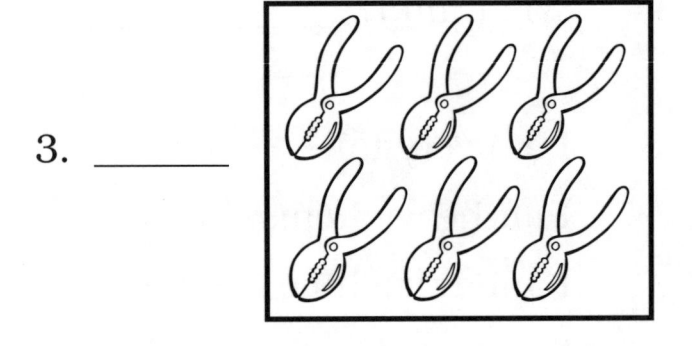
4. _____ 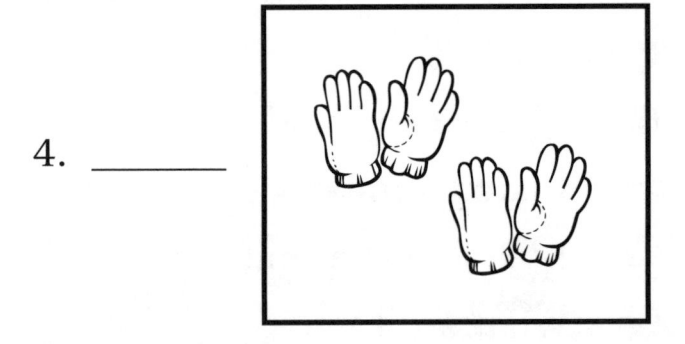
5. _____ 
6. _____ 
7. _____ 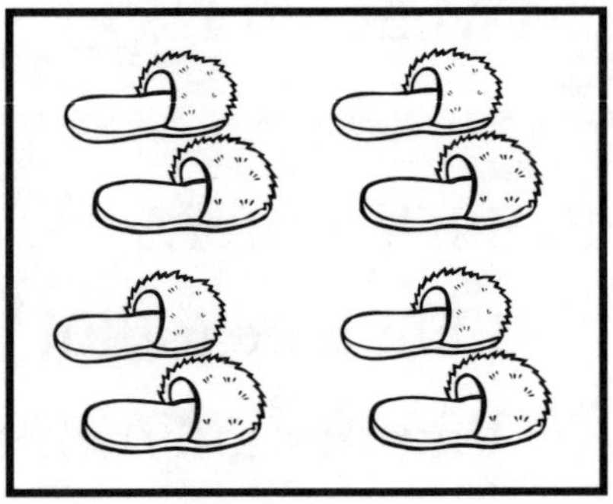
8. _____

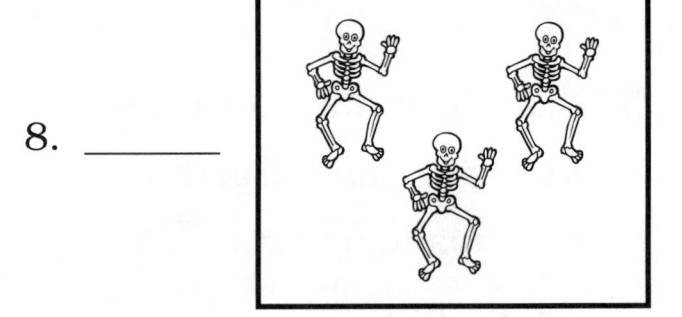

Homework Partner   Date   Speech-Language Pathologist   S,R,L Blend Phrases

Spinner Action

Directions: Read/say aloud the picture–words below. If you prefer, glue this page to construction paper for added durability. Cut out the arrow/dial. Use a brad to connect the dial to the circle. Spin the spinner. When you land on a picture, read/say the word aloud, using your best blend sounds.

- the baby blanket
- a long dress
- the purple plum
- my wet swimsuit
- the wood floor
- the red stop sign
- yummy fruit
- the pretty swan

Homework Partner　　　Date　　　Speech-Language Pathologist

S,R,L Blend Phrases

Phrase Race

Directions: Read/say aloud the picture–words below. Then, cut out the markers. Flip a coin (heads=1, tails=2) to determine how many spaces to move. As you move, read/say each phrase aloud, using your good blend sounds. First player to reach the finish wins.

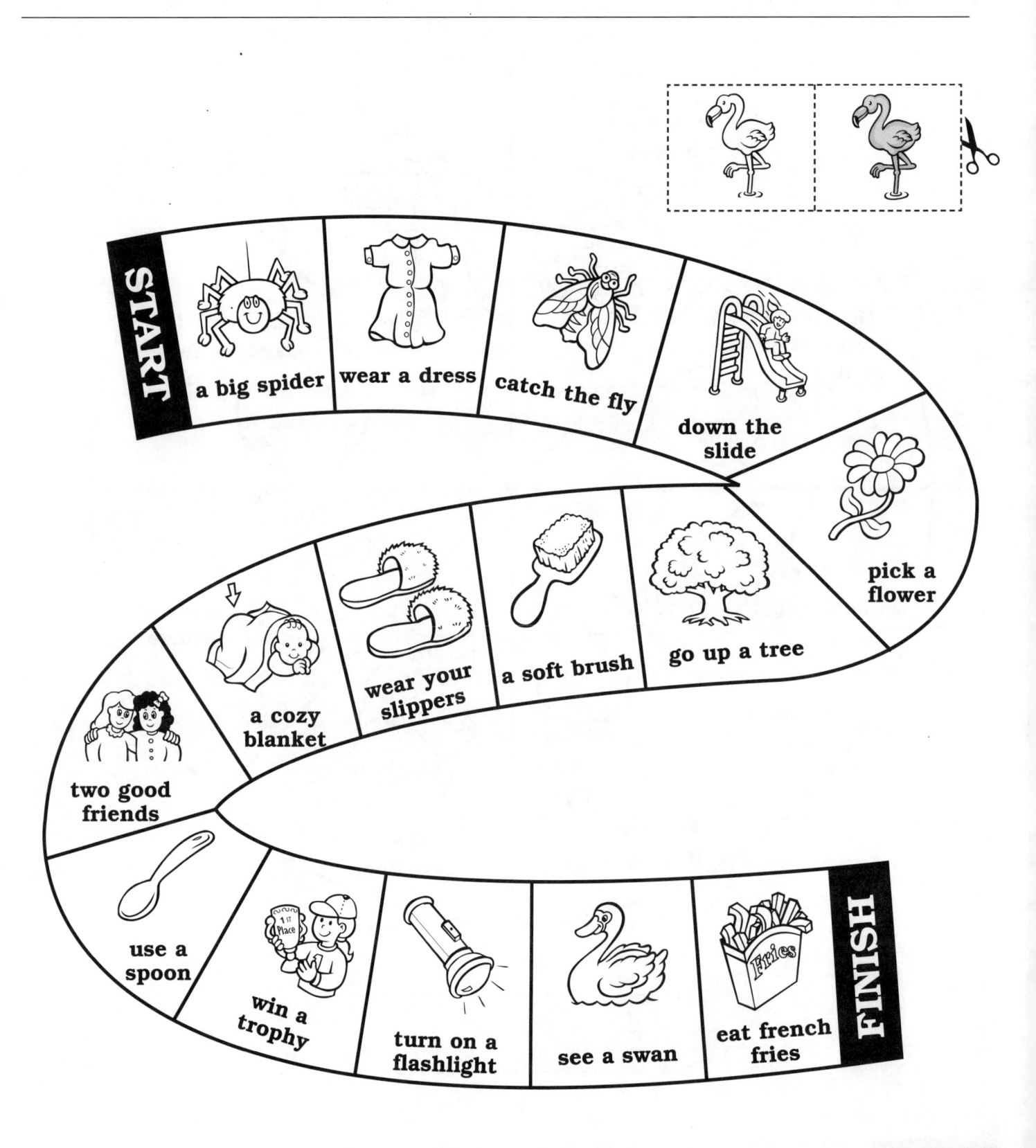

START
- a big spider
- wear a dress
- catch the fly
- down the slide
- pick a flower
- go up a tree
- a soft brush
- wear your slippers
- a cozy blanket
- two good friends
- use a spoon
- win a trophy
- turn on a flashlight
- see a swan
- eat french fries

FINISH

Homework Partner Date Speech-Language Pathologist

S,R,L Blend Phrases

Where is It?

Directions: Read/say aloud the picture–words below. Then, cut out all the cards below keeping A and B separate. Choose two pictures and make up phrases using "on," "under," or "over" ("boat on clam"). Use your best blend sounds.

A	A	A	A
boat	cowboy	baby	bathtub
crib	robot	spider web	bee

B	B	B	B	B
star	broom	clam	swan	frog
flag	glue	snowman	train	stick

Homework Partner   Date   Speech-Language Pathologist   S,R,L Blend Phrases

269

Story Loop

Directions: Read/say aloud each picture-word. Make up a story using all of the pictures in the circle. You can start anywhere in the circle and go in either direction, but you must always end where you started to complete the loop. Say your story aloud, using your good blend sounds.

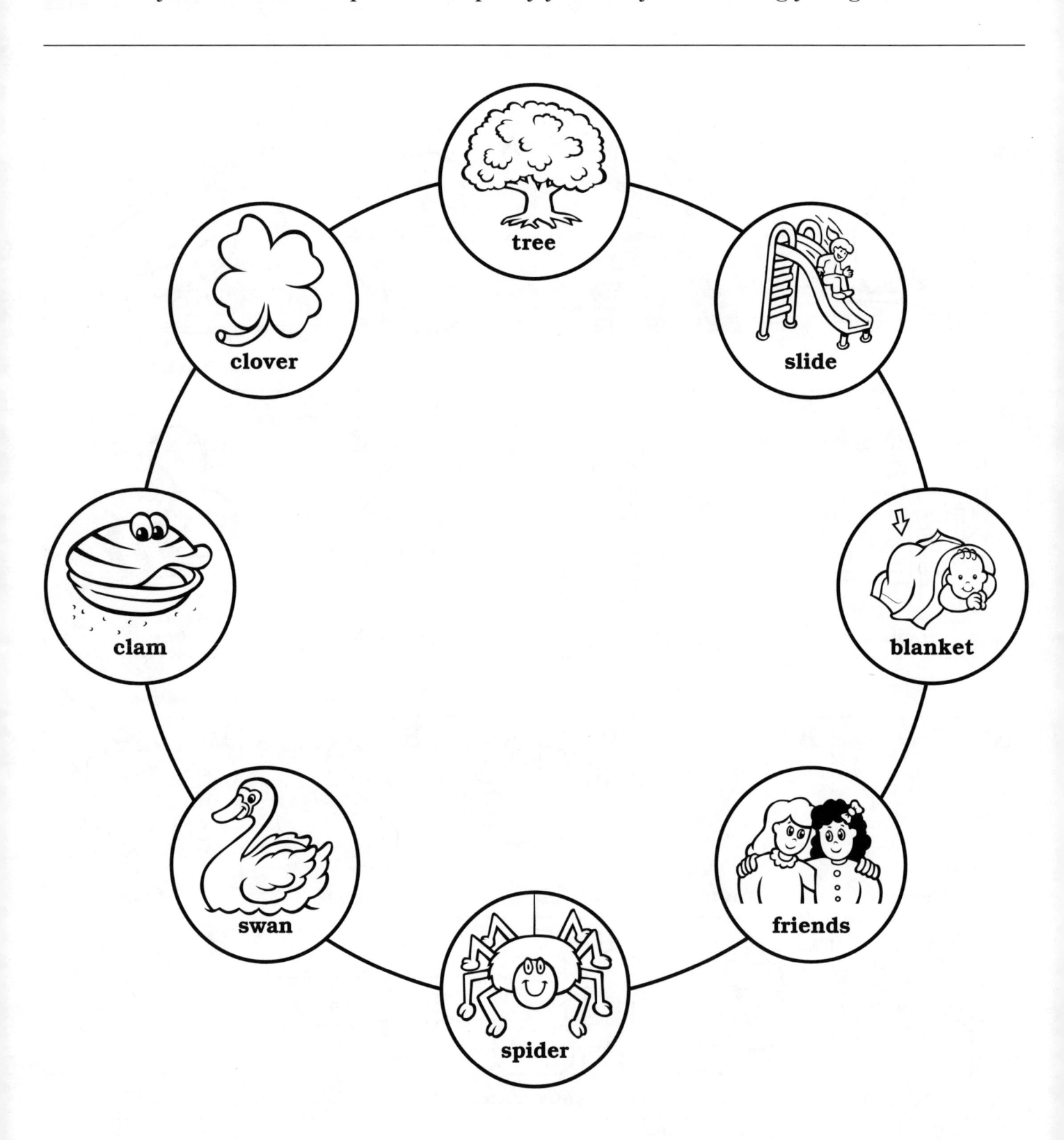

- tree
- slide
- blanket
- friends
- spider
- swan
- clam
- clover

Homework Partner   Date   Speech-Language Pathologist

S,R,L Blend Sentences

270

Sentence Completion

Directions: Read/say aloud the picture–words below. Then, cut out the pictures. Find the picture that best completes the sentence and glue/tape or place it under the correct phrase. Read/say the sentences aloud, using your good blend sounds.

You are baking a...	You grow a...	Mom knit a...	I like to wear...	Dad likes his...
Catch the...	I move as slowly as a...	The artist colored with a...	The winner won a...	Please eat the salty...

| crayon | bread | snail | skunk | pretzel |
| truck | trophy | flower | sweater | glasses |

Homework Partner   Date   Speech-Language Pathologist

Yes or No?

Directions: Read the questions. Then, put an X in the correct boxes. Say your answers aloud in sentence form. ("Yes, a spider makes a web.") Remember to use your best blend sounds.

	Yes	No
1. Does a spider make a web?	☐	☐
2. Do you eat a slide?	☐	☐
3. Do you wear slippers?	☐	☐
4. Do you sit on a drum?	☐	☐
5. Can you braid your hair?	☐	☐
6. Do you ride a tricycle?	☐	☐
7. Can you cover yourself with a blanket?	☐	☐
8. Is glue used to write?	☐	☐
9. Do you use a sleeping bag when you camp?	☐	☐

Homework Partner   Date   Speech-Language Pathologist

S,R,L Blend Sentences

Awards

Super Job!

This S Award is Presented to

_____
Name

_____
By   SLP

On _____ Date _____

You did it!
Great
R Sound!

Presented to _____

By _____ SLP

On _____ Date

L Award

_____'s L is the best!

Presented to

_____

_____ _____
SLP   Date

Excellent

276 · #BK-290 Webber® Artic Fun Sheets • ©2001 Super Duper® Publications • www.superduperinc.com • 1-800-277-8737

Ama-Z-ing Work!

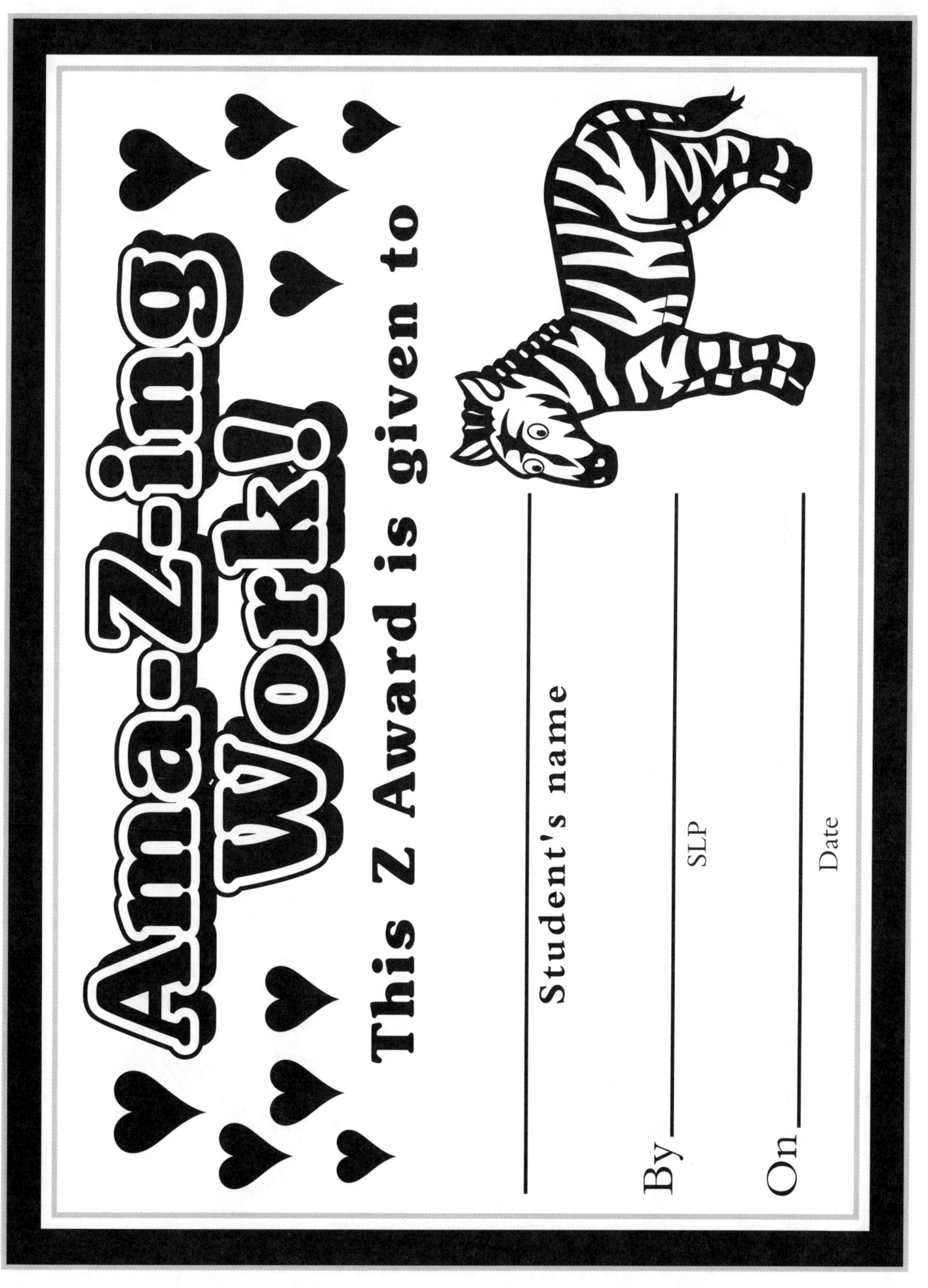

This Z Award is given to

_____
Student's name

_____
By   SLP

_____
On   Date

#BK-290 Webber® Artic Fun Sheets • ©2001 Super Duper® Publications • www.superduperinc.com • 1-800-277-8737

My Blends are Super Duper!

This Award is Presented to

_____
Student's name

_____
By   SLP

_____
On   Date

Activity Answers

Pg 5   1. sun   2. seal   3. seven   4. sandwich   5. cereal   6. seatbelt   7. silly   **secret word:** sandals

Pg 7   A. sun   B. cereal   C. sailboat   D. Santa   E. seatbelt   F. sock   G. seven   H. saw

Pg 14   1. The sock is blue.   2. My dog had seven puppies.   3. I ate a bowl of cereal.   4. The clown was silly at the carnival.
5. I made a peanut butter and jelly sandwich.   6. You should wear your seatbelt in the car.   7. He wears sandals when it is hot.
8. I need a saw to cut the board.

Pg 49   1. B,   2. A,   3. B,   4. B,   5. A

Pg 72   A. 5,   B. 4,   C. 7,   D. 10,   E. 9,   F. 2,   G. 1,   H. 3,   I. 8,   J. 6

Pg 74   1. balloon   2. apple   3. B   4. whale   5. socks   6. pencil   7. camel   8. bulldozer

Pg 110   1. The baby has a rattle.   2. Do you hear a bird singing?   3. Wish upon a star.   4. Don't go out in the rain.
5. I like your new earrings.   6. Pick a blue flower.

Pg 125   1. The fat lobster pinched my toe.   2. The mother fed her cubs   3. The runner's legs hurt after the race.
4. The oak tree dropped a leaf.   5. The baby sits in daddy's lap.   6. Every Sunday is laundry day.   7. He knocked over the lamp.
8. May I have lemon in my tea?

Pg 137   1. The camel has two humps.   2. My cat hurt its tail.   3. I picked the red apple.   4. The owl sleeps in the day.
5. The dog chased the ball.   6. He saw a whale in the ocean.

Pg 164   1. I ate jellybeans at Easter.   2. She hit her heel on the chair.   3. The baby sat on Santa's lap.   4. Don't pop the red balloon.
5. How many spots does a leopard have?   6. The fisherman caught the whale.

Pg 189   1. He read the Three Little Pigs.   2. The monkey ate the bananas.   3. We cut apples to make the pie.   4. I can't find my tennis shoes.
5. Dad gave Mom a rose.   6. The hen laid six eggs.

Pg 190   1. The boy fell on his knees.   2. Please make me a cheese sandwich.   3. The boys went camping and hiking.
4. The three girls love to play dress-up.   5. We have five toes on each foot.   6. The farmer milked the cows.

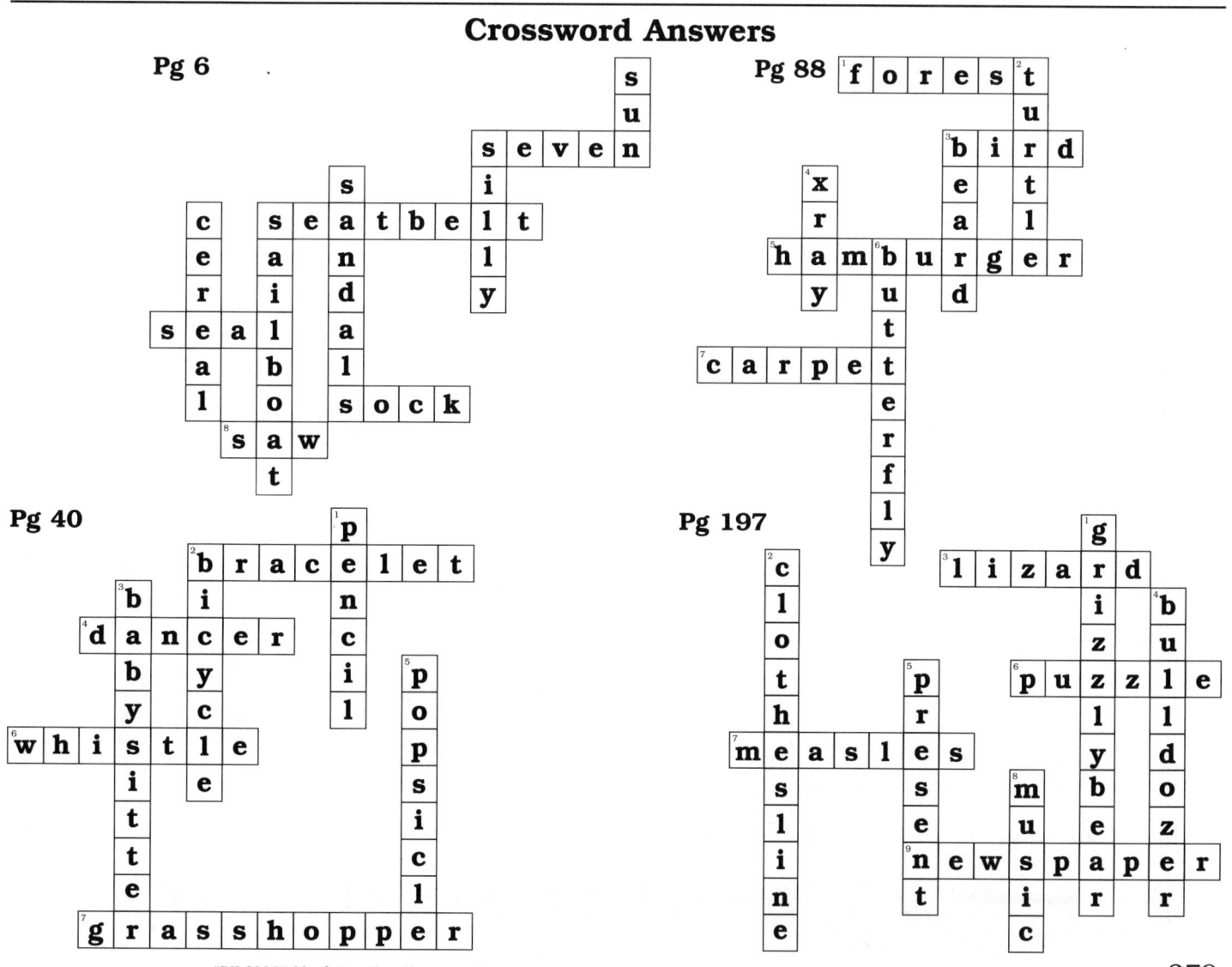

Crossword Answers

Pg 6, **Pg 88**, **Pg 40**, **Pg 197**

Word Search Answers

Pg 11

Pg 76

Pg 96

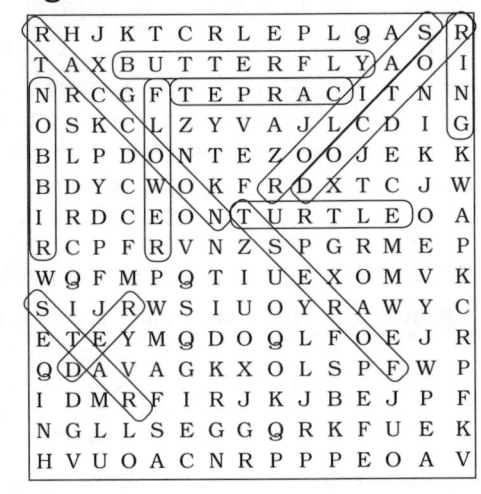

Pg 214

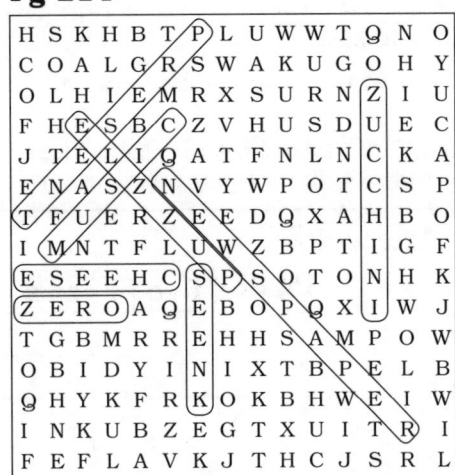

Pg 255

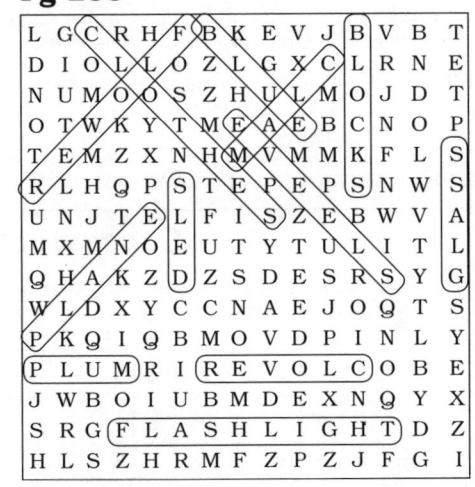

Maze Answers

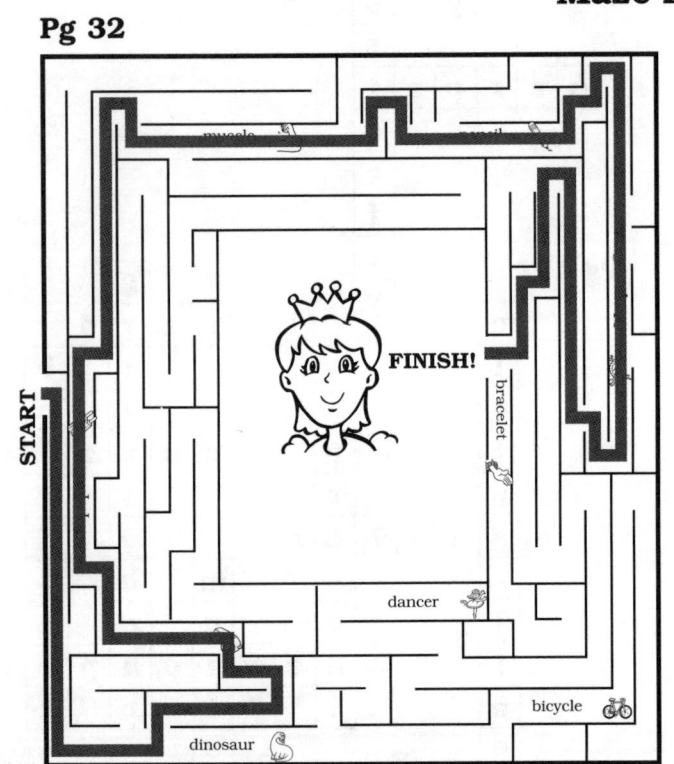

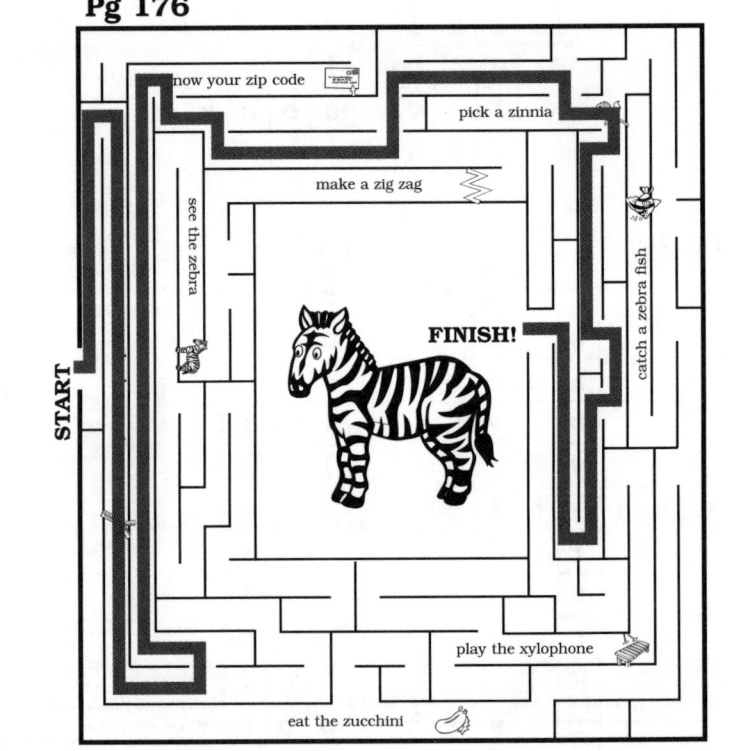

Pg 32

Pg 176